पुरातत्त्व
PURĀTATTVA

Bulletin of the Indian Archaeological Society

No. 9 1977-78

Editor
B.K. Thapar

D.K. Printworld (P) Ltd.
New Delhi

Cataloging in Publication Data — DK

[Courtesy : D.K. Agencies (P) Ltd. <docinfo@dkagencies.com>]

Purātattva : bulletin of the Indian Archaeological
Society, no. 9, 1977-78 / editor, B.K. Thapar.
p. cm.
Includes bibliographical references.
ISBN 8124602859

1. Archaeology — India — Periodicals. 2. India
— Antiquities — Periodicals. 3. India — Civilization
— Periodicals. I. Thapar, B.K. II. Indian
Archaeological Society.

First Published in 1980
First Reprinted in 2005
ISBN 81-246-0285-9
Price for volume 9 (1977-78): Rs. 800 US $ 40

Reprint authorised by
Indian Archaeological Society
New Delhi - 110 016

Purātattva is published annually.

Manuscripts (whether in the form of articles or notes or book reviews) offered for publication should be sent to the Editor, Purātattva, Indian Archaeological Society, B-17, Qutab Institutional Area, New Delhi - 110 016.

Published and printed by:
D.K. Printworld (P) Ltd.
'Srikunj,' F-52, Bali Nagar
New Delhi – 110015
Phone : (011) 2545 3975, 2546 6019 Fax : (011) 2546 5926
E-mail : dkprintworld@vsnl.net
www. dkprintworld.com

PURATATTVA

NUMBER 9, 1977–78

CONTENTS

PURATATTVA

NUMBER 9 1977-78

Editorial

Readers of the *Puratattva* would recall that on the occasion of the Centenary Celebration af the Archaeological Survey of Indian in December 1961, an International Conference on Asian Archaeology was organised. At the closing Plenary Session of this Conference a unanimously accepted Resolution was moved that the Conference on Asian Archaeology should meet, if practicable, at intervals of approximately five years. Pursuant perhaps to this Resolution-two Conferences, one at Colombo in Sri Lanka and the other at Bahrain, were held, after which no such Conference has been convened by any Asian country and the resolution of 1961, has remained unimplemented, Meanwhile in 1970, an association of South Asian Archaeologist in Western Europe was founded to provide a forum for scholars based in Europe who specialise in Prehistoric and Historic archaeology of the Indian Sub-continent and its Iranian and Burmese borderlands. This Association *inter alia* decided that a Conference on South Asian Archaeology should be held biennially. Five Conferences of this Association have so far been held, very regularly indeed : Cambriege, 1971; Amsterdam, 1973; Paris, 1975, Neples 1977; and Berlin, 1979. Excepting the last one, the Proceedings of these Conferences have also been published. Perusing the Papers presented at these Conferences one finds that the excavations conducted at some of the sites in the Indo-Pak boarderlands have a great relevance to Indian Archaeology. Among these, perhaps five sites stand out more prominently; Shortugai in the oxus valley of Afghanistan; Mehrgarh in the Kachi plain of Pakistan; Shahr-i-Sokhta in Iranian Siestan; Umm ar-Nor, an Island of the Abu Dhabi coast; and Bahrain. Of these, four sites indicate perceptible interrelationship with the Indus Civilization : Shortugai shows a basal Harappan Culture evolving into a later Phase with intrusive Central Asian Cultures of the second millennium B.C. The occurrance of a tyhical Indus seal along with shell bangles, carnelian beads and chart blades confirms the Harrappan character of the occupation. At Mehrgarh and the nearly mound of Nowsharo the evidence points to an evolution right from the pre-pottery neolithic to the Harappan. While these two sites throw fresh light on the origin and the dynamics of the Indus Civilization, the sites in the Persian

Gulf and the Iranian Siestan Indicate the economic mercantile character of the indus Civilization. To date, from Bahrain there is one Indian gaming piece of lapis lazuli which is identical with the innumerable pieces discovered at several Harappan sites together with lapis lazuli pendants which appear to be of Indian origin. These objects are ascribable of the Akkadian Period. As regards the Harappan civilization a direct Dilmun-Meluhha contact is, textually speaking, less tangible although it seems to be corroborated by archaeological evidence. During the last three years or so there have been three International Seminars on the Indus Civilization : Simla, 1977; Karachi. December, 1978-January, 1979; and Srinagar, 1979. The discussions and the papers presented at these Seminars have underlined the necessity for further work on the Indus Civilization, More sites of the Harappan affiliation should, therefore, be excavated in India. Other problems of Indian archaeology which have relevance to the work done outside the country relate to (a) the identifiable cultural remains of the Aryans and (b) the Megalithic Culture. As regards the former, a seminar was held in Dushambe in 1977 on the Ethnic Problems of the Early History of the Peoples of Central Asia and India in the second millennium B. C. On the Megalithic Culture, the only Seminar so far held was in 1968 at Varanasi, subsequent to which much work has been in the Peninsular. Both the above-mentioned problems need re-assesment periodically as fresh evidence comes to light.

With a view to solving the various problems of Asian archaeology as also to indicating lives on which future research should be carried, it seems necessary that we should revive the Resolution adopted in 1961 to set up a permanent secretariat for the purpose of summoning future sessions of Asian Conference. If scholars based in Europe can hold Conference of South Asian Archaeology biennialy we in South Asia should not lag behind in holding regular Conferences.

Handaxe and Chopper-Chopping tool radition : the ideas of two culture theory of Early Palaeolithic in Asia*

A. P. Khatri

(Received on 3 May 1975)

1. INTRODUCTION

THE prehistoric research in Asian countries is picking up again. With the outbreak of World War II in 1939, prehistoric activities ceased to flourish in Asia. Since the fifties, however, there has been enough activity and many new facts have come to light which tend to reduce the old theory of Chopper-Chopping tools and Handaxe-Cleaver Complex as two separate Lower Palaeolithic traditions to a mere film-flam.

1.2 During the past four decades, World prehistory in general has undergone drastic changes. In Europe and Africa particularly, there has taken place a complete metamorpohsis in the conceptual framework of prehistory. For instance, the parallel phyla theory of Breuil is accepted no more (Breuil, with Koslowski, 1931, 193, Breuil, 1939). The seven-fold Acheulian succession in northern France (Breuil 1912, 1939) is discarded. Leakey's evolutionary scheme of eleven stages of Chelles-Acheul culture at Olduvai Gorge (Leake, L.S.B. 1951) has been proved invalid by his own wife's excavations (M.D. Leakey 1972). The Pluvial-Interpluvial hypothesis is no more fashionable. The climato-stratigraphic approach is considered no more practical (Butzer *et al.* 1972). The latest in lake Rudolf findings in Ethoipia have pushed back the date of the emergence of tool-making man to 2.6 million years (Issac *et al.* 1971). Gone are the days when man's appearance on the face of the earth was considered utmost to one million years. Even the modern Man, the *Homo sapien* is now being thought of 60,000 years old instead of 35,000 years (Bordes 1972, 315). The earliest ancestor of Man is now thought to be *Ramapithecus*, the creature who lived in the Himalayan foothills of north India and in East Africa 8-12 million years ago in the Miocene (Simons, 1961, 1964, Khatri 1973). Such have been the sea changes in our thinking regarding human evolution and development of lithic cultures during the past four decades. There is no reason for the *status quo* to continue in Asian prehistory and for the thought process to remain static.

2. IMPORTANT DEVELOPMENT

2.1 Five important events/discoveries have taken place during the past twenty years which have materially affected the outlook in Asian prehistory. These have, to a large extent, invalidated the theory propounded by Movius in 1940's about the two independent traditions in the early palaeolithic in the Old World. These five discoveries are :

(i) Paolo Graziosi's re-investigation of the Indus-Soan valley sites in the north-west of India in 1954-55 (Graziosi 1964) and his refutation of

* This paper was presented, read and thoroughly discussed in the Pre-Congress symposium on' Early Palaeolithic in South and East Asia' held in Montreal, Canada on August 28-31, 1973. This symposium was a part of the activites of the IXth International Congress of Anthropological and Ethnological Sciences which took place from August 28 to September 8, 1973, in Chicago, Illionois U.S.A. In this connection, please see, p. 3. of the *Early Paleolithic in South and East Asia* (1978) Ed. Fumiko Ikawa Smith published in World Anthropology Series by Mouton Publishers. The Aague, Paris

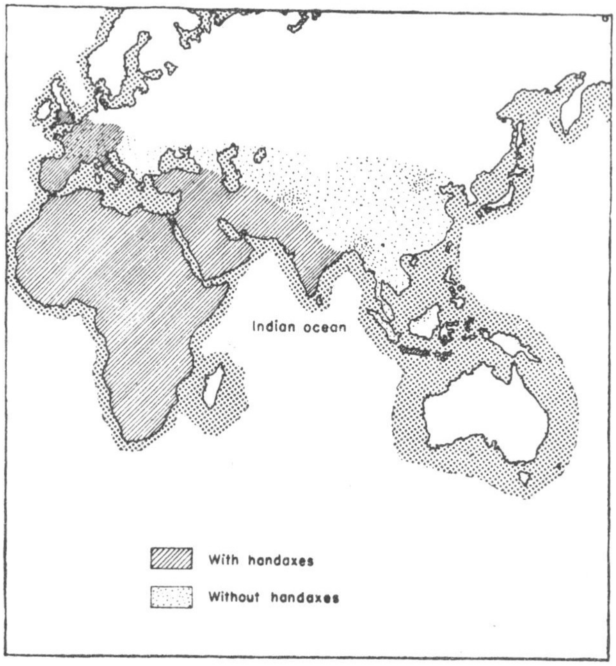

Fig. 1 (After (Bordes)

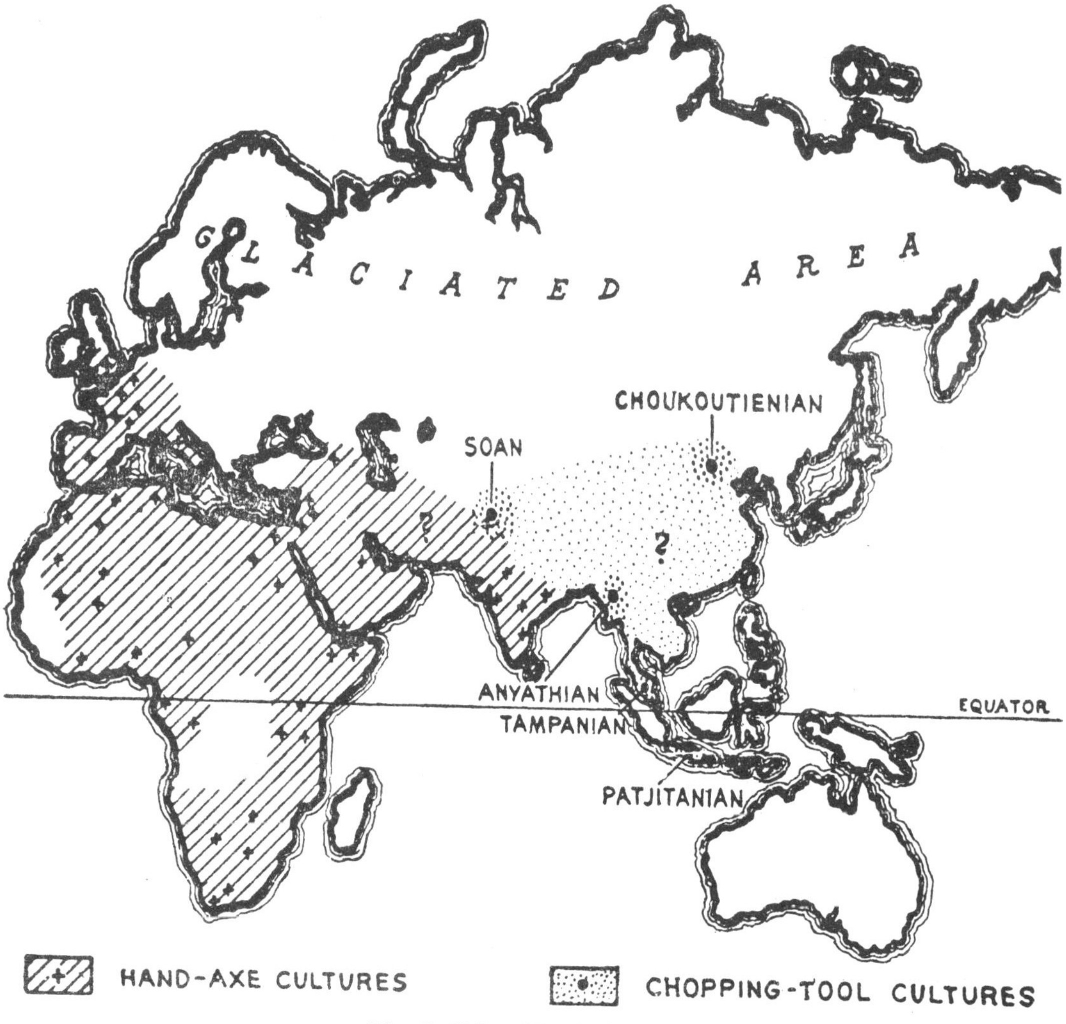

Fig. 2 (After Movius)

Paterson's results arrived in 1935 (De Terra and Paterson 1939).

(ii) Khatri's investigations in the rift valley of the Narmada river in Central India and the discovery of Mahadevian Pebble-tool Industry (Khatri 1963b) consisting of purely Choppers, Chopping tools and *incipient* handaxes.

(iii) Discovery of Handaxes in Vietnam (Boriskovsky, P.I. 1962 a, b), China (Chang, K. C. 1960), Japan (Serizdwa and Ikawa, 1960) and in Indonesia (von Koenigswald 1939; and Movius 1944, 1948).

(iv) Discovery of purely 'non-handaxe' (Chopper-Chopping tools) sites in Europe (Kretzoi and Vertes 1965; Vertes 1964 ; Bordes 1968 : 48) and

(v) Madam Leakey's excavation of living floors in the Olduvai Gorge during 1960-63 (Leakey M. D. 1972)

2.2 We shall discuss these points after we present the theory and the reasons militating against it.

3. SALIENT FEATURES OF THE THEORY

3.1 There are six pillars (Movius 1944, 1948) on which this theory stands. These are :

(i) The hand-axe-cleaver complex and Chopper-Chopping tools made on pebbles represent two separate Stone Age traditions.

(ii) They occupy two very clear cut demarcated zones. The handaxe occupying Africa and Europe while chopper-Chopping tools occupying the Asian mainland (Figs. 1 and 2).

(iii) The Early Soan (India), Anythian (Burma), Tampanian (Malaya); Patjitanian (Java) and Chukoutien (China) are the outstanding examples of cultures belonging to Chopper-Chopping tool traditions.

(iv) Peninsular India is the last out-post of the great handaxe culture.

(v) Wherever Handaxe and Chopper-Chopping tools are found together, that means the fusion of two separate cultures and confluence of streams belonging to two traditions.

(vi) These two Stone Age cultural traditions were practiced by two different races in two separate lands—Pithecanthropus-like man in Asia and Heidelberg-type of man in Europe.

4. REASONS FOR REJECTING THIS THEORY

4.1 The theory of Handaxe and Chopper-Chopping tools as two separate Stone Age traditions or cultures can be clearly traced to Breuil's parallel phyla theory which was quite popular in Europe in 1930s. As a matter of fact, the two-tradition theory is an adaptation of Breuil's theory. The Western prehistorians trained in French and English schools of that time, had it as an important part of their mental equipment. According 'to parallel phyla concept', there was a flake-tool tradition (Clactonian - Levalloisian) and a Core-biface tradition (Abbevillian-Acheulian) and each of them developed in a parallel manner completely independent of each other. It was even thought that paleo-anthropic stock of fossil man was responsible for introducing flake tools and men of neanthropic stock practiced the core-biface complex. The 'mixed' assemblages of handaxes and flakes were considered as a result from contacts and migrations of different racial elements. Now, when Paterson, the prehistorian and geologist in the Yale - Cambridge Expedition, on behalf of Cambridge University, U.K. in 1935, dealt with the Soan material, he interpreted consciously or unconsciously his observations on the Soan in north-west India which fitted in very well with the most popular conceptual framework available at that time in Europe. As a matter of fact it will not be wrong if we say that Paterson's interpretation of Soan prehistory and Movius' theory covering whole of Asia is a mirror copy of Breuil's theory. The book published in 1962

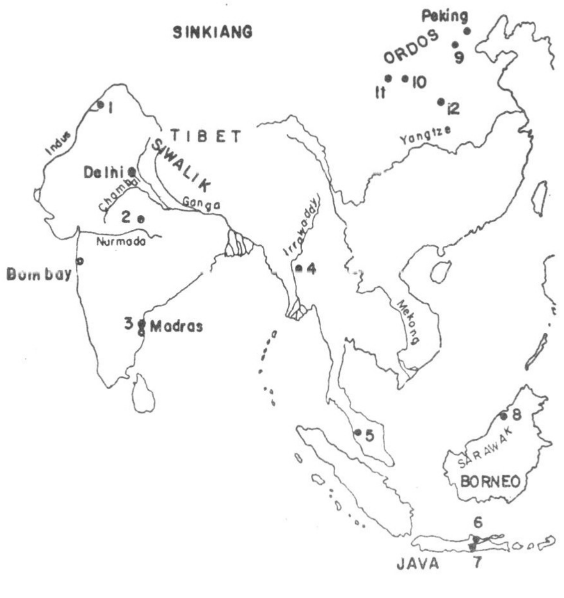

FIG. 3.

1. Soan 2. Mahadev-Piparia 3. Madras 4. Irrawadi Sites 5. Kota Tampan 6. Tinil 7. Patjitan 8. Nyah Cave. 9. Choukoutien 10. Sjara-Osso-Gol 11. Shui-Tong-Kou 12. Tngtsun.

by Pakistan Government on the *Soan-the Palaeolithic of pakistan,* the manuscript of which was prepared by Paterson and Drummond fifteen years before its publication, further confirms this. The book was completely out of date even at its time of writing Movius (1944) took the clue from Paterson and applied it to whole of Asia though fully conscious of the inconvinient fact of the occurrence of handaxes in Java. The point is, that when Breuil's original theory is now consigned to the dust bin then how this theory of Handaxe and Chopper-Chopping tools developed on that pattern can stand the test of time and can be found relevant after the lapse of thirty years.

4.2. Paolo Graziosi, Professor of Anthropology in the University of Florence (Italy) reinvestigated the area in the summer of 1954 between the Jhelum and Indus rivers to the east and west and the Soan and Haroy rivers to the south and to the north in north-western Punjab, as a part of the anthropological programme carried out by the Italian Scientific Mission. In his opinion, the surprising clearness of the chronological charts of the alluvial deposits and the terrace system of the Punjab rivers in relation to glaciations and interglaciation, as prepared by De Terra, Teilhard do Chardin and Paterson leaves one rather perplexed, especially in regard to the simple. systematization of the various lithic cultures (Graziosi 1964 : 8)

'This perplexity is also present when one is on the site and wishes to classify the artifacts on the basis of their physical state in relation to their typology, and place them in the perfect stratigraphical and chronological structure presented by the Anglo-American authors.'

He further states that charts which are not only chronological but also typological and which synchronize the geo-chronological succession of the alluvial formation.

'If on one hand these appear to be suggestive and acceptable but on the other hand these are excessively schematized and therefore are not always satisfying to any one who strives for clarity and symmetry in statements regarding natural phenomena.'

He does not agree that in the Early Soan, Choppers and Chopping tools made on pebbles are genetically apart, from the Abbevillian-Acheulian handaxes and have developed independently. He concludes that the opinion expressed by De Terra, Paterson and Chardin 'that from a genetical point of view, the 'Soan' pebble culture should be considered separatelly from the handaxes' is wrong. In short we can sum up his observations on the Soan tools as follows :-

(a) Flake implements, pebble tools, handaxes, and cleavers are found alongside each other. That means that unifacial and bifacial industries are found at the same time mixed together.

(b) Pre-Soan, the oldest culture of the Punjab, as claimed by De Terra and Paterson and belonging to the second glacial age and consisting of large, massive flakes with little retouch does not exist.

(c) Flake technique from the genetic point of view cannot be separated from the pebble tools and the handaxes.

(d) The handaxes and cleavers are clearly derived technically and morphologically from wedges and large flakes,etc. There is a direct connection between handaxes, cleavers and pebble tools.

Now the above observations on the palaeolithic situation in the Soan valley in the periglacial area of the Himalayas are such that even a prehistorian standing on the bank of a river in Central and Southern India, abounding in rich palaeolithic sites along its riverine course, will speak the same language. There is no doubt that the situation in the Potwar region regarding palaeolithic archaeology is not at all different from what it exists in other parts of India.

4.3 On techno-morphological grounds, it can be demonstrated that the handaxe is the successor of the Chopping tool and therefore these two types cannot be genetically set apart.

4.4 In the Narmada valley in Central India, the development of the handaxe from the Chopping tool through various intermediary stages can be convincingly demonstrated in the Mahadevian Pebble tool Industry (Plates I to XI). This industry was discovered from Mahadev-Piparia, its type site (Fig. 5) by the writer in 1960. This site is an immensely rich factory site where tens of thousands of tools are found lying in the river bed. All the conceivable stages of the development of the handaxe from the Chopping tool can be seen at this factory site. Besides this, the Mahadevian Pebble tool industry occurs *in situ* at the basal most horizon of red clay indicating that it is the earliest palaeolithic Industry of the Narmada valley belonging at least to the early Middle Pleistocene (Khatri, 1963 b). The discovery of the Mahadevian culture has given a convincing proof that the handaxe has developed from the Chopping tool and both of them constitute a single culture rather than two separate, independently evolving entities.

4.5 In Central India, at sites of Lalitpur, Multanpura near Mandsaur, Jhalawar. Bhanpura. Besla, Rampura,

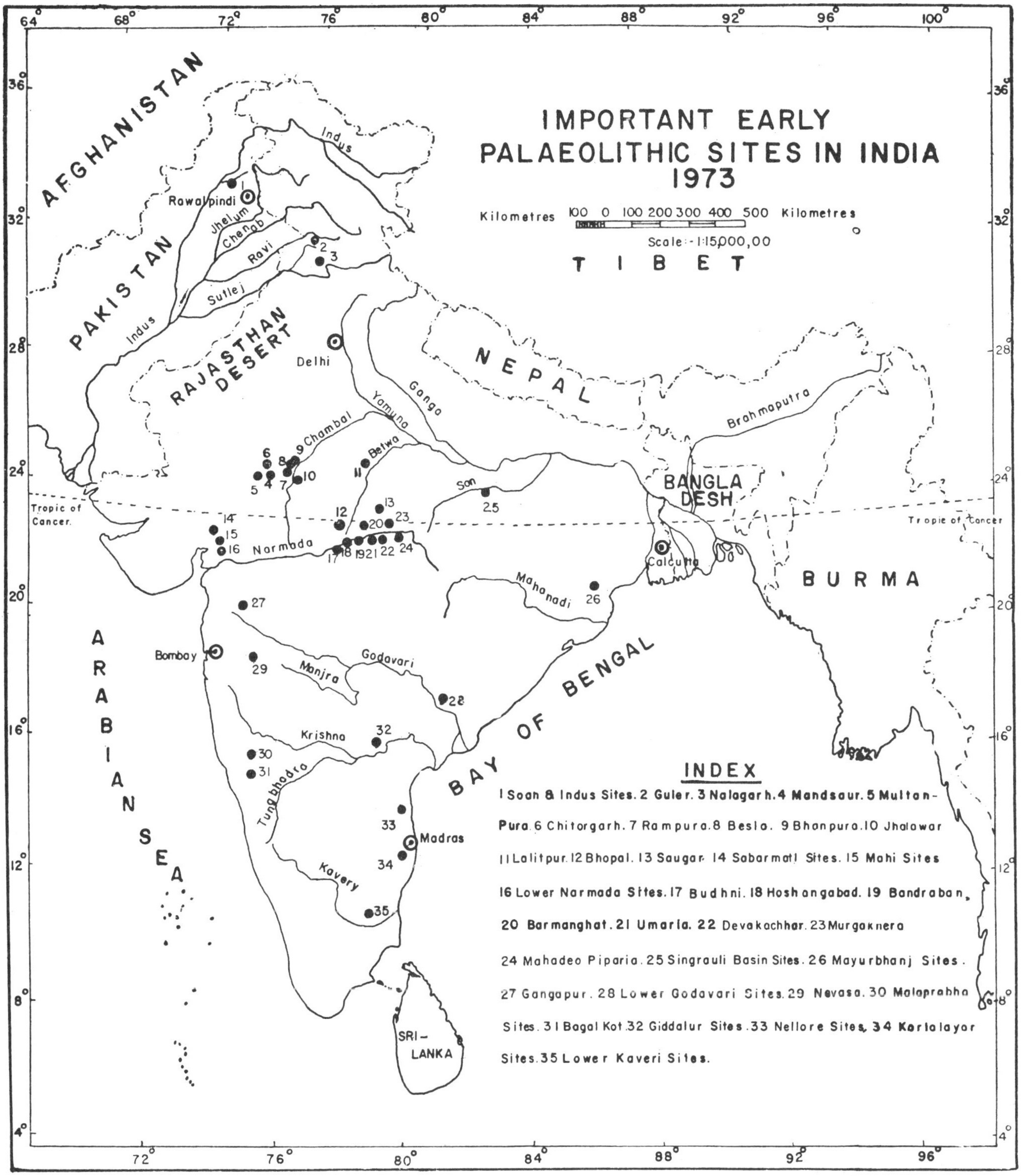

FIG. 4.

Chitorgarh (Fig. 4), the Lower Palaeolithic industries have handaxes, cleavers, chopping tools and Choppers occuring at the same cultural level with no difference in manufacturing technique. The same is the case at sites further down in the south in Karnatak, Andhra Pradesh, Tamil Nadu, Orissa and Mirzapur in eastern Uttar Pradesh. It is absurd to seek and search the meeting frontiers of two opposite cultural traditions, one coming from the east and another from the west everywhere at all these places.

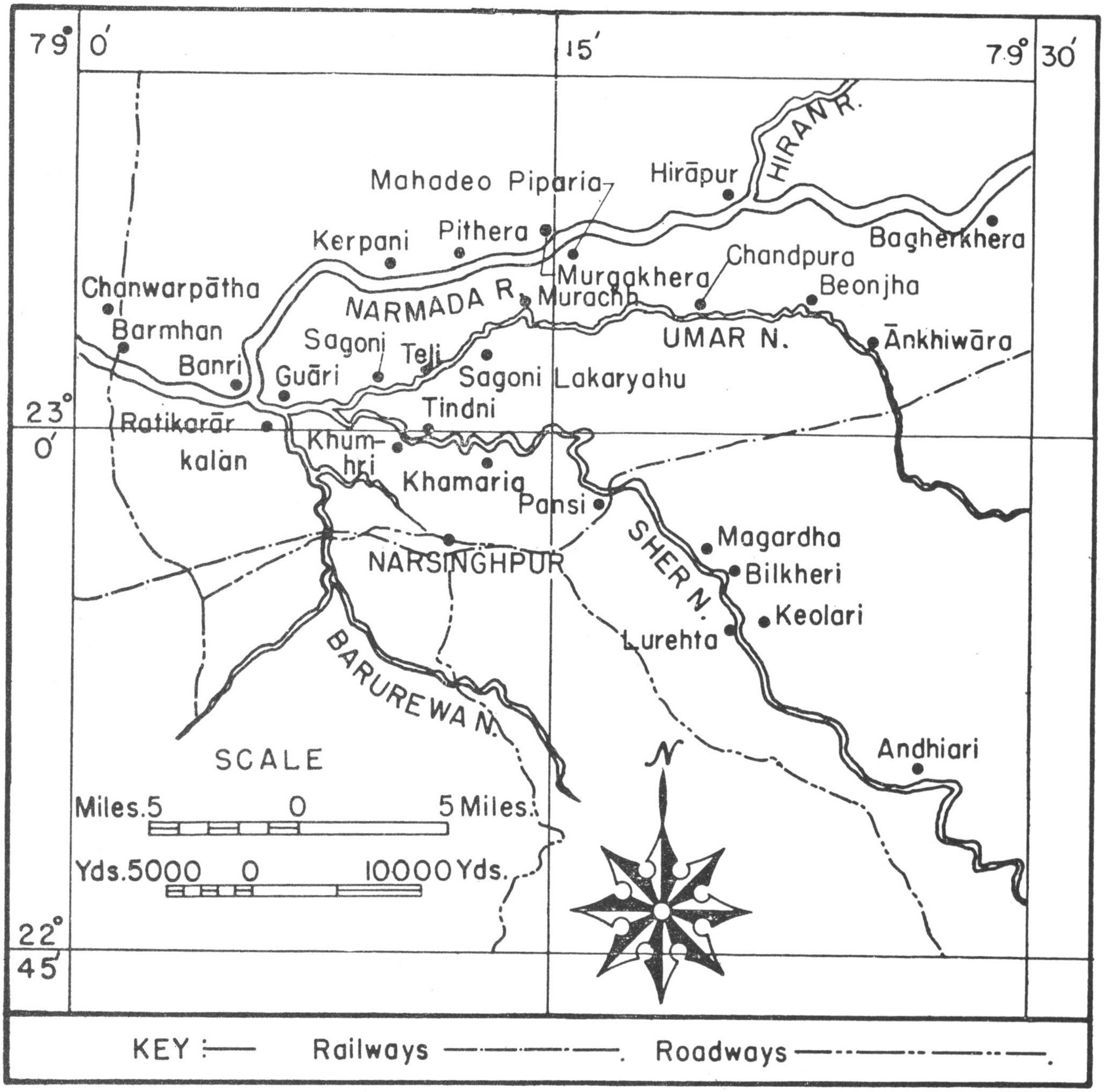

FIG. 5.

4.6 There is no difference at all between the sites like Morgah, Gola, Riwat, Khasla, Chauntra and Chhocar investigated by Graziosi in 1964 between Rawalpindi and Jhelum in north-west India and the sities in Central southern India as far as typological components of the early palaeolithic industry is concerned.

4.7 The discovery of handaxes in Chopper-Chopping tool Zones of Movius in the east and Chopper-Chopping tools ('non-handaxe cultures' of Bordes) in the West in Europe has made complete nonsense of the Movius theory. The Chopper-Chopping tools have been found in Europe in the Vallonet cave at Roquebrune-Cap-Martin on the Mediterranean coast in France in 1958 and at the traventine quarry near Ve'rtesszollos, west of Budapest in Hungary in 1964 showing that Chopper-Chopping tools made on pebbles are not only peculiar to Asia but are there down right in the heart of Europe too !

4.8 The recent discoveries of handaxes in Vietnam (Borskovsky, P.I. 1962 a & b), Japan (Serizdwa and Ikawa 1960), and China at Tingstun and in the Fenho complex in Shansi and Honan province (Chang, K.C.

1960) and previously known Patjitanian handaxes in Indonesia (Koenigswald 1939 and Movius 1944. 1948) have proved that the last out-post of the Great Handaxe culture is not south India but far beyond. The handaxes in Java were already known in 1936. It was also recognised that they were so similar to handaxes found in Penninsular India and in Africa that if they would have been found in that part of the world, they would have been taken as handaxes in true Acheulian tradition without any hesitation. But to give an aura of creditability and authenticity to the theory of two separate, independently evolving cultural traditions, the true nature of these tools were contested and the inconvenient fact of the existence of true handaxes in the supposed Chopper–Chopping tool zone was explained away as a local development in Java. They could not be derived from India because Burma with Anyathian Chopper-Chopping tools and hand-adzes came in the way while no question arose of its being derived from the farther east from China and Japan because no handaxes were found there at that time. The author is fully convinced that Patjitanian handaxes are true handaxes. Bordes (1968 : 82) has also expressed a similar opinion.

4.9 The author had an opportunity to examine the Burmese palaeoliths of Early Anythian from Upper Burma at the Peabody Museum in the University of Harvard and at the University Museum at Philadelphia in 1970. He found many incipient handaxes in that material. Movius has infact described a specimen (Movius 1943, p. 359. Fig. 58, No. 8) which he called Pointed double sided Chopper which if flaked on the lower surface would have been classified as a handaxe.

4.10 In north-western Malaya also, the Tampanian Lower Palaeolithic Industry has tools which Mrs. Ann Sieveking (1962, p. 65) calls 'Points'. These are infact handaxes though Ann Sieveking does not admit that. In Movius terminology these Tampanian points will be called Proto-handaxes. In any case, It is very clear that in Malaysia also, there are handaxes and the Lower Palaeolithic is very similar to that of Java from Patjitan (Bordes 1968, P. 69).

4.11 At Olduvai Gorge in Tanzania, the excavations conducted in Beds I and II during 1960-63 by M.D. Leakey has demonstrated that Choppers, pebble tools, etc, form only one element of the tool-kit of the Oldowan. They are of course in majority but cannot be considered alone (M.D. Leakey 1972). Bifaces also from a part of the tool kit even at Oldowan level.

4.12 The recent techniques in prehistory of obtaining the over-all picture from the total assemblage by excavating sealed deposits and living floors is a clear advance from the methods practiced in 1940s. To find out the different elements constituting the tool-kit of the early Man at a particular time-level and abolishing the practice of making out a particular tool as an all important index fossil to the exclusion of the predominant element of an industry was responsible for revising the eleven stages Chelles-Acheul succession in Olduvai Gorge as develoed by Leakey (Leakey, L.S.B. 1951).

4.13 Recently, it has been demonstrated (Bordes 1972 : 315) that there is no relationship between physical characteristics of Man and an Industry or a culture. It is considered futile to seek identity between biological and cultural evolution. In Europe the Neanderthal man and Mousterian culture went together but the recent work at Qafzeh has shown that Mousterian artefacts are the work of 'modern' man. Similarly, to assign particular racial group for Handaxes or Chopper-Chopping tools will be considered wrong in the light of modern thinking.

5. SUMMING UP

5.1 It has been clearly and convincingly demonstrated in the foregoing pages that the two-culture theory of Handaxe and Chopper-Chopping tools, having distinct indentity, is a fallacy which has been perpetuated rather too long in Asian prehistory. When the Breuil's two phyla theory has no place in modern European prehistory then by what stretch of imagination its mirror image which the Movius theory is, can remain valid. The work done in Asia since the fifties of the present century have demolished the two separate zones which handaxes and Chopper-Chopping tools were supposed to have according to Movius. The handaxes found in Vietnam, Japan, China and in Java of course, have established that peninsular India was not the last out-post of the Great handaxe culture. Moreover the recent methods and concepts being developed in prehistory in Africa and Europe make it necessary to revise our old conclusions and look critically at theories which have become almost sacrosanct. It has been shown satisfactorily that handaxes and Chopping tools are not genetically separate but are part of the same culture. The handaxe has rather developed from the chopping tool as demostrated at Mahadev-Piparia in the Narmada valley in Central India.

Alimen, M.H. and Chavaillon, J. 1962 Position stratigraphique et evolution de La Pebble Culture an Sahara nord-occidental, in *Actes du IVe Congress Panefricain de Prehistoire et de l' Etude Quaternaire* (ed. G. Mortelamans and J. Neguin) 3:3-26

Bailloud G. 1965 'Les gisements paleolithiques de Melka Kontoure, Addis Ababa, *Cahiers de L' Institut Ethiopien d' Archeologie*, vol. 1

Bonnet, Andre' 1961 La Pebble Culture' in *situ* de l' Idjerane et les terrasses de piedmont du Sahara Central. *Bull. Soc. Prehist* France 48 (1-2) : 51-61

Bordes, F. 1968 *The Old Stone Age*. World Univ. Library

1972 *The Origin of Homo Sapiens:* Proceedings of the Paris Symposium 2-5 September 1 9 6 9, UNESCO, Paris, Ecology and Conservation Series 3 : 1-321.

Boriskovsky, P.I. 1962a Exploration of ancient sites of the stone age in the Democractic Republic of Vietnam. *Soviet Archaeology*, Moscow (U.S.S.R. Academy of Sciences) 2 : 17-25

1972b Archaeological discoveries in Vietnam, *Herald of the Academy of Science of U S.S.R.* Moscow 4 : 98-101

Breuil, H. 1912 "Les, subdivisions du Paleolithique Superieur. etlur signification *Compt. rend. du Congres International d Archaeologie Prehistorique*, 14th Session, Geneva 2nd. ed. Lagny. E. Grevin.

1939 The Pleistocene succession in the Somme Valley. *Proceedings of the Prehistoric Society*, n.s. *5* : *33-38*.

Breuil, H and Koslowski, L. 1931 Etudes de Stratigraphic Paleolithique dans le Nord de la France, La, Belgigue et 18 Angleterre, Anthropologic XLI : 449-88

1932 Ibid. XLII : 27-47, 291-314

1934 Ibid. XLIV : 249-90

Breuil, H, and Lantier, R. 1951 *Les Homme de la Pierre Ancienne (Paleolithique et Mesolithique)* paris: payot.

Butzer K.W., Issac G.L. et al 1972 Radiocarbon Dating of East African Lake Levels. *Science* 175 : 1069-1076

Chang. Kwang Chih 1960 New Light on Early Man in China, *Asian Perspectives* 2 (2) : 41-62

Chavaillon J. 1967 La Prehistoric Ethiopienne a Melka Kontoure, *Archeologia* 19 : 56-63

Chavaillon J and Taib, M. 1968 Stratigraphie du Quaternaire de Melka Kontoure (Valle de l'Aouache, Ethopie): Premiers resultants, *C.R. Acad.* Sci : 266-1210-12.

Clark, J.D. 1962 The Problem of the Pebble Culture. *Atti Del Vi Congresso Internationale Delle Scienze Preistoriche E Protohistoriche I Relazioni Generali*, 1 : 265-71

Dani A.H. 1966 Prehistoric Pakistan : Studies in *Prehistory*, Bruce Foote Memorial Volume. Calcutta. 71-76

De Terra H and Paterson T.T. 1939 *Studies on the Ice Age in India and associated Human cultures*. Carnegie Institute of Washington 493 : 1-354 Washington.

1943 Research on Early Man in Burma *Trans : Amer. Phil. Soc.* Philadelphia, 32 (3) ; 265-464

Flint, R F. 1963 Pleistocene Climates in low latitudes. *The Geographical Review* 43 (1) : 123-129.

Garrod. D.A.E. 1966 A Pebble Industry of Early Wurm Age from Abri Zumoffen, South Labanon. *Studies in Prehistory* Bruce Foote Memorial Volume, Calcutta 41-48.

Graziosi, P. 1964 *Prehistoric Research in Northwestern Punjab*. Scientific Report, Halian Expeditions to the Karakorum (k²) and Hindukush. (Prehistory – Antrhropology 1 : 1-52, P.1.95, Leiden)

Heekeren H.R. Van 1955 New Investigations on the lower Paleolithic Patjitan Culture in Java. *Bull. Arch. Service of the Republic of Indonesia* 1 : 1-12

1957 *The stone age of Indonesia.*

1960 The Tjabenge Flake Industry from South Celebes. *Asian Perspectives* 2 (2): 77-82

Heider K.G. 1960 A Pebble Tool Complex in Thailand. *Asian Perspectives* 2 (2) : 63-67

Issac G.L., Leakey R.E.F. et al 1971 Archaeological Traces of Early Hominid Activities, East of Lake Rudolf, Kenya. *Science* 173 : 1129-1134

Khatri A.P. 1957 Paleolithic industry of River Shivna, *Bull. Deccan College Post Graduate Research Institute,* Taraporewala Volume 18 : 160-169

1958 The Stone Age cultures of Malwa (Central India) a Ph. D thesis, Poona University.

1958 The Stone Age Tools of the Gambhiri Basin (Rajasthan). *Bombay University Journal*; 26 (4) : 35-49

1960 Exploration for the Remains of Early man in India, *Proceedings of the Indian Science Congress.* Roorki (48th Session)

1961 Stone Age and Pleistocene chronology in the Narmada basin (M.P.) *Anthropos* 57 (3-4) : 519-530

1962 Origin and Development of Series II Culture in India, *Proceedings Prehistoric Society of Great Britain* 28 : 191-208

1963 a A Century in Prehistoric Research in India. *Asian Prespectives 6* (1-2) : 169-185

1963 b 'Mahadevian' : An Oldowan Pebble Culture of India. *Asian Prerspectives* 6 (1-2): 163-169

1963 c Prehistoric Cultures of Malwa (Central India). *Anthropos* 58: 458-506

1963 d Recent Exploration for the Remains of Early Man in India. *Asian Perspectives,* VIII (1-2) : 160-82

1966 a The Pleistocene Mammalian Fossils of the Narmada River Valley and Their Horizons. *Asian Perspectives* 9 : 113-133

1966 b Origin and Evolution of Hand Axe Culture in the Narmada Valley (Central India) in *studies in Prehistory*. Robert Bruce Foote Memorial Volume, Calcutta. 96-121.

1975 The Early Fossil Hominids and Related Apes of the Siwalik Foot-hills of the Himalayas : Recent Discoveries and New Interpretation. *Palaeo anthropology, Morphology and Palaeoecology* (ed. Russel H, Tultle) : Mouton Publishers, The Hague, Paris : 31-58

Koenigswald, G. H. R. Von. 1936 Early Palaeolithic Stone Implements from Java. *Bull. Raffles Museum* 1 : 52-60

1949 The discovery of Early Man in Java and Southern China. *Studies in Phys. Anthrop.* No. 1 Early Man in the Far East. Amer. Assn. Phys. Anthrop. 83-101

1956 *Meeting the Prehistoric Man*. Thames and Hudson. London.

1960 Preliminary Report on a Newly discovered Stone Age Culture from Northern Luzon. Philippines. *Asian Perspectives*. 2 (2) : 69-70

Kretzoi M, and Vertes, L. 1965 Upper Biharian Pebble Industry Occuptation Site in Hungary *Current Anthropology* 6 : 74-87

Krishnaswami, V. D. 1947 Stone Age India, *Ancient India* 3: 11-49

1953 Progress in Prehistory, *Ancient India* Special Jubilee Number 9 : 53-79

Krishnaswami, V. D. Soundara Rajan, K. V. 1951 The lithic tool Industries of the Singrauli basin. *Ancient India* 12 : 58-93

Lal, B.B. 1956 Palaeoliths from the Beas and Banganga Valleys, Punjab. *Ancient India* 12 : 58-92

Leakey, L. S. B. 1951 *Olduvai Gorge*. Cambridge University Press.

1953 *Adam's Ancestor*, 4th Edition, London

1961 *Progress and evolution of Man in Africa* London

Leakey, M. D. 1966 A review of the Oldowan Culture from Olduvai Gorge, Tanzania. *Nature*, London 210 : 462-6

1966 Primitive artifacts from the Kanapoi Valley. *Nature*, London 212 : 579-81

1967 Preliminary Survey of the Cultural material from Bed I and II, Olduvai Gorge, Tanzania. In Background to Evolution in Africa (ed. W.W. Bishop and J. D. Clark : 417-446. Chicago University

1970 Early artefacts from the Koobi Fora Area. *Nature*, London 226 : 1228-30

1970 Stone artefacts from Swartkrans *Nature*. London 225 : 1222 - 25

1971 *Olduvai Gorge : Excavations in Beds I and II, 1960 - 63* Cambridge Univ. Press, London.

Mohapatra, G. C. 1966 Preliminary Report of the Exploration and Excavation of Stone Age Sites in Eastern Punjab. *Bulletin Deccan College Research Institute*, Poona 25 : 221-237

Movius H. L. Jr. 1943 The Stone Age of Burma. *Trans. Amer. Phil. Soc.* 32 : 341-439

1944 *Early Man and Pleistocene Stratigraphy in Southern and Eastern Asia*. Papers Peabody Museum, Harvard Univ. *19* : 1-125

1948 The Lower Palaeolithic Cultures of Southern and Eastern Asia. *Trans. Amer. Phil. Soc. 38* : 329-420

1949 *Lower Palaeolithic Archaeology* in *Southern Asia and the Far East* Amer. Assoc. Phys. Anthr. 17-81

1955 Palaeolithic Archaeology in Southern and Eastern Asia, exclusive of *India Journal of World Prehistory* 257-82; 520-53

1956 New Palaeolithic sites near Ting-Tsun in the Fen river, Shansi Province, North China, *Quaterneria*, 111

1957 Pebble tool terminology in India and Pakistan. *Man in India*. 37 (2) : 149-156

1960 Introduction to *Asain Perspectives*. Special Palaeolithic Issue. Hong Kong *2* : (2) : xi-xiv

1962 Old World Prehistory: Palaeolithic in *Anthropology Today* Ed. Sol. Tax 122-151

1967 Review of P. Graziosi book *Prehistoric Research in Northwestern Punjab* in *Asian Perspective* 10 : 167-168

Paterson, T. T. 1962 *Soan. The Palaeolithic of Pakistan* Memoir, Department of Archaeology in Pakistan 2 : 1–172

Prufer, O. 1956 The Prehistory of the Sirsa Valley, Punjab, *India Quarterly* 7/8 : 91-123

Sankalia, H. D. 1957 Is the Soan a Flake Industry ? *Jour. Asia. Soc. Bengal. 22* (2) : 161-162

Sen, D. 1954 Lower Palaeolithic Cultures Complex and Chronology in India. Presidential Address Section of Anthropology and Archaeology. *Proceeding* Indian Science Congress (41st Session) Hyderabad -1-19.

1955 Nalagarh Palaeolithic Culture *Man in India 35* (3) : 176-84

1957 The Soanian and the Pebble tool complex in India. *Man in India* 37 (2)

1969 Pebble Chopper-Chopping tools and Flakes in India and Pakistan; a review in the light of recent finds in Europe and Asia. *Anthropology and Archaeology*. Essay in commemoration of Verrier Elwin Ed. Pradhan, M. C. *et al.* 287-295

Serizdwa, C. and Fumiko 1960 The oldest Archaeological Materials from Japan. *Asian Perspectives* 2 (2) : 1-40

Sieveking A. 1960 The Palaeolithic Industry of Kota Tempan, Peralk, North-western M a l a y a. *Asian Perspectives* 2 (2) : 91-102

Simons, E. L. 1961 The Phyletic position o f Ramapithecus. *Postilla 57* : 1-9

1964 On the Mandible of Ramapithecus. *Proceedings National Acadamy of Sciences* 51 (3) : 528-535

Solheim, W. G. 1960 The Present status of the Palaeolithic in Borneo. *Asian Perspectives* 2: (2): 83-90

1962 Regional Report on Southeast Asia Section on Vietnam, *Asian Perspecitves* 6 (1-2)/23-32

Soundara Rajan, K. V. 1965 Is 'Soan' A Separate Culture' ? in Indian *Prehistory* Proceedings of the symposium held in Poona in 1964, 1-14

Te-Kun; Cheng 1959 *Prehistoric China*. Archaeology i n China Vol. 1 Cambridge, W. Heffer and Sons

1966 *New Light on Prehistoric China* (Supplement to Vol. 1 of Archaeology in China, Cambridge and Tornto.

Tweedie, M.W.F. 1942 Prehistory in Malaya, *Jour. Royal. Asiatic Soc*. 1-13.

1953 The stone age in Malaya, *Jour. Royal Asiatic Soc* 26 : 1-90

1955 *Prehistoric Malaya :* Background to Malaya Series *6*. 1-43

Vertes, L. 1964 Neuere Ausgrabungen and palaolithische Flunde in der Hohle Von Istallosko'. *Acta archaeologica,* Budapest

1964 'Tata' *Archaeologica humgarica.* Budapest.

Jamalpur : A Typological Variant Within the Middle Palaeolithic Culture-complex of India

P. C. Pant & Vidula Jayaswal

Lecturers in Archaeology
Banaras Hindu University, Varanasi (India)

(Recevied on 16 May, 1976)

1. INTRODUCTION

OWING to its unique techno-typological features the industry of Jamalpur can legitimately claim to represent an important variant within the Middle Palaeolithic culture complex of the Indo-Pakistan sub-continent. Since long, prehistorians have been thinking in terms of techno-typological and regional variations within the Middle Palaeolithic phase (Sankalia 1965), and a few genuine attempts have also been made in this direction (Rao 1968-69 ; also Jayaswal 1974). Even a cursory examination of the Jamalpur tool-kit brings out the uniqueness of this industry. It is a collection from the surface, made by the authors during two hurried visits to the site in the years 1968 and 1972. Nevertheless, its extraordinary techno-typological traits prompted us to write on this industry, without waiting for a detailed investigation of the site, which we very much wish to undertake in near future.

1.2 The town of Jamalpur (District Monghyr, Bihar) is situated on the Patna-Howrah railway. The palaeolithic site of this place is on a flat top of a small hill, locally known as *Kalipahar*, about one kilometre to the east of the Jamalpur Railway Station from where it is easily approachable (Fig. 1). The hill is familiar to the local population for a small shrine of the Goddess Kali which apparently gives it its name.

1.3 The topography of the area is a mixture of alluvial plain, laid by the river Ganga about 11 km to the north of Jamalpur, and the south-eastern hilly tract, an extension of the Kharagpur range, which itself is an outcrop of the Chotanagpur plateau. Geologically, this hill consists of the Dharwar formation of the Archean system. The basic rock is schist, which at times is interrupted by the dykes of other rocks. The dykes of quartzite provided the source material to the palaeolithic occupants of Jamalpur for tool fabrication.

1.4 The morphology of the *Kalipahar* hill top is very simple. There is a small range of comparatively higher hills on the east and north-east, while the western and south-western part is in the form of a flat pain, which is occasionally disturbed by erosional activities of the rain water. The flat surface of the hill top has a slow gradient from the north-east to the south-west. Only a few metres south of Kali shrine there is a tank which gets its supply from the rain water. It is the only source of water at the hill top. There is another tank at the eastern foot of the hill.

1.5 The potentiality of this place being a prehistoric habitat was recognized as early as 1926 by the Brahmcharis, when two neolithic celts were obtained during an excavation of a tank at Jamalpur (Brahmchari, U. N. and S C. 1929). Nearly four decades later, R.C.P. Singh made a small collection of palaeoliths from *Kalipahar (Indian Archaeology 1960-61—A Review pp.* 5-6). In 1961, L. N. Singh of the Banaras Hindu University brought a small collection from the same locality (*Indian Archaeology 1961-62—A Reveiw*) and showed it to one of the authors. Taking clues from

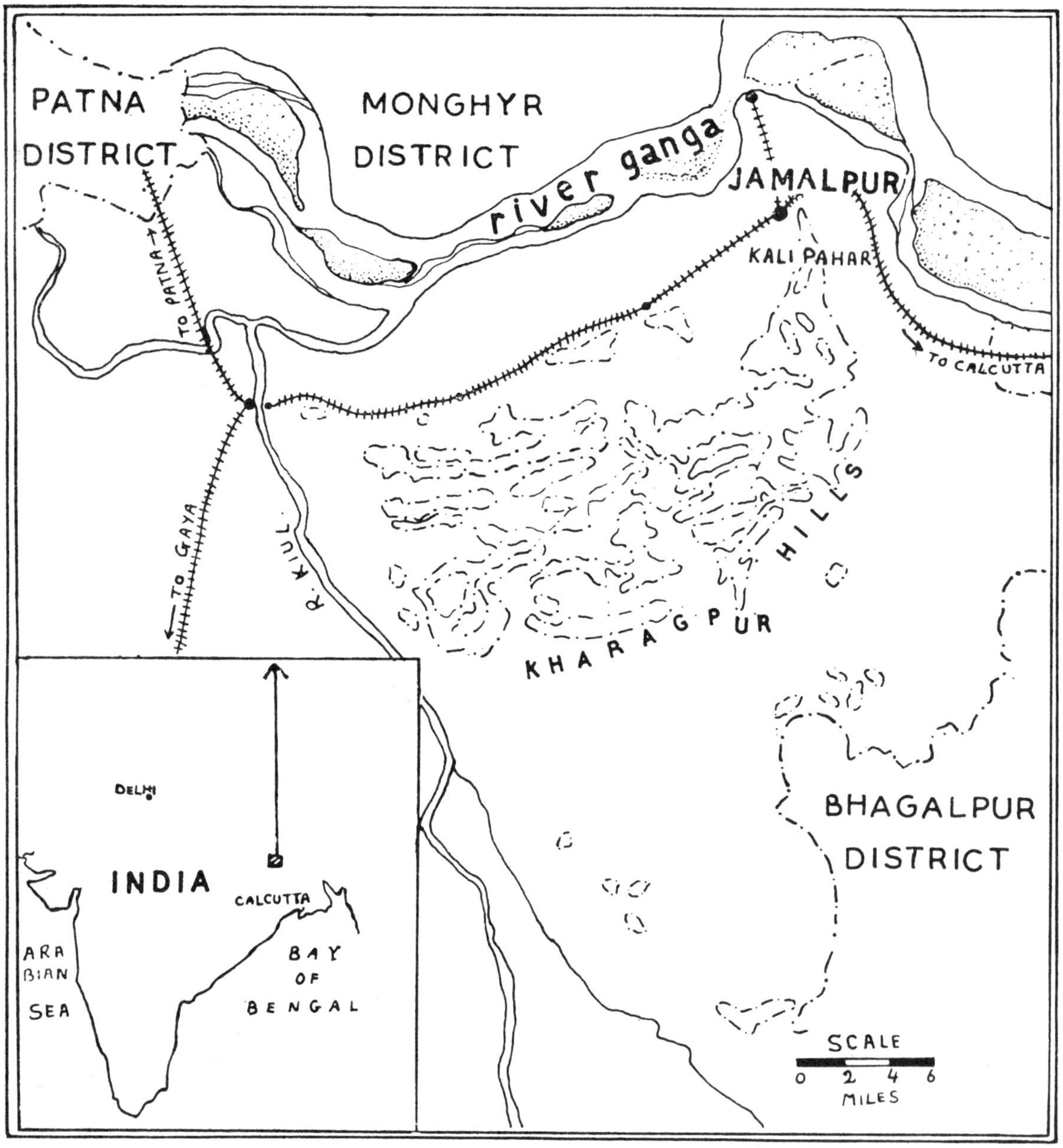

FIG. 1

these discoveries the present authors visited the site in 1968. During this short visit only a limited area of this extensive site was explored, from where a large number of artefacts were picked up. The importance of the site was immediately impressed upon us, but even our second visit in 1972 was only for a very short period. A detailed study of the area is still awaited.

1.6. The artefacts occur in two different modes at this site. Firstly, there are small tools of fine grained quartzite of darker shades, which appear on the surface of the plain in the form of big clusters. Such clusters are so rich that almost every piece of quartzite is an artefact. Majority of them is also retouched. Secondly, there are a few bigger artefacts, which occur around the shrubs of the uplands of the plain, nearby slopes and the bed of the rain-gullies. These are also made of quartzite, but in most of the cases the stone is rough and light yellow in colour. Apparently, they look like two different groups of tools. Considering the fact, however, that there is no stratigraphical confirmation of this division and even the techno-typological distinctions between the two are too small to be pushed very far, the two groups have been dealt here as a single industry.

1.7 With a view to understanding the nature of the tool clusters, a very small trench, measuring 2 X 1 m was dug at one such place during our first visit. The deposit, composed of the soils formed by the disintegration of rocks, hardly exceeded 1 m but it yielded as many as thirty-two artefacts, which are techno-typologically similar to the smaller tools of the area. It was observed that the artefacts are found within a radius of about two hundred metres from the tank of the flat hill top. This indicates that the tank, which is the only source of water here, probably also served the needs of the palaeolithic man.

2. `TYPOLOGY

2.1 As mentioned in the opening paragraph the industry of Jamalpur distinguishes itself from the other Middle Palaeolithic industries of the sub-continent on account of it's unique typological characteristics. Broadly the industry may be divided into the following :

TABLE 1

S. No.	Artefact type	No.	Percentage
1.	Finished tool	607	84.28
2.	Unretouched blank	31	4.29
3.	Core	76	10.54
4.	Undetermined	7	0.97
	Total	721	99.80

2.2 The first three among them deserve detailed treatment. The term 'undetermined' includes those artefacts, which, due to their irregular shape and working, do not form any particular type. It may be noted that this term is quite different from 'diverse' used by Bordes (1961 ; 43). By using the term undetermind we wish to express our disagreement with Bordes who thinks that those tool-types which are scarce in an industry should not find a place in its typological table and should be placed under the head 'diverse'. The finished tools are of following types :

TABLE 2

Sl. No.	Tool-types	Nos	Percentage
1.	Chopper	8	1 32
2.	Chopping tool	2	0 33
3.	Handaxe	16	2.64
4.	Jamalpur axe	20	3.29
5.	Jamalpur knife type A	20	3.29
6.	Jamalpur kinfe type B	16	2.64
7.	Jamalpur knife type C	12	1.94
8.	Knife	24	3.95
9.	End scraper with tip	8	1.32
10.	End scraper with retouched sides.	43	7.08
11.	End scraper	25	4.11
12.	Gratoir eventail	1	0.16
13.	Gratoir unguiforme	2	0.33
14.	Keeled scraper	1	0.16
15.	Middle burin	24	3.95
16.	Middle gouge burin	1	0.16
17.	Side burin	8	1.32
18.	Transversal burin	5	0.82
19.	Beaked burin	2	0.33
20.	Double burin	2	0.33
21.	Pseudo burin ('de siret')*	3	0.50
22.	Alternate beaked burin	13	2.14
23.	Notched tool	22	3.62
24.	Denticulate	29	4.78
25.	Convex side scraper	25	4.11
26.	Straight side scraper	19	3.13
27.	Concave side scraper	7	1.15
28.	Side scraper with zig-zag edge	28	4.62
29.	Transverse scraper	18	2.97
30.	Angle scraper	12	1.98
31.	Double side scraper	54	8.90
32.	Convergent scraper	7	1.15
33.	Flake with chopped off top and retouched corners	18	2.64
34.	Raclette	4	0.66
35.	Point	3	0.50
36.	Borer	3	0.50
37.	Awl	2	0.33
38.	Tranchet	8	1.32
39.	Thumb nail scraper	1	0.16
40.	Chisel edged tool	1	0.16
41.	Flake with retouched top	7	1.15
42.	Partially retouched flake	77	12.68
43.	Partially retouched blade	8	1.32
	Grand total	607	99.88

*Though a result of accidental flaking, pseudo burin has been intentionally included in this table of finished tools with a view to emphasising its occurrence in Jamalpur industry. To the best of our knowledge, it has not been noticed so far in any of the palaeolithic industries of India

2.3 It may be noted that the above table includes some new types. Besides, there are some other types which have hardly been noticed in the palaeolithic industries of India. They need to be explained in some detail.

2.4 *Jamalpur axe* (No. 4). This tool is invariably made on a flake detached from a prepared core. The working edge is generally formed by the intersection of a transversal preparation scar on the core. A typical Jamalpur axe contains a few half negative-scars on the dorsal surface and thorough working from the sides towards the centre on the ventral surface. The working end may or may not be retouched, and the bold working of the ventral surface is always confined to the lower portion. The working edge is narrow as well as broad. The type resembles to some extent with the axe made on flake found in the Maglamosian culture of North Europe (Clark 1936). Both typical and atypical (3) forms are present in the industry.

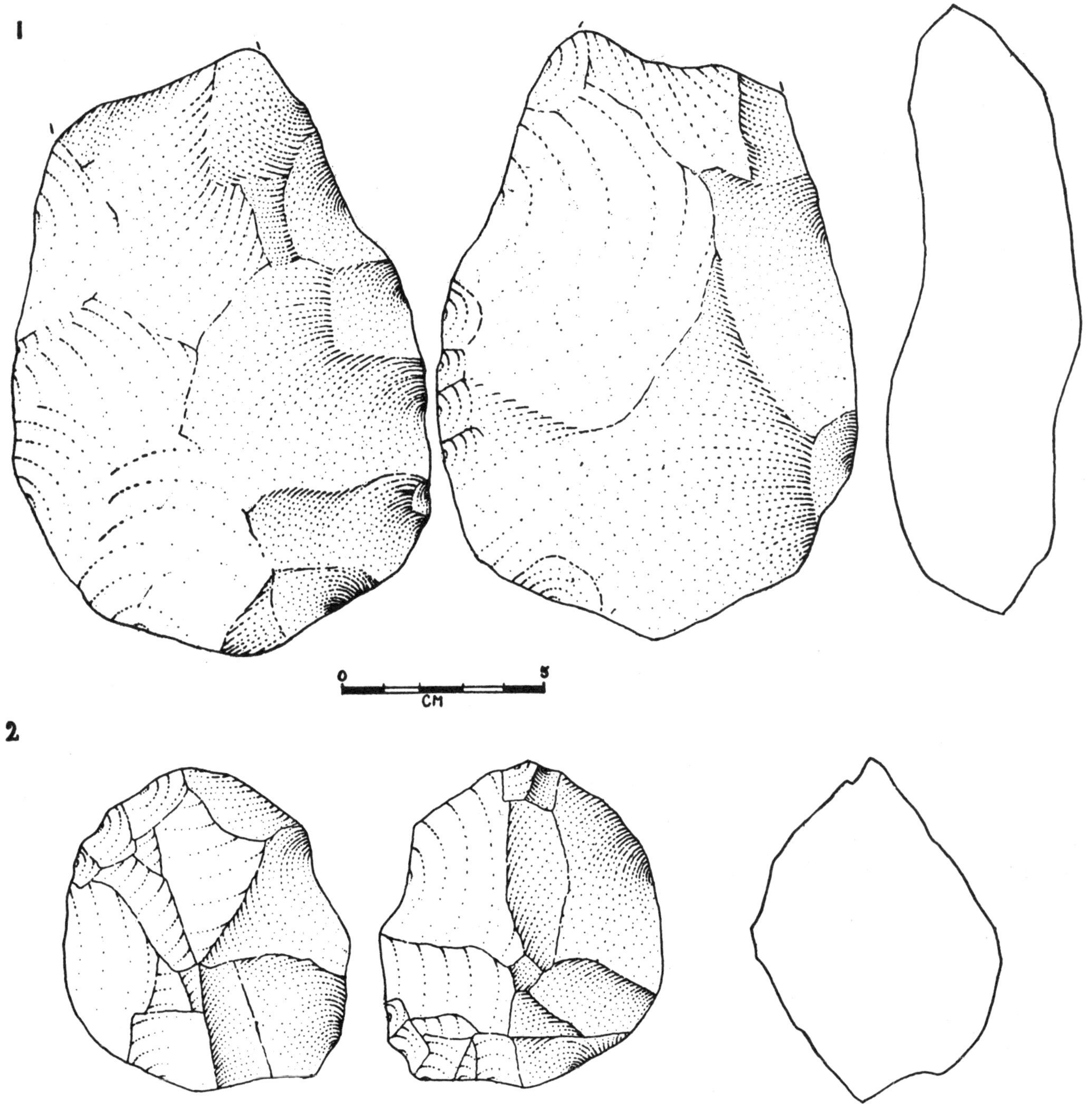

FIG. 2. 1, Handaxe ; and 2, Mousterian core

2.5 *Jamalpur knife* (Nos. 5-7). This tool has not been reported so far from any of the palaeolithic industries of India. Hence the name Jamalpur knife. It differs from a simple knife on account of it's unusual blunting on the back. While the blunted side of an ordinary knife is invariably convex with almost perpendicular retouch all through the side, in the case of a Jamalpur knife it is either blunted on the upper part of the side, which is generally oblique, or it is thick on account of an intentional breakage and peculiar position of the core preparation scars on the flake.

Three different types of this tool have been recognized on the basis of the mode of blunting the back.

2.6 *Type A*—It is a Levallois or a prepared non-Levallois flake or a blade with obliquely blunted upper part of a side. This abrupt retouch covers nearly half or more of the side, which shows a mild carination due to it's obliqueness. The other side is generally unifacially retouched, but the specimens having bifacial and alternate retouching are also not wanting. This side does not show any uniformity. It is convexo-concave, straighto-convex, straight or denticulate.

2.7 A few specimens are also end scraper (1), double burin (1), denticulate (1), and with retouched base (3). Five out of twenty are atypical.

2.8 *Type B*—In this case one of the sides has been thickend, presumably by intentional breaking of the flake. One of the specimens is made on a flattish nodule. The retouch on the working side is usually unifacial in this case also. At times it is bifacial (2), bold (1), alternate (1), or partly from dorsal and partly from ventral (2). The side is either convex (8), straight (4), or denticulate (4). Some of the tools of this type are also end scraper, (2), denticulate (3) and notched at the base (5). Two specimens are atypical.

2.9 *Type C*—In the case of this type the side has not been thickened by any secondary working. It is thick as a primary preparation of the core, continuation of the prepared striking platform up to the side or cortex. The other side is either unifacial or alternately retouched. This side is mostly convex (seven out of twelve), but concave (1), concavexo-concave (1) and denticulated examples are also there. One tool of this type is also a borer and five others are denticulates.

2.10 *Ogival end scraper/end scraper with a tip* (No. 9). To the best of our knowledge this tool type is peculiar to the Jamalpur industry in India, although it has been noticed in some palaeolithic industries of Europe (Bosinski & Hahn 1973). It is made on elongated Levallois flakes (7) or a prepared non-Levallois flake. The end scraper type retouch appears mostly on distal end (6) but occasionally on the proximal (2) as well, resulting in a convex working end with a slight carination or a diffused tip in the middle. Since this feature appears on as many as eight specimens, it may be regarded intentional.

2.11 *End scraper with retouched sides and pointed base (Gratoir eventail or Pfannenkratzer)* (No. 12) This is a short and broad end scraper made on a flake or blade. The other end, lying just opposite scraper end, is pointed and both the sides are retouched. The convex scraper end is rather unusually broad and is at times termed as 'fan shaped'. There is only one speciman of this type in our collection.

2.12 *End scraper with pointed base (Gratoir Unquiforme* No. 13). There are two specimens of this type which differ from Gratoir ewential on acconnt of its unretouched sides.

2.13 *Pseudo-burin or 'de siret'* (No. 21). The term 'de siret' is generally applied to the specimens which are in fact result of accidental flaking. According to Bordes, it happens sometimes that during the removal of a flake two perpendicular planes of flaking are produced. The second separates the flake in the two more or less equal parts. The burin point in this case is formed by the intersection of the perpendicular fracture at the normal flaking planes (Bordes 1961 : 32).

2.14 *Alternate beaked burin* (No. 22). Made on a flake or blade this type has an oblique burin edge formed by the intersection of two inversaly retouched notches. In other words, the working on these notches is alternate one being worked from the dorsal, and the other from the ventral surface, and a small burin edge is formed at the meeting point of the two. This tool type was previously classified by Bordes as 'alternate burinated point' (Bordes 1961 : 37). Alternate beaked burin of Bordes was called 'Burinscisean' by Terrade (1912).

2.15 The twelve specimens of the type in the Jamalpur industry reveal four sub-types, *i.e.* atypical (4), with retouched base (2), with retouched sides (2), and simple alternate burin (4). The working in the case of atypical ones is unifacial and not alternate.

2.16 *Notched tool* (No. 23). Notched tool, as the name suggests, has one or more intentionally made notches on one or more sides. Bordes recognized three types of notches among the Mousterian industries of Western Europe. They are true notches, Clactonian notches and those formed as a result of utilization (Bordes 1961 35).

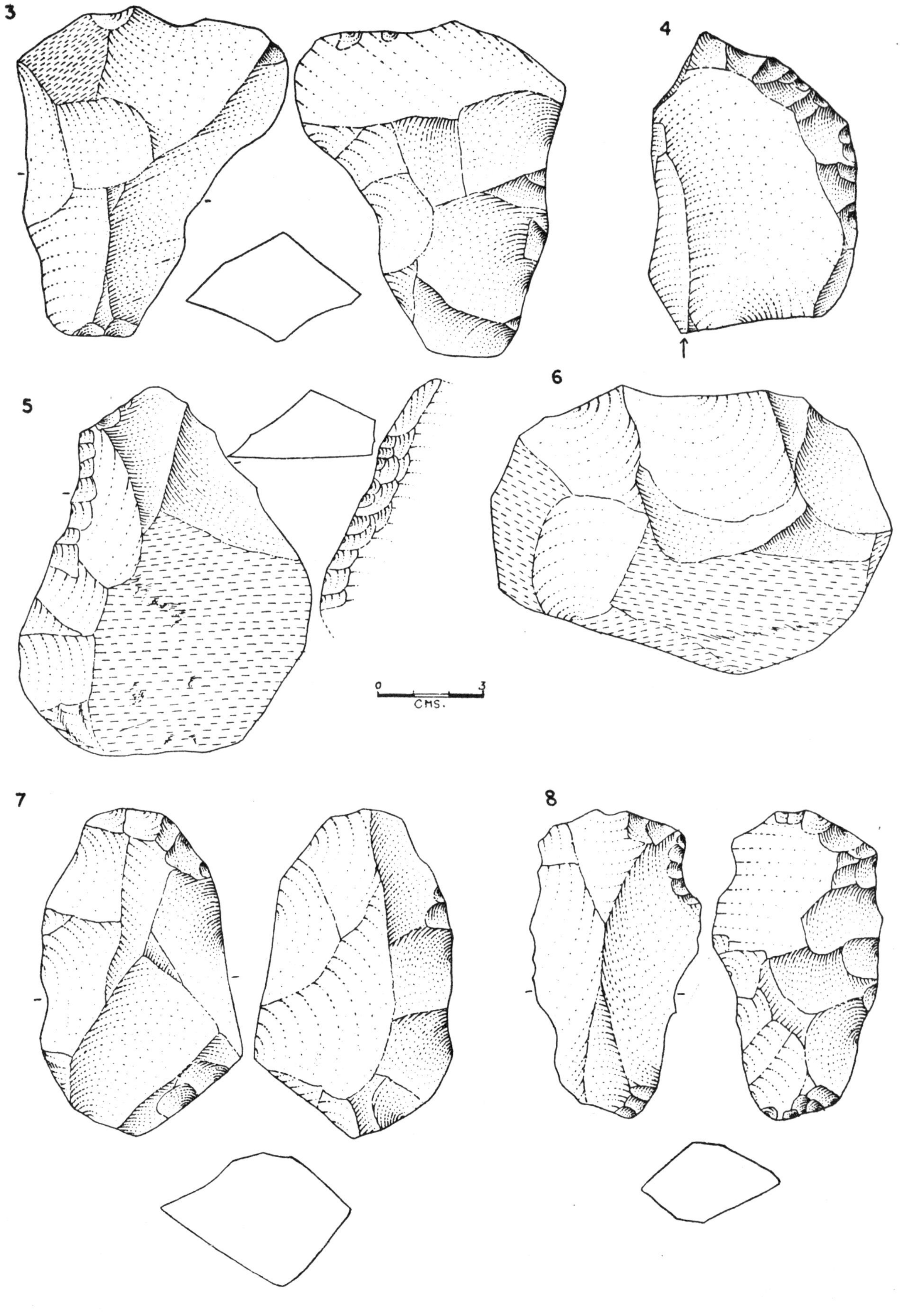

FIG. 3. 3, Jamalpur axe 4, convex side scraper on a care rest ; 5, knife ; 6, chopping tool ; 7, handaxe ; and 8, Jamalpur axe type C.

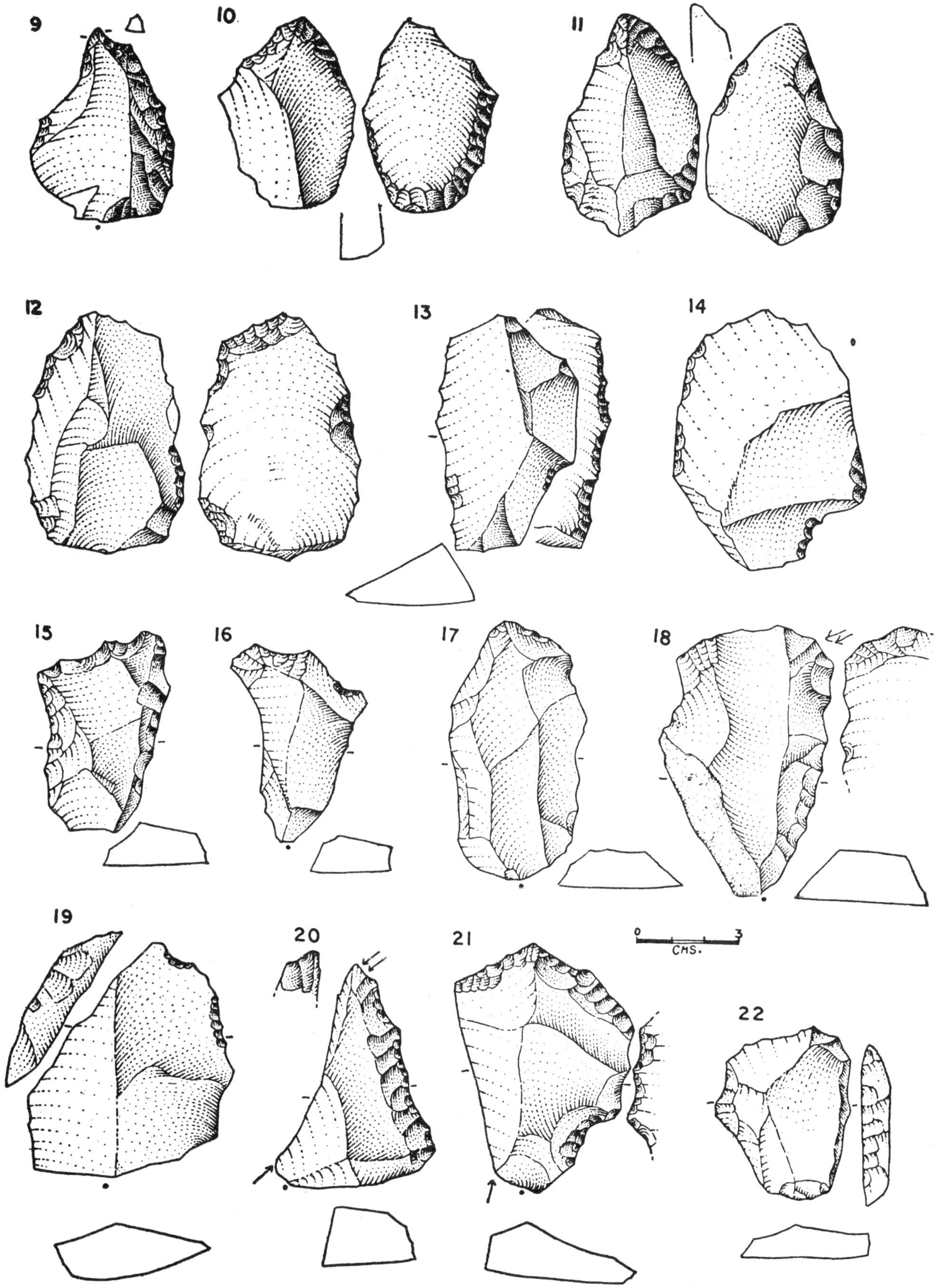

FIG. 4. 9, Borer on Levallois point ; 10-11, end scrapers ; 12, double side scraper with retouched top ; 13, knife ; 14, Jamalpur knife atypical ; 15, tranchet ; 16, tranchet atypical ; 17, Levallois blade ; 18, burin ; 19, Jamalpur knife type A ; 20, knife with middle burin edge ; 21, end scraper with a tip ; and 22, end scraper with blunted side.

2.17 In our collection it is always a true notch formed by a carefull retouch. Invariably, the notch does not cover more then one third of the length of a side.

2.18 *Denticulate* (No. 24). These are tools made of flakes or blades, presenting on one or several margins a series of continuous notches produced either by small retouch or by large notches of Clactonian type (Bordes 1961 ; 36). Fifteen specimens of our collection correspond to the Bordes' sub-type (a) *i e.*, simple (11) or double denticulates (4). There are four transversal denticulates (sub-type B) which have retouched top (2) and base (1). Besides, we have also an extra sub-type in which all the eight specimens are retouched all along the edges. Most of the specimens are either alternately (13) or unifacially retouched (11). The examples of bold retouching (2), retouching partly from the dorsal surface and partly from the ventral (2) and those having unifacial retouching on the one and the alternate on the other (1), can also be observed. Serial number 28—side scraper with zig-zag-edge differs form the earlier two types on account of It's wavy edge, whice may be a result of either a few diffused notches on one or more sides or retouching partly from the ventral surface. In this case it may be noted that these notches are quite separated from each other and not continuous.

2.19 *Convergent scraper* (No. 32). These are double side scrapers, of which the two retouched sides converge normally at the distal and in an angle which is more than 50°. The sides are generally somewhat convex. Some of these are included in points by a few scholars (referred to by Bordes 1961 ; 27).

2.20 In all the seven specimens of our collecton, one side is retouched from the dorsal surface and the other from the ventral.

2.21 *Flake chopped off top and retouched corner* (No. 33). This is indeed a peculiar type which can be distinguished from other broken flakes only with some difficulty. The most important feature in this case is that the top of the flake has been at first intentionally chopped off and the two corners created by the breakage have been lightly retouched. Consequently the specimen obtains the shape of a rough square or short rectangle. In some cases, one (5) or both (3) sides are also retouched, and a few (5) are also denticulates. The retouch is mostly unifacial (10), but at times it is alternate (5), and in one case it is partially from the dorsal and partially from the ventral surface.

2.22 *Raclette* (No. 34). Raclette, according to Bordes, is a tool made generally on thin flakes, and rarely on blades and bladelets. The retouching is abrupt to very abrupt on one or more sides often alternately. They appear in Mousterian of the Acheulean tradition in France particularly (Bordes 1961 ; 37).

2.23 Two of the four specimens of Jamalpur industry are retouched on both the sides. The rest are either retouched on one side (1) or on the upper half portion of both the sides (1). The retouching is either unifacial, alternate, or half from the dorsal and half from the ventral surface. One specimen has an end scraper edge and is also a denticulate.

2.24 *Chisel-edged tool* (No. 40). It is a thick elongated type with a square cross-section. One of the ends is chisel-like.

3. TECHNIQUE

3.1 The dominant technique employed for detaching blanks is Levallois, followed by non-Levallois prepared core technique (proto-Levallois ?).[1] A few massive cores, prepared in Levallois, are of particular interest. In many cases, sides have been bifacially prepared and big flakes have been detached from both dorsal and ventral surfaces. Besides these, there is an appreciable number of flakes detached from unprepared and partially prepared cores. Those specimens which do not show any prior preparation may be the first few flakes taken off from the nodule or lump of stones. This supposition is supported by the fact that there is no corresponding core in the industry. However, there are six partially prepared cores, five of which bear a few preparation scars on their dorsal surface also. All the six have prepared striking platforms. In some cases, it was noted that thick flakes have been converted into flake or blade cores. It appears that there was some sort of shortage of proper raw material which is indicated by the presence of small thin core rests, core rejuvenating flakes and thick flakes converted into cores. Although the Jamalpurians were aquainted with the technique of manufacturing blades, as is evident from a few blades and blade-cores of the industry, yet they manufactured their tools mostly on flakes. Among the Levallois and non-Levallois prepared flakes a good number is broad. Almost all the flake types have been converted into various tool types. This means that no particular tool type is associated with any specific flake type, as evident from the table given below.

1 We found the term proto-Levallois rather ill-defined. Hence the term 'non-Levallois' prepared core technique has been preferred instead. Some of the blanks grouped under this category may be proto-Leavallois of others.

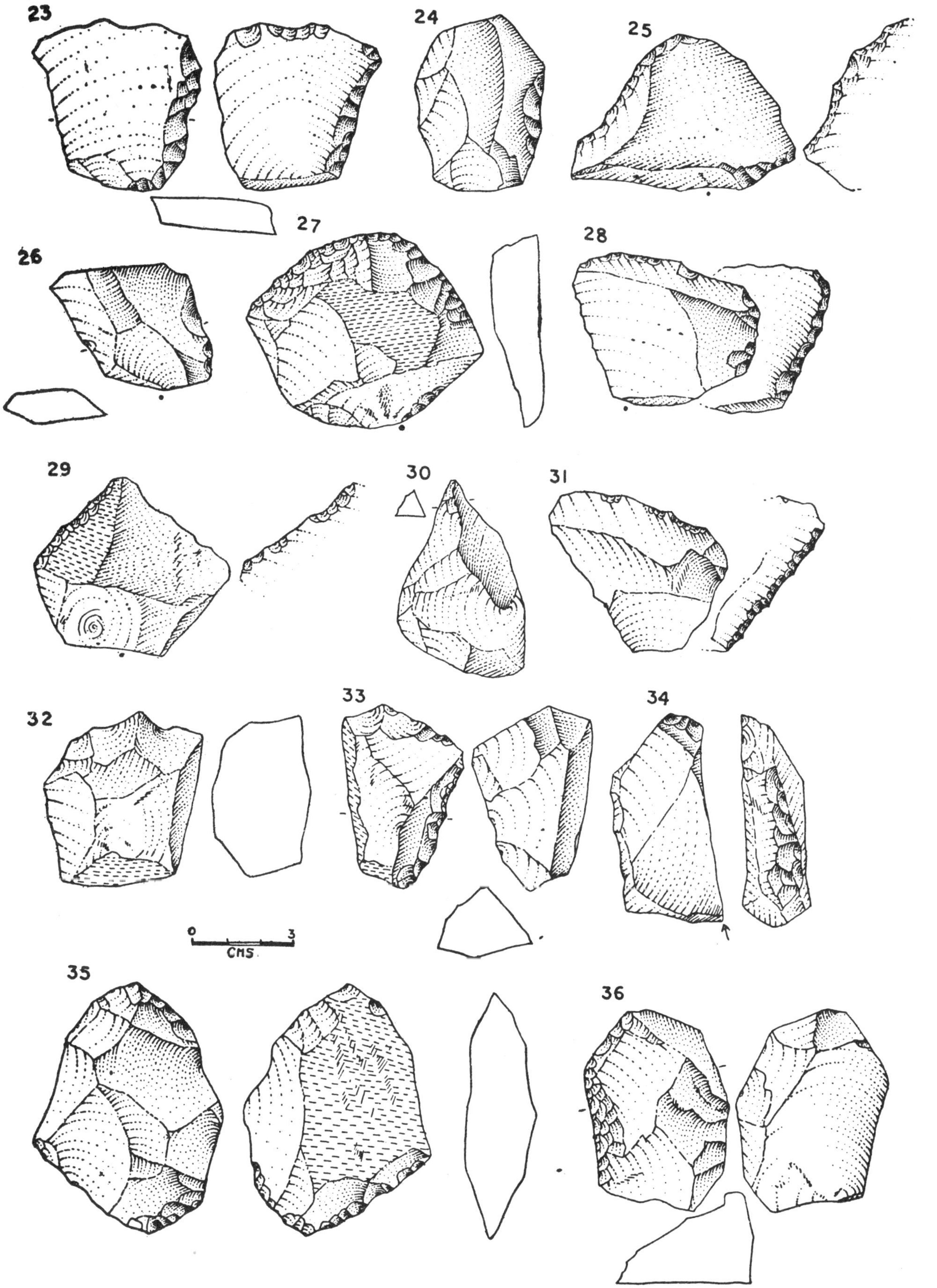

FIG. 5. 23, Tranchet ; 24, flake with retouched top and denticulated side ; 25, transversal scraper with denticulated edge ; 26. blade with chopped off top and retouched corners ; 27, transversal scraper ; 28, angle scraper with denticulated edge ; 29, convergent side scraper ; 30, awl ; 31, denticulated ; 32, small chopper ; 33, side scraper ; 34, side burin with blunted edge ; 35, Jamalpur axe ; and 36, side scraper.

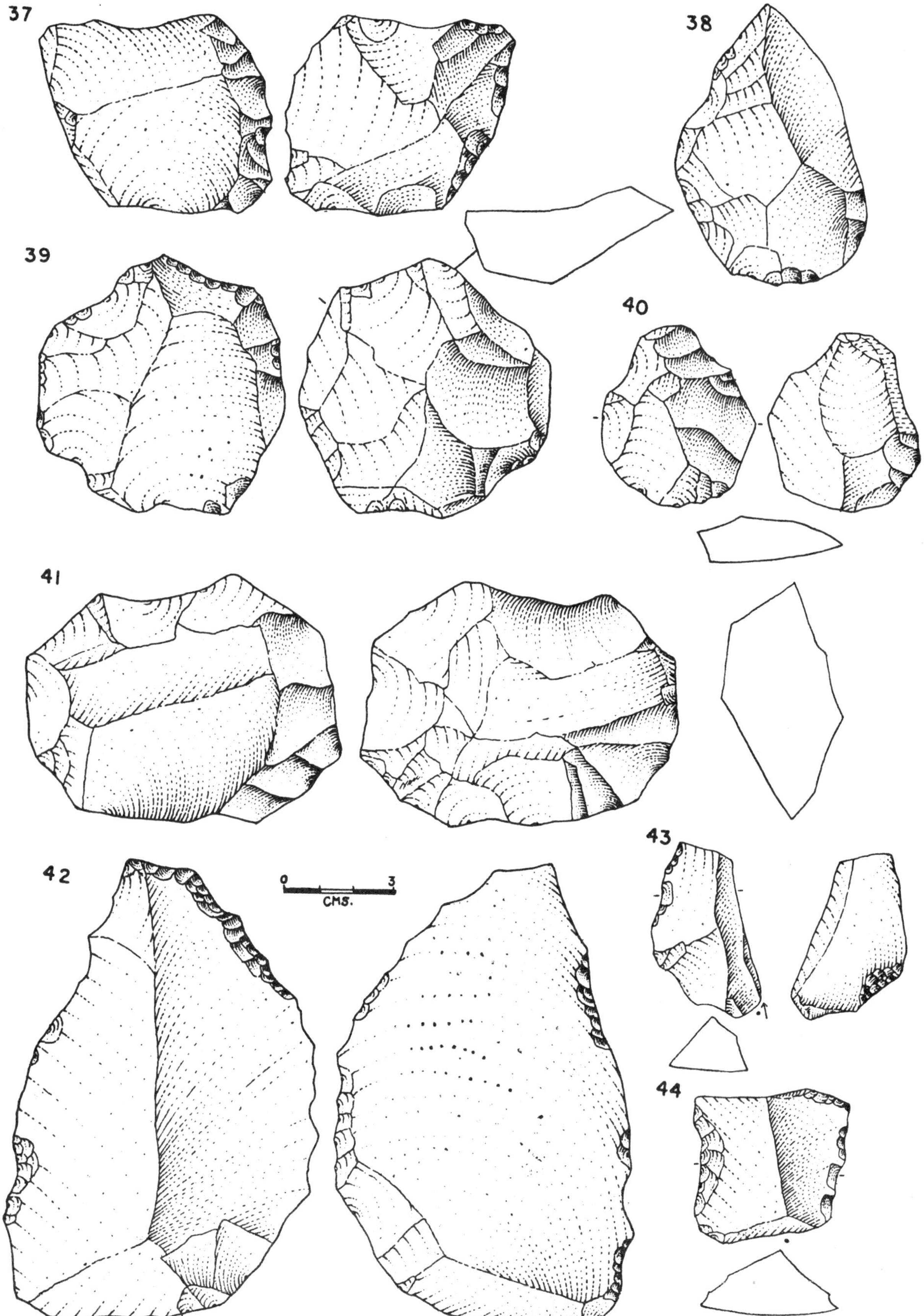

FIG. 6. 37, 39, 41, Levallois core ; 38, Jamalpur knife ; 40, core with partial retouching ; 42, double side scraper denticulated ; 43, pseudo-burin 'de siret' ; 44, blade with chopped off top and retouched corners.

TABLE 3

DISTRIBUTION OF BLANK TYPES WITHIN MAIN TYPOLOGICAL GROUPS

No.	Artefact Types	Blank—Types								Cores	Total
		Non - Levallois			Levallois			Blade	Undet. Flake		
		Unpre.	Pre.	Part Pre.	Fl.	Po.	Bl.				
1.	Chopper–Chopping	2	—	—	—	—	—	—	—	8	10
2.	Handaxe	—	—	—	—	—	—	—	9	7	16
3.	Jamalpur axe	—	—	—	—	—	—	—	20	—	20
4.	Jamalpur Knife A, B, C	2	14	—	10	—	—	—	22	—	48
5.	Knife	2	8	—	8	—	2	1	3	—	24
6.	End & Keel scraper	5	8	—	50	—	—	6	11	—	80
7.	Burin	—	13	1	20	—	—	1	7	—	42
8.	Pseudo-burin	—	—	—	2	—	—	—	1	—	3
9.	Alternate beaked burin	2	4	—	6	—	—	—	1	—	13
10.	Notched tool	3	8	—	8	—	—	1	2	—	22
11.	Denticulate tool	—	10	—	16	2	—	—	1	—	29
12.	Side scrapers	7	15	2	27	1	—	—	19	8	79
13.	S. No. 29, 30 & 41	5	9	1	17	—	—	—	5	—	37
14.	Double side scraper	6	15	—	28	—	—	—	10	2	61
15.	Flake with chipped top	1	7	—	1	—	—	1	6	—	16
16.	Raclette	—	1	—	2	—	—	—	1	—	4
17.	Point	—	2	—	1	—	—	—	—	—	3
18.	Borer & Awl	—	1	—	1	2	—	—	1	—	5
19.	Tranchet	—	2	—	3	—	—	—	3	—	8
20.	Thumbnail scraper	—	—	—	—	—	-	—	2	—	2
21.	Partially retouched blank	17	23	—	33	—	—	8	4	—	85
22.	Unretouched blank	1	8	4	6	—	—	2	10	—	31
	Grand Total	53	148	8	239	5	2	20	138	25	638
	Percentage	8.31	23.20	1.25	37.48	0.78	0.31	3.13	21.63	3.92	99.99

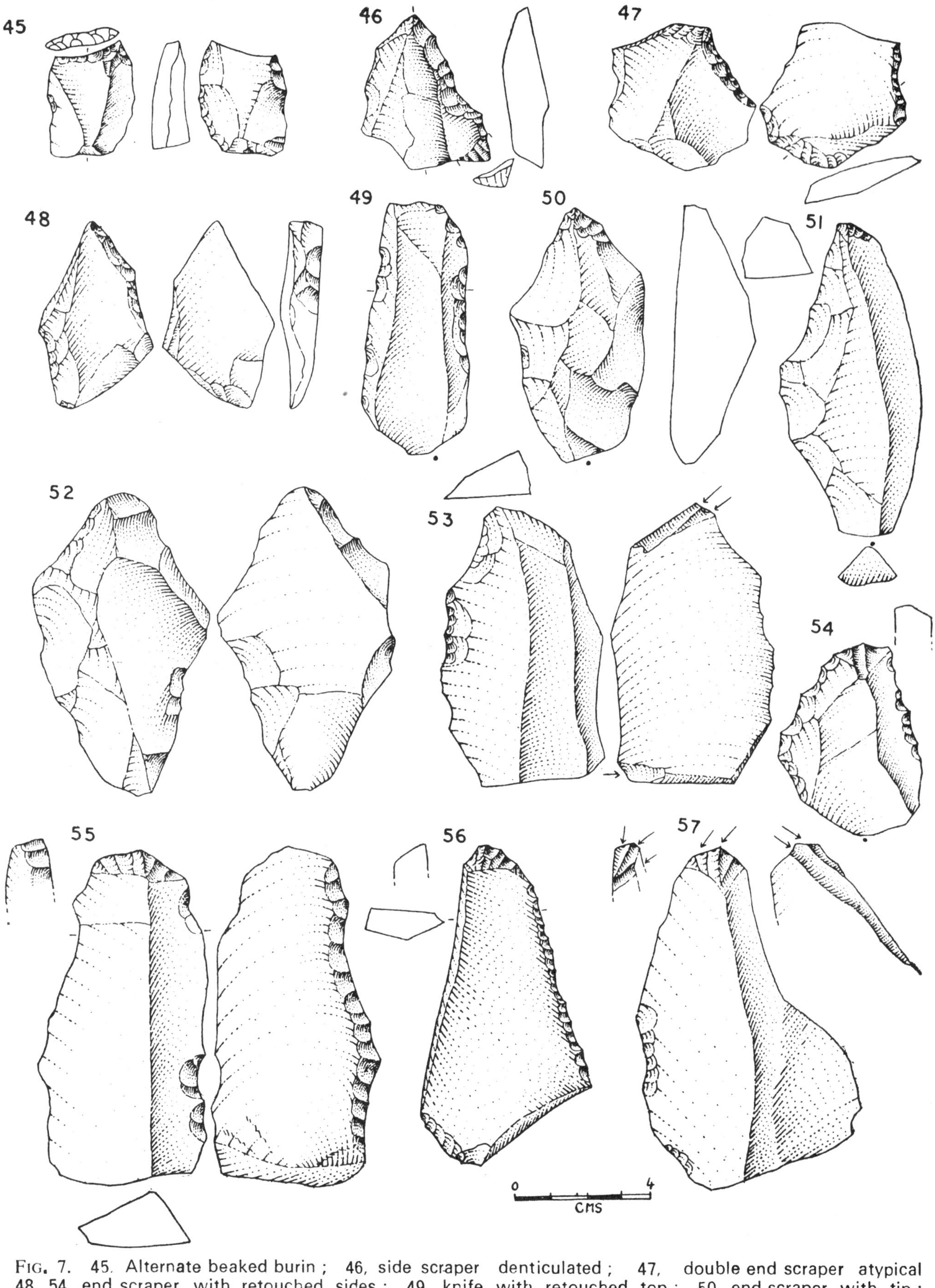

FIG. 7. 45. Alternate beaked burin ; 46, side scraper denticulated ; 47, double end scraper atypical 48, 54, end scraper with retouched sides ; 49, knife with retouched top ; 50. end scraper with tip ; 51, 56, end scraper on Jamalpur knife, 52, double convergent scraper ; 53, middle burin on knife ; 55, end scraper on knife ; 57, middle gauge burin.

3.2 The following table shows the numerical position of the various blank types in the Jamalpur industry.

TABLE 4

DISTRIBUTION OF BLANK-TYPES

Blank-types	Nos.	%
Non-Levallois unprepared & partially prepared flake	53	11.1
Non-Levallois prepared flake	148	31.1
Levallois flake	239	50.3
Levallois point	5	1.1
Levallois blade	2	0.4
Blade	20	4.0
Core rejuvenating flake	8	1.7
Total	475	99.9

3.3 There is considerable number of undetermined blanks, which, if included in the table, will minimize the actual significance of the individual blank-types. Hence the proceeding table excludes the undetermined blanks.

TABLE 5

PROPORTION OF CORE-TYPE

No.	Types	Nos.	%
	I. NON-LEVALLOIS—A		
1.	Unprepared dorsal & prepared striking platform	1	
2.	Partially prepared	5	
3.	Irregular	3	
4.	Flake converted into irregular core	4	
	Total	13	17.1
	II. NON-LEVALLOIS—B		
5.	Prepared	18	
6.	Core rest	3	
	Total	21	27.6
	III. LEVALLOIS		
7.	Flake core	23	
8.	Massive Levallois core	3	
9.	Flake core rest	3	
10.	Flake converted into core	4	
11.	Blade core	1	
	Total	34	44.7
12.	IV MOUSTERIAN CORE	5	6.5
	V BLADE CORE		
13.	Blade core	2	
14.	Flake converted into blade core	1	
	Total	3	4.0
	Grand total	76	99.9

4. SECONDARY WORKING

4.1 It is very interesting to note that almost all the blanks show some sort of secondary work on them. Out of the total number of six hundred and thirteen, only thirty-one are devoid of any mark of secondary work. Bold secondary working is rather scarce in this industry. Retouching is unifacial, bifacial, alternate and partly from the dorsal and partly from the ventral surfaces. Many specimens show a combination of two or more types of retouch. In some cases one side has been unifacially retouched and the other alternately. As the table given below will indicate, unifacial retouch is most common, followed by alternate retouch. Bifacial retouch is rare.

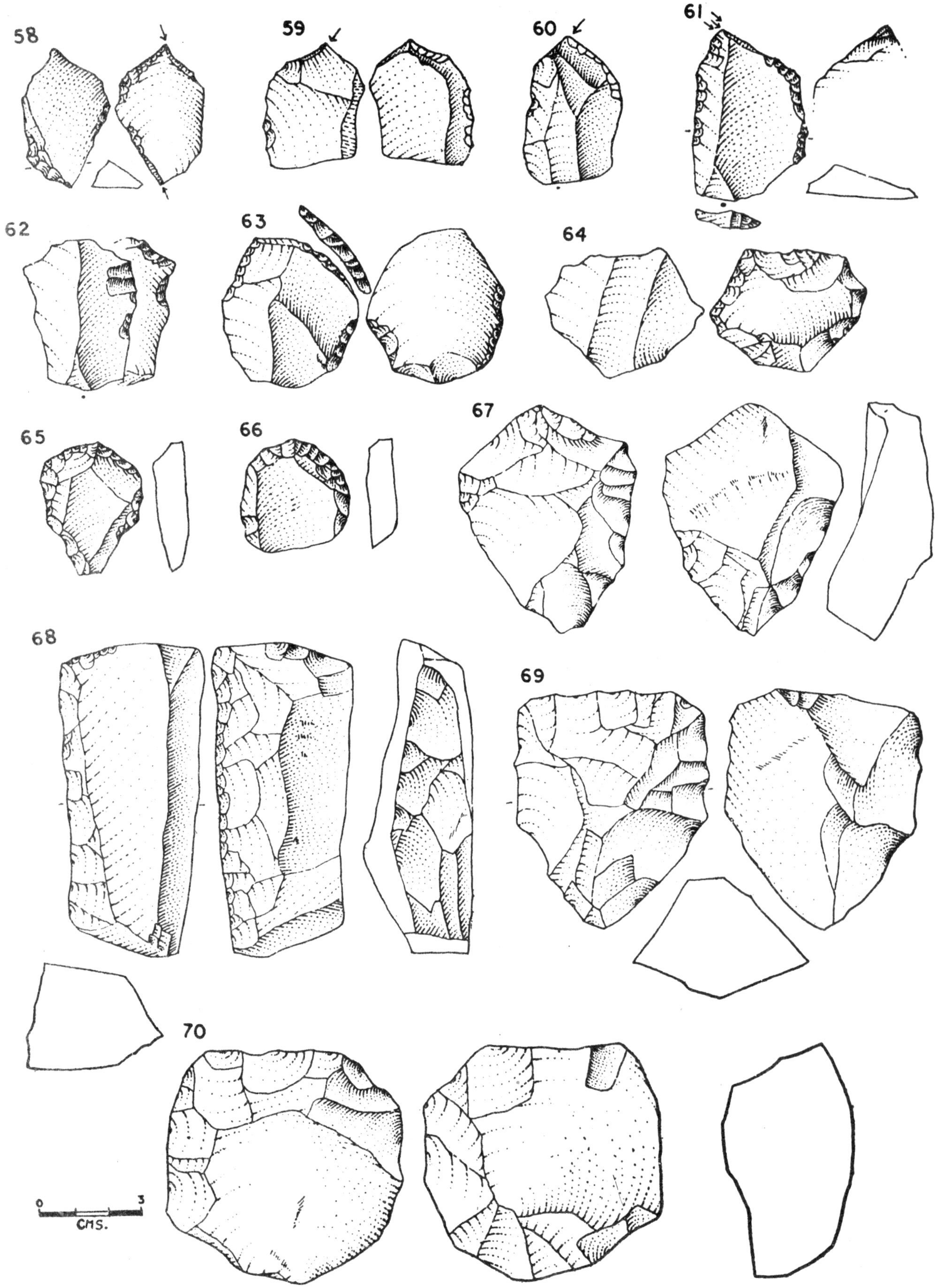

FIG. 8. 58, Double burin ; 59-60, alternate beaked burin ; 61, middle burin with a retouched side ; 62, notched tool ; 63, Jamalpur knife type A ; 64, knife ; 65, grattoir eventail ; 66, thumb nail scraper ; 67, double-end-scraper ; 68, chisel ; 69, Jamalpur axe, and 70, Levallois core.

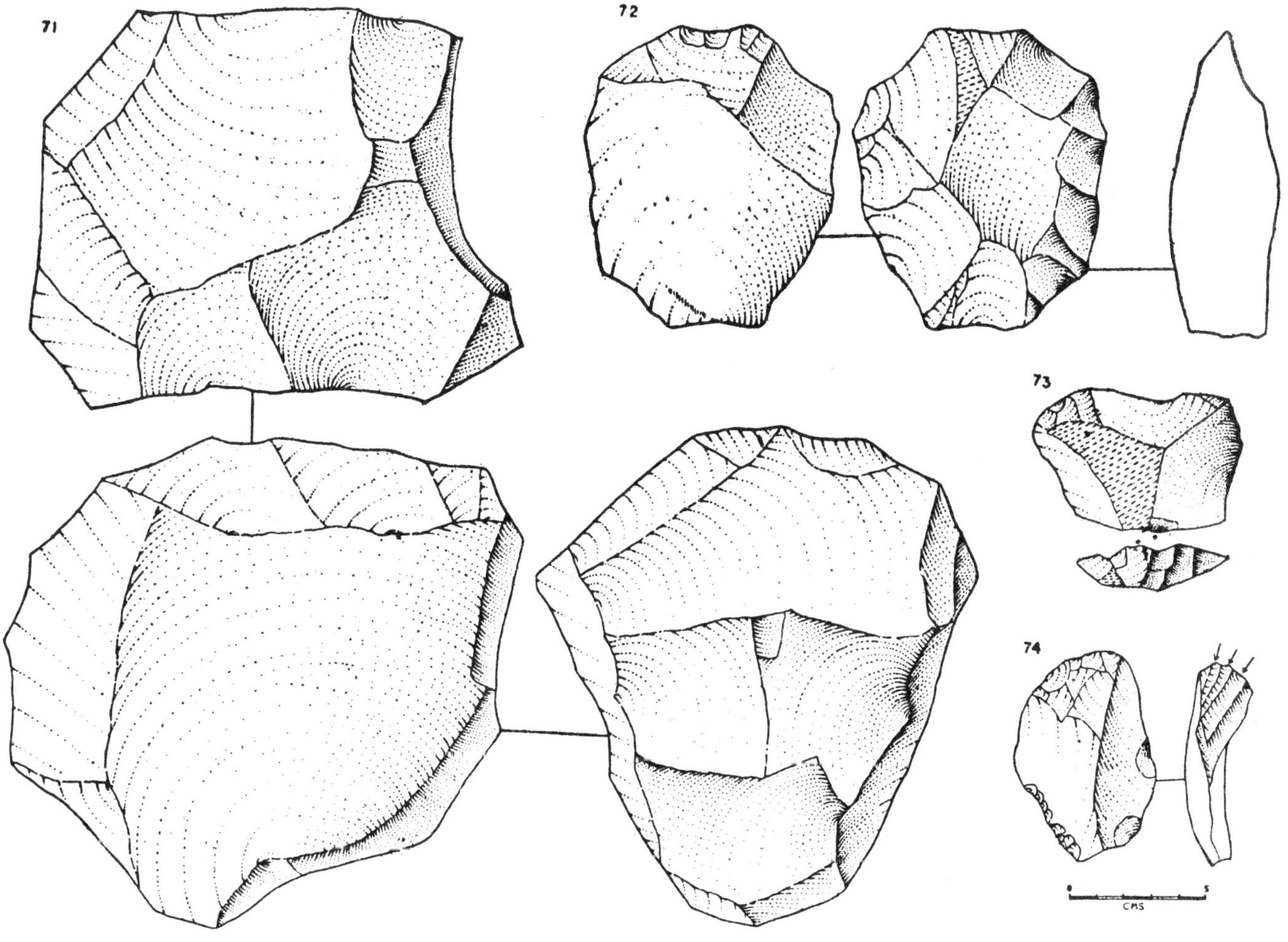

FIG. 9. 71, Massive Levallois core ; 72, unfinished core ; 73, partially-prepared flake ; and 74, middle burin.

TABLE 6

DISTRIBUTION OF THE MODE OF RETOUCHING ON FINISHED TOOLS

Ty. No.	Tool type	Unifacial	Bifacial	Alternate	Partly dorsal Partly vent.	One side unifacial & other alternate.
I.	Chopper-chopping	8	—	2	—	—
II.	Handaxe	—	16	—	—	—
III.	Jamalpur Axe	32	3	11	1	—
IV.	Jamalpur knife	8	—	—	—	40
V.	Knife	9	—	3	—	12
VI.	End & keel scraper	67	—	—	—	13
VII.	Burin	25	—	6	5	3
VIII.	Pseudo-burin	—	—	—	2	—
IX.	Alternate beaked burin	4	—	8	—	—
X.	Notched	2	—	12	8	—
XI.	Denticule	13	—	13	2	1
XII.	Side scraper	49	3	14	13	7
XIII.	Transversal scr. + flake with ret. top	17	—	4	4	—
XIV.	Double side scraper	24	3	6	—	—
XV.	Flake with chopped off top	10	—	5	1	—
XVI.	Raclette	1	1	1	1	—
XVII.	Point	3	—	1	—	—
XVIII.	Borer & awl	2	—	2	1	—
XIX.	Tranchet	8	—	—	—	—
XX.	Thumb nail scraper	1	—	—	—	—
XXI.	Angle & convergent scraper	13	—	1	1	4
XXXII.	Partially retouched blanks	47	3	15	20	—
	Grand Total	343	29	104	59	80
	Percentage	55.7	4.6	16.9	9.5	13.0

4.2 It was noticed that almost all the specimens have been retouched at an angle more than 55°. Generally, the retouch is of ordinary regular type, which is mostly found on side scrapers. Besides, high angle retouch (more than 80°) was also prevalent in the form of abrupt and occasionally as end-scraper type retouching. In some cases, the retouch is limited to margins only. It has been termed as nibbling in the following table. Scali-form retouch (Quina type) is also visible on a few specimens.

TABLE 7

NATURE OF WORKING ON FINISHED IMPLEMENTS

No.	Types	Miscellaneous	Bold	Ordinary	Nibbling	Quina	Perpendicular	Burin
I.	Chopper–chopping	—	10	—	—	—	—	—
II.	Handaxe	16	—	—	—	—	—	—
III.	Jamalpur axe	20	—	—	—	—	—	—
IV.	Jamalpur knife	—	2	40	6	—	20	—
V.	Knife	—	—	22	2	—	24	—
VI.	End & keel scrapers	—	—	65	9	—	80	—
VII.	Burins	—	—	20	7	—	4	43
VIII.	Pseudo-burin	—	—	1	—	—	—	3
IX.	Alternate beaked burin	—	—	5	—	—	—	12
X.	Notched tool	—	2	15	5	—	—	—
XI.	Denticule	—	2	27	—	—	—	—
XII.	Side scraper	—	10	56	9	4	—	—
XIII.	Transversal scraper & Flake with retouched top	—	—	21	11	3	—	—
XIV.	Double side scraper	—	11	41	8	3	—	—
XV.	Flake with chopped off top	—	—	6	—	—	—	—
XVI.	Raclette	—	—	—	—	—	4	—
XVII.	Point	—	—	3	—	—	—	—
XVIII.	Borer & awl	—	—	5	—	—	—	—
XIX.	Tranchet	5	—	3	—	—	—	—
XX.	Thumb nail scraper	—	—	—	—	—	1	—
XXI.	Angle & convergent sc.	—	—	13	1	4	—	—
XXII.	Partially ret. blank	—	7	63	10	—	—	5
	Total	41	44	416	58	14	138	58
	Frequency	5.33	5.72	54.09	7.54	1.82	17.94	7.54

4.3 As mentioned earlier we do not find Clactonian notches in the Jamalpur industry, nor there are notches formed as a result of utilization. The true notches are the result of a deep flake scar followed by careful retouching at an angle which is normally more than 75°. This retouch is unifacial as a rule. But it needs to be clarified that in many cases when the specimens bear more than one notch, one is from the dorsal and the other from the ventral surface. Denticulation is mostly a result of alternate retouching, but it is also done by careful unifacial retouch in many cases.

TABLE 8

DISTRIBUTION OF NOTCHING AND DENTICULATION

Tool - Types	Un-notched	Notched		Denti-culation	Total
		1 – 2 :	3 or more		
Concave scraper	1	3	1	2	7
Convex scraper	6	13	4	2	25
Side scraper with zig-zag edge	4	11	6	7	28
Straight side scraper	12	5	2	—	19
Double side scraper	12	14	14	14	54
Denticulated tool	—	—	—	29	29
Notched tool	—	10	13	—	23
Transeversal scraper	8	5	2	3	18
Convergent scraper	4	3	—	—	7
Angle scraper	4	1	2	5	12
Flake with retouched top	4	2	1	—	7
Flake with chopped off top	6	3	2	5	16
Jamalpur knife	10	9	10	19	48
Knife	7	3	7	7	24
Raclette	2	1	—	1	4
Thumb nail scraper	2	—	—	—	2
Grattoir eventail	1	—	—	—	1
End scraper with retouched side	21	17	10	12	50
'De siret' with retouched side	1	—	—	—	1
Burin with retouched side	7	8	10	5	30
Borer & Awl	2	1	2	—	5
Point	1	2	1	—	4
Tranchet	5	1	2	—	8
Partially retouched blank	53	21	5	—	79
TOTAL	173	123	94	111	501
Percentage	34.5	24.5	18.7	22.1	99.9

5. RESUME

5.1 The above details clearly indicate the techno-typological uniqueness of the Jamalpur industry. In the absence of any stratigraphical evidence reliance had to be placed on typology. On this consideration it is clearly a Middle Palaeolithic industry. But on the same consideration it distinguishes itself from other similar industries of the Indo-Pakistan sub-continent for having an-appreciable number of various types of end-scrapers, notched tools and denticulates. It needs to be emphasised that out of a total number of five hundred and one specimens, three hundred and twenty-eight show either notches or denticulation, although most of them exhibit dominant features of various other tool types. The table 8 indicates the distribution of notches and denticulation among differnt tool groups. In respect of this uniqne characteristic and overwhelming use of the Levallois technique the Jamalpur industy shows close affinities with the Middle Palaeolithic industries found in the region of the river Belan in southern Uttar Pradesh (Jayaswal & Pant 1973). But it has also quite a few new types in It's tool-kit, such as the Jamalpur knife, the ogival end-scraper, etc. Besides, to the best of our knowledge, Jamalpur is the only industry in the sub-continent which has such an appreciable proportion of end-scraper, although various types of side scrapers still dominate. It the notching and denticulation only are to be taken into consideration the Jamalpur industry generally agree with the Denticulate-Mousterian of France but widely differs from it in respect of other typological details.

6. ACKNOWLEDGEMENT

6.1 We express our sincere thanks to our friend and colleague Dr. J.N. Tiwari, Reader in the Department of Ancient Indian History, Culture and Archaeology, Banaras Hindu University, for going through the manuscript and making necessary corrections.

REFERENCES

Bordes, F. (1961), *Typologie du Paleolithque Ancien et Moyen*, Publications du l 'institut de Prehistoire de l' universite de Bordeaux, Memoire No. 1 Bordeaux.

Bosinski, G. & Hahn, J. (1973), 'Der Magdalenean-Fundplatz Andernach (Martinsberg)', *Rheinische Ausgrabungen*, Band 11, Bonn.

Brahmchari, U.N. & S.C. (1929), 'Two Neolithic Stone implements found in the tank at Jamalpur (Monghyr), *Journal of the Asiatic Society of Bengal*, (New Series). XXII.

Clark, J.G.D. (1930, *The Mesolithic Settlement of Northern Europe*. Cambridge.

Indian Archaeology 1960-61—A Review, (1961) Ed. Director General of Archaeology in India, New Delhi.

Indian Archaeology 1961-62—A Review, (1964), Ed. Director General of Archaeology in India, New Delhi.

Jayaswal V. (1974), 'A Techno-typological Rewiew of the Middle Palaeolithic Cultures of India', *Puratattva*, No. 7.

Jayaswal, V- & Pant, P.C. (1973). 'Statistical Studies with reference to Techniques of Manufacture of Palaeothic Artefacts' in Agrawal & Ghosh (Eds), *Radiocarbon and Indian Archaeology*, Bombay.

Rao, S. N. 1968-69), 'Regional Variations in the Indian Middle Stone Age Culture with spscial reference to Nalgonda in Andhra Pradesh', *Puratattve*, No. 2.

Sankalia, H. D. (1965), 'Middle Stone Age Cultures in India and Pakistan', *Science*.

Terrade, A. (1912), Le Burinci-seau de la station mousterienne de Catigny (Oise)', *Memories de la Prehist. Franc*.

Recent Advances in the Study of the Indus Script*

Iravatham Mahadevan
Joint Secretary
Ministry of Industries, New Delhi.

(Received on 7th March 1979)

1. INTRODUCTION

THE Indus Script still remains undeciphered. However, there is a growing understanding of the script, thanks to the steadily increasing number of published texts as well as recent compilations of concordances and statistical tabulations (Parpola *et al* : 1973 ; Mahadevan : 1977). It has now become possible to establish some objective results which, while they still fall far short of an actual decipherment of the script, can nevertheless serve to indicate the direction of further research. This paper deals with some of these results obtained mainly on the basis of my recently published work *'The Indus script: Texts, Concordance and Tables'*, (Archaeological Survey of India, 1977), referred to hereafter as *ISTCT*. I shall confine myself in this paper to two fundamental questions relating to the Indus Script, namely, direction of writing and word division, concentrating more on methods rather than on results. Text numbers are cited as in *ISTCT*.

2. DIRECTION OF THE INDUS SCRIPT

2.1 It is widely accepted that the normal direction of the Indus script is from right to left. However, Fairservis (1976, 1977) has challenged this view and has argued for a left to right direction. This calls for a re-statement of the problem especially in the light of recent advances made possible by computerisation of the texts and the background data.

2.2 The direction of the script can be discovered by a study of the external features of the writing like cramping or overflow of end signs, as well as from the internal evidence of sign sequences. It is my view that a conclusive proof of the direction of the script can be obtained only by a combination of both the approaches and by a comparative statistical study of the frequency and distribution of signs.

2.3 In the study of external features of the writing, an early lead was given by Marshall (1931 : 40) who pointed out the overflow of one sign at the left end of the text in *1052* (pl. I-A) and the cramping of the left end sign in *1060*, both indicating a right to left direction. He also showed that the one and half lines of text in 1*247* (pl. I-B) written as a loop opening to the right (thus : ) must be in the *boustrophedon* mode with the first line starting at the right and the second line continuing from the left. Gadd and Smith (Marshall : 1931 : 410) showed that the disposition of the adial line *4254* (pl. I-C) along the top, left and bottom edges of the rectangular side (thus ; ) proved that the inscription ran in an anti-clockwise, that is right to left direction. Alekseev (in Knorozov *et al* : 1965, 1968; tr. by Zide and Zvelebil : 1976 : 18)-has collected a number of examples where the signs at the left end of the lines undergo occasional cramping, dimunition in size, angular rotation or vertical displacement suggesting that the writing terminated at the left. B. B. Lal (1966 : 52)

*Paper presented at the X International Congress of Anthropological and Ethnological Sciences, New Delhi, December 1978.

produced the most important piece of external evidence by demonstrating from a study of overlapping incisions on pottery graffiti (pl. I-D) from Kalibangan that the inscriptions in question must have been incised from the right.

2.4 It is, however, necessary to stress that such external evidence does not by itself constitute conclusive proof of the direction of writing. The limitation of the method lies in the fact that we know, by mere observation, that lines of the script run in either direction, as may be seen from the examples in Fig. 1. Hence all the external characteristics relied upon to prove a direction are, atleast in theory, reversible and will, in such cases, lead to the opposite conclusion *unless the results are correlated to the internal evidence provided by sign sequences.*

2.5 Let me illustrate this point, with special reference to Lal's method of overlapping incisions on pottery graffiti. Fig. 2 shows two pairs of indentical inscriptions. In each pair, one inscription is from a seal (impression) and the other is incised on pottery, and the lines in each pair run in opposite directions. If these pottery graffiti had overlapping incisions, they must indicate a direction of writing which is known to be at variance with that occuring on the vastly greater number of sales (impressions). This might lead to an erroneous conclusion, if the *normal* direction of the script is sought to be deduced merely from the overlapping incisions. In such cases, the results should be corrected by applying the test of sign sequences which will show that these graffiti are incised in the reversed direction.

2.6 The method of overlapping incisions to determine the direction of the script suffers from yet another, and somewhat surprising, limitation. It now appears that it is even possible for the direction of *writing* to be at variance from the direction of *reading.* Evidence for this curious situation is furnished by B. B. Lal himself (1967-68 : 15), though he does not seem to be aware of the problem. In this paper Lal has published an inscribed potsherd excavated by him at Kalibangan. The inscription* (Pl. I-E) consists of four signs written with bold and deep incisions made before firing the pottery. Lal has made an analysis of the sequence of overlapping incisions between the two middle signs as well as of the component parts within each sign and proved that the inscription is *written* from right to left. However, the test of sign sequences makes it certain that this inscription (as incised in the original) has to be *read* from left to right. The direction of this text becomes evident when the sign pairs occurring here are compared with those in the Table of pairwise frequencies in *ISTCT* (Table II : 724). Similarly the sign group formed by the three signs at the left (of the original) can be compared with identical or similar sign groups listed in *ISTCT* (Concordance : 466-67). The results are shown in Fig. 3. It will be seen that only a left to right reading (of the original) is productive. It may also be mentioned here that the pairs and the triplet arranged in the reversed order (that is, read from the right in the original) are not recorded even once in *ISTCT*. It is therefore certain that this inscribed sherd from kalibangan has to be read from the left (in the original) even though it may have been incised from the right as shown by Lal. A plausible explanation of the riddle may be that the potter or the scribe copied the text from a seal (original) which would have been engraved from the left, but wrote from the right according to the normal practice in direct writing. Whatever may be the true explanation, the point to be noted here is that the results of the study of overlapping incisions cannot be applied mechanically to determine the direction of the script without due regard to internal evidence provided by the sign sequences.

2.7 Hunter (1934 : 37) was the first scholar to apply systematically the statistics of sign sequences as internal evidence to elucidate the direction of the script. It is instructive to compare his handling of the evidence of the seals *1052* and *1247* (pl. I-A,B) with that of Marshall. In dealing with the overflow sign in *1052*, he does not rely merely on the fact that it is found below the left end of the line for want of space. He points out that it is the most common left end sign and that if placed at the right end of the upper line, it does not form a known combination with the adjacent sign. In dealing with the text in *1247*, his argument does not rely on the looping of the line at the left end, but on comparison of sign sequences in similar texts which show that the only tenable reading of *1247* is in the *boustrophedon* mode starting from the right end of the upper line. By adopting the combinatory method he is able to show that most of the second lines in 2-line texts are to be read only from the right and are not *boustrophedon*

*This is included in *ISTCT* as no. 8221. Unfortunately the text has been incorrectly copied, as  (as unusual variant of ) was confused with  and || with | owing to the indeterminate length of the strokes in the original. As a result, the evidence of sequence was not perceived and the text was copied from the right on the basis of overlapping incisions. The text has to be corrected as indicated in this paper (Fig. 3).

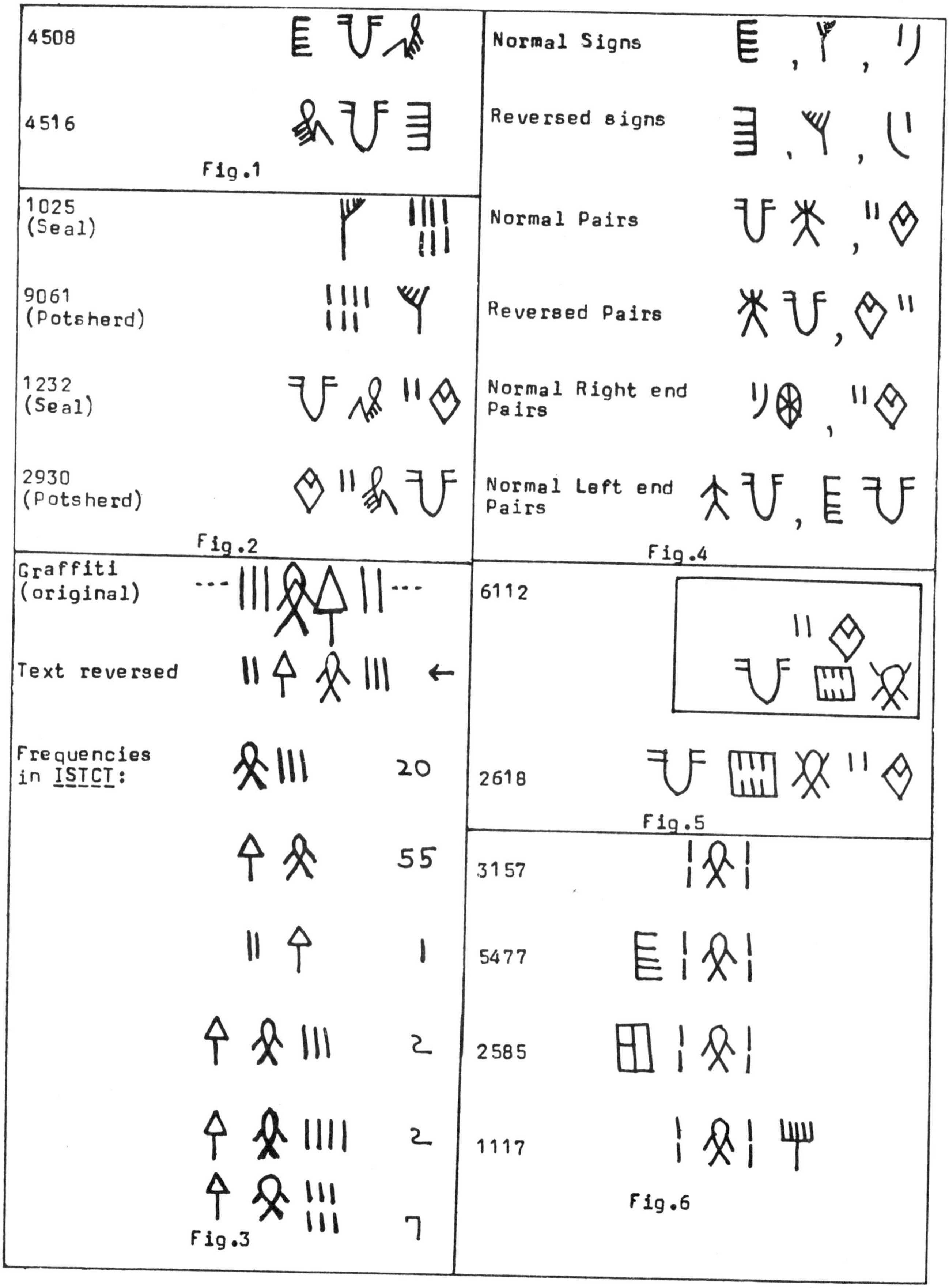
4508
4516
Fig.1
1025 (Seal)
9061 (Potsherd)
1232 (Seal)
2930 (Potsherd)
Fig.2
Graffiti (original)
Text reversed
Frequencies in ISTCT:
20
55
1
2
2
7
Fig.3
Normal Signs
Reversed signs
Normal Pairs
Reversed Pairs
Normal Right end Pairs
Normal Left end Pairs
Fig.4
6112
2618
Fig.5
3157
5477
2585
1117
Fig.6

Figs. 1–6

and that there are many single-line inscriptions, especially from Harappa, which are to be read from left to right. Hunter still remains the best guide in this matter.

2.8 Ross (1939 : 554) also applied the test of sign sequences to elucidate the direction of the text in *1247* (PP. I-B). He shows that while a 2-line inscription can be read theoretically in 8 possible ways (by reading each line from left *or* right and by reading top *or* bottom line first), there is only one tenable reading of *1247* (first the upper line from the right and then the lower line from the left) when the sign sequences are compared with similar single-line texts. However, Ross's "extremely rigorous treatment" is marred by his axiom that "the direction of all single-line inscriptions is the same as the direction of that line of multilinear inscriptions which is to be read first". This is just not true as there are many single line inscriptions running demonstrably in either direction. It will be nearer the actual state of affairs to say that the line to be read first in a multi-line inscription will be in the normal direction of the script. At least no exception is known to this modified rule. Ross's objection to considering the upper line as the first line of a multi-line inscription in an undeciphered script is not also justified, as no exception to this arrangement is known in any script, ancient or modern.

2.9 An independent and complete proof starting from first principles for the direction of the Indus Script has been attempted by me earlier in *ISTCT* (Introduction : 10). It is based on the premise that the only universal characteristic which determines the direction of a script is the sequence of signs reflecting the fixed order of speech in the language. This order remains the same whether the written text runs from the right or the left or in the *boustrophedon* mode, and whether we look at a seal or its impression. External evidence is necessary only to identify the fixed order of the more frequent sequences which will then enable us to determine statistically the normal direction of the script. Such external evidence is provided by three sets of "direction markers" viz.,

(i) Orientation of asymmetric signs which can be observed to change along with the direction of the line ;

(ii) Terminal signs and sign groups which occur with greater frequency at the left end or right end positions ;

(iii) Sequence of the more frequent sign groups ;

In each of these categories, the 'normal' direction and the 'reversed' direction are established purely on a statistical basis. It may be clarified that, the terms 'normal' and 'reversed' are neutral to actual direction and are merely based on the frequency of occurrences. Examples of these "direction-markers" are given in Fig. 4.

2.10. The statistical data is then applied to "split sequences", which are identical inscriptions occurring both in single lines and as two lines one below the other on the same side of an inscribed object. If we assume (on the basis of universal experience) that the upper line is written first and the lower line thereafter, we can establish the order of the signs in the corresponding single-line text. It then follows that all other lines containing this sequence have to be read in the same direction. This is a cumulative process and it is possible by means of interlocking evidence in respect of orientation of asymmetric signs, sequence of sign groups and the positional distribution of the more frequent terminal signs and sign groups to establish conclusively the normal direction of the script. The method of 'split seqences' is illustrated in Fig. 5. Assuming that in *6112* (Pl. I-F) the upper line is read first, it follows that the single-line text in *2618* (Pl. I-G) has to be read from right to left. The importance of this example lies in the fact that  is the most frequent right end pair and  the most frequent left end sign in the script. Hence it follows that the normal direction of Ihe script is from right to left.

2.11 The statistical study in *ISTCT* (p. 14 and Tables VI and VII)) shows that about 83 per cent of the lines run from the right and about 7 per cent from the left. (The rest are mostly single-sign or doubtful due to damaged signs.) writing in the *boustropheden* mode is rare, though 18 examples are listed in *ISTCT*. The evidence seems to suggest that the second line runs in the reversed direction generally when the first line has an incomplete sequence (e.g. 1247, 6402).

2.12 The recent work of Fairservis (1976, 1977) proposing a new model for the decipherment of the Indus Script proceeds on the assumption that the normal direction of the Script is from left to right. This does come as a surprise in view of the near-unanimous snd well-established view based on the labours of a long line of scholars for nearly half a century that the normal direction of the script is from the right. It is unfortunate that Fairservis takes hardly any notice of the previous work in the field in this respect. He wrongly cites (Fairservis : 1976 : 33) the Soviet scholars in support of his own view that the script runs from the left. The Soviet Scholars have clearly stated their position (Knorozov: 1968 : 99) that the script runs from right to left. Fairservis has perhaps been misled by the Soviet practice of referring to the original seals (which normally run from the left) rather than to the seal impressions (which normally run from the right).

2.13 Fairservis (1977 : 6) advances three arguments in support of his view. His arguments may be summarised and briefly countered as follows :

(1) Many Graffiti show a slant to the right. Such slants are common to the writing which is written from left to right.

Graffiti on pottery may show a slant depending on the curvature of the surface and the angle in which the potter or the scribe held the vessel while incising the signs. In this respect the few pottery graffiti are not representative of the norm of writing which can be more clearly from hundreds of beautifully carved and well preserved seals.

(2) The signs in column 5 of the grid (Fairservis : 1976 : Tables 1-75) are positionally so regular that one might presume that they start an inscription rather than end it. It is in fact unlikely that the bulk of the inscriptions would end in the same column.

This is a curious argument considering that the grid itself is so arranged by Fairservis : As the Concordances would show, it is possible to arrange the occurrences of any sign under a regular column. The observed positional regularity is nerely a reflection of the set word order found in the Indus texts. It is possible for the bulk of the inscriptions either to begin or to end with the same signs (or columns) if they have stereotyped beginnings or endings, a state of affairs which is not at all unlikely in ancient seal-inscriptions.

(3) The tables of Pair-wise frequencies compiled by Fairservis (1976 : Tables 57-59) demonstrate left to right reading. Right to left ordering of these signs produced far lower frequencies in all cases.

The *absolute* frequency of a sign pair must remain constant in whichever direction it is read. What fairservis means perhaps is that if the pairs are tabulated in a left to right order, the *relative* frequency of corresponding pairs in the reversed direction would be much less in such a tabulation. This argument would also hold good if the entire arrangement is reversed as in the Finnish Concordance and in *ISTCT*. In these tabulations where the right to left order is followed, the occurrence of corresponding reversed pairs in left to right order is quite rare. This is therefore a circular argument which proves nothing.

2.14 The position taken up by Fairservis in the matter of direction of the script forces him to read the lower lines in the 2-line inscriptions as the first lines (Fairservis : 1977 : Appendix IV : 14, 16, 141 and 142). He does not however explain why Harappans chose to write from bottom upwards, an arrangement of lines not known in any other script. Fairservis is also quite inconsitent in this respect. In many other cases, he reads the upper line as the first line (ibid : 41, 66, 99 and 175) without offering any explanation for the variation. He denies (1976 : 40) the existence of *boustrophedon* inscriptions, but does not explain how *1247* would be read by him. In fact if his method of reading is adopted this inscription would not only start from the lower line, but also in the reversed direction (in his system), neither of which is at all likely.

2.15 It is unfortunate that the wrong choice of direction has rendered the model of decipherment set up by Fairservis *ab initin* invalid. In general it can be stated that in the light of the clear evidence in favour of a right to left direction, no attempted decipherment of the Indus Script based on a left to right direction can be taken seriously.

3. WORD DIVISION IN THE INDUS SCRIPT

3.1 Broadly speaking there are two competing schools of thought about the nature of the signs of the Indus Script, one regarding them as word signs and the other as phonetic signs. I shall briefly summarise the arguments and present the results of my recent work based on the material available in *ISTCT*. The conclusions will be based purely on the analysis of the script and will take no account of linguistic speculations.

3.2 The earliest analysis of "the mechanical nature" of the script was undertaken by Smith (in Marshall : 1931 : 415). He analysed three texts and recorded the following findings :—

1120 : "A series of intelligible expressions"
1314 : "A series of 5 signs, each having a separate meaning".

1435 : "The evidence points to the inscription being a succession of separate words".

He also analysed the positional distribution of one sign () and found that there was a general probability that it possessed "a meaning in and by itself" and that, on the whole, it seemed a separate word, atleast in most cases. He made the perceptive observation that this sign could not be a syllable "for, it should then appear in more varied positions". He concluded that most of the signs studied by him had meanings by themselves and that some were probably ideograms in that they conveyed a word as an idea and were therefore not used in syllabic values.

3.3 Hunter (1934 : 126) formulated the following criteria in deciding on word division in the script :

(i) That the combination (of signs) is found in a number of cases relatively larger in proportion to the total occurrences of one its members ;
(ii) That the first member of the combination is demonstrably independent of any signs found preceding the combination; and
(iii) That the last member is demonstrably independent of any signs found following the combination.

After carrying out the analysis, Hunter concluded that "no sign of common occurrence (with one exception) is *not* found as a single word". In view of this finding, Hunter's "words" containing two or more signs are perhaps better described as "phrases". It should also be noted here that these results are independent of Hunter's linguistic speculations viewing the signs as phonetic syllables and hence the Harappan language as monosyllabic, as these deductions do not necessarily follow from his own formal analysis and are in any case unproved.

3.4 The Soviet Scholars (Knorozov *et al* : 1965, 1968 ; tr. Zide and Zvelebil : 1976) analysed the texts by computer techniques involving interval statistics and were able to segment the inscriptions into 'blocks' corresponding to dafinite grammatical units like words and word combinations. The 'blocks' are regarded as comprising word signs standing for roots, attributes grammatical suffixes.

3.5 The Finnish scholars (Parpola *et al* : 1969) arrived at similar results by analysing inscriptions with the same words but different word order, and near-indentical inscriptions. Their basic principle in dividing the inscriptions into words is that each of the supposed words should be verifiable from elsewhere either separately (forming the whole of an inscription) or in other contexts so that the neighbouring words can also be ascertained by similar means. In all their subsequent publications, the Finnish scholars have proceeded with their interpretation of the script on the basis of word signs; but a consideration of the linguistic aspect of their work is outside the scope of the present paper.

3.6 I undertook an independent verification of these results utilising the much larger textual material as well as the concordance and the statistical tabulations now available in *ISTCT*. The procedures followed by me are extremely simple and logical and can easily be verified by other scholars from the published material.

Method (1) :

3.7 The first step is to collect single-sign texts from well-preserved and complete inscribed objects. It will be seen from the concordance in *ISTCT* that 43 signs occur as single-sign texts, which must therefore be regarded as self-contained and independent linguistic units, namely, 'words'. A special category of the single-sign texts which can be readily identified as words, consists of 'numerals' (two to ten short strokes arranged in one or two tiers) incised on the rims of pottery and on the blades of bronze weapons for obvious inventory purposes.

3.8 The second step is to compile two-sign texts in each of which one sign is already identified as an independent word on account of its solitary occurrence elsewhere. In these cases, the remaining sign must therefore be regarded as a separate word. This technique is illustrated in Fig. 6. The search is then extended progressively to longer texts containing three or more signs, of which all but one are already established as word signs, thus proving that the remaining sign must also be an independent word.

Method (2) :

3.9 Another method is to list pairs of texts which are identical but for the presence of one additional sign at either end. The additional signs in these cases must therefore be independent 'words' (including grammatical morphs like case endings, suffixes and other particles). For example, *ISTCT* lists 24 pairs of identical texts but for the presence of one additional sign () at the left end in one of the texts in each pair. See the examples in Fig. 7.

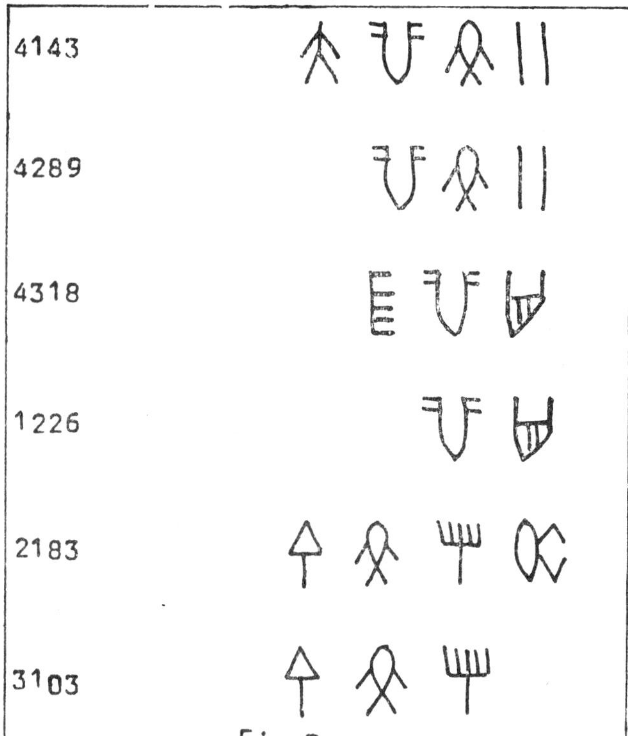

Fig.7

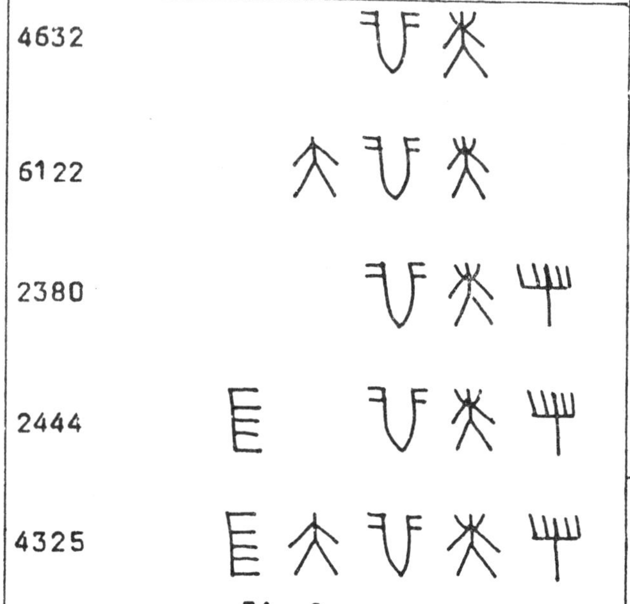

Fig.8

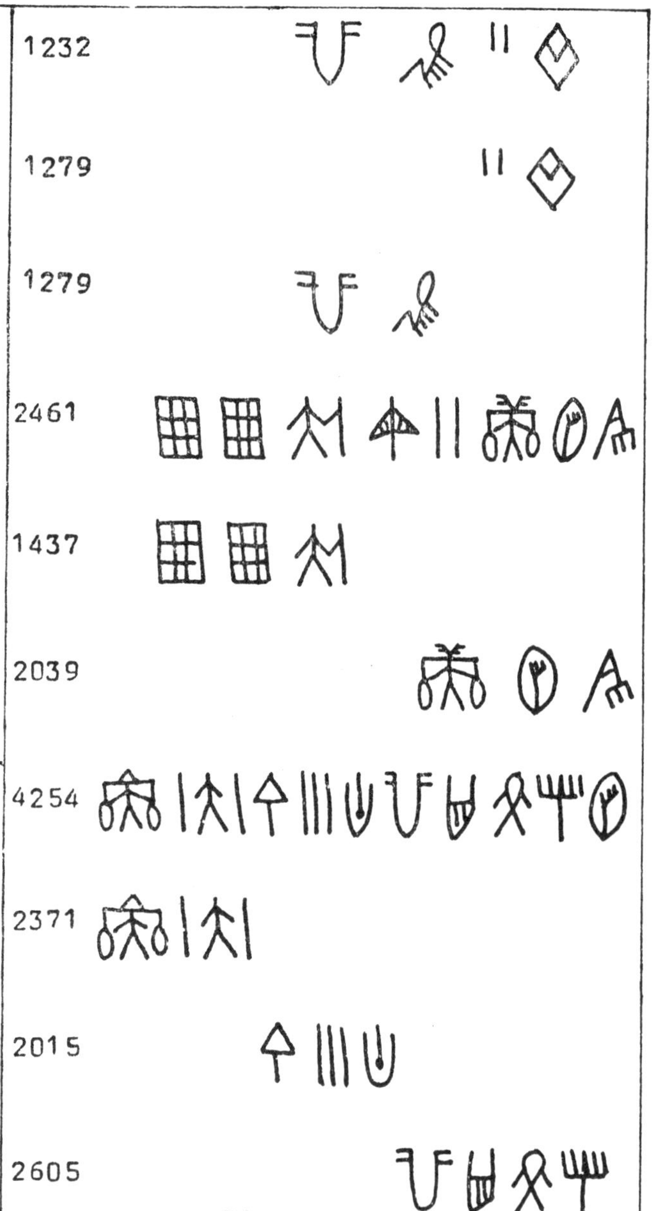

Fig.9

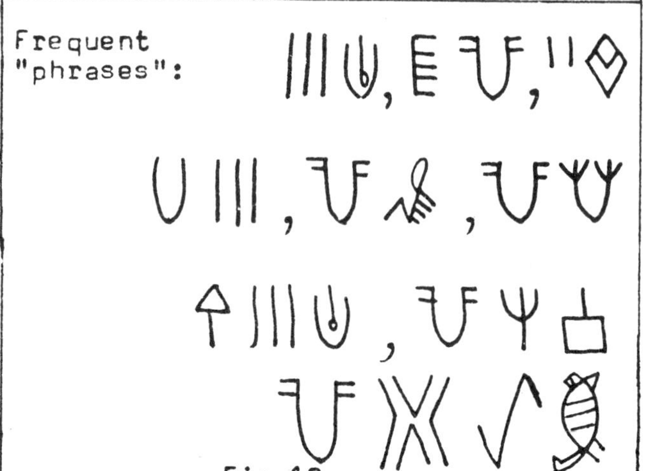

Fig.10

FIGS. 7—10

3.10 Another extension of this method is to search for pairs of near-identical texts which vary only by the addition of single signs in the medial positions. These are to be considered as independent words. The method can be extended further by comparing pairs of near identical texts which vary only by the substitution of one sign in a text by another in the other text. Such substitutions prove the independent character of both the signs in question.

Method (3) :

3.11 Another method is to search for sets of texts which are built up by the progressive addition of one sign at a time at either end, Hunter (1934 : 127) has already cited one such interesting set. For another, see Fig. 8. such texts clearly prove the independent word values of each sign occurring in them.

Method (4) :

3.12 A few signs occur with very high frequencies and form stable pairs with a large number of other signs. Analysis shows that these few high-frequency signs are integral units having some independent meaning or grammatical function. Examples of such signs are given below :

It therefore follows that the other members forming stable pairs with the above signs must be separate words. This is a particularly productive method in view of the very high frequency of these "suffixes" and the very large number of stable pairs formed by them.

3.13 The methods described above are overlapping and the results are cumulative. They prove that, almost without excepton, the signs in the Indus Script are word signs wih specific meanings or grammatical functions and cannot be treated as mere phonetic units with alphabetic or syllabic values as suggested by scholars like S.R. Rao (1973 : 127).

3.14 The next step is to segment the texts into 'phrases' consisting of stable combinations of two or more words or compound words. Two methods were followed by me for the purpose :—

Method 1 :

A longer text can be shown to consist of two or more shorter texts appearing as complete texts elsewhere, clearly indicating the points of segmentation. See Fig. 9 for examples.

Method 2 :

With the help of pairwise frequencies, it is possible to isolate "phrases" (generally containing 2 to 4 signs only) with high frequencies forming integral linguistic units.

It is possible, by following these methods, to segment all but few of the texts included in *ISTCT* into separate phrases and words. Fig. 10 contains some illustrative "phrases" with high frequencies.

4. CONCLUSION

4.1 In conclusion, I should like to stress two general points about the results summarised in this paper. Firstly, they are totally independent of any theory about the language of the Harappans and will remain valid for any successful decipherment of the script. Secondly, as the foregoing discussions show, my methods are in continuation and extension of those already employed by the earlier investigators in the field and the results are also in general conformity with their findings. The significance of the present work lies in its independent verification and confirmation of the results as well as in the application of the methods to the entire corpus of known texts to test their validity. The results thus from a secure base for further progress towards the eventual decipherment of the Indus Script.

REFERENCES

Fairservis, JR.W.A. 1976. *Excavations at the Harappan site of Allahdino : The seals and other inscribed material.* Papers of the Allahdino Expedition, No. I. New York.

———1977. *Excavations at the Harappan site of Allahdino : The Graffiti. A model in the decipherment of the Harappan script.* Papers of the Allahdino Expedition, No. III. New York.

Hunter, G. R. 1934. *The script of Harappa and Mohanjodaro and its connection with other scripts. Studies in the* History of Culture No. 1. London : Kegan Paul, Trench, Trabner and Co.

Knorozov, YJ. V., Alekseev, G.V., Probst, M.A., Kondratov, A.M., Fedorova, I.K. and Volcok, B.Ya., 1965. *Preliminary Report on the investigation of the Proto-Indian Texts,* (in Russian), Moscow.

Knorozov, Yu. V., Volcok, B. Va., and Gurov, N.V. 1968. *Proto-Indica : Brief report on the investigation of the Proto-Indian Texts* (in English), Moscow. Tranlated and edited by Zide, Arlene R.K. and Zvelebil, Kamil, 1976. The Hogue : Moton.

Lal, B.B. 1966. The direction of writing in the Harappan Script. *Antiquity* : 9 (1966).

———1967-68. A further note on the direction of writing in the Harappan Script. *Puratattva, Bulletion of the Indian Archaeological Society :* 1 (1967-68)

Mahadevan, Iravatham, 1977. *The Indus Script : Texts, Concordance and Tables,* Memoirs or the Archaeological Survey of India No. 77, New Delhi.

Marshall, Sir John. 1931. *Mohenjo-daro and the Indus Civilization* (3 Vols,) London : Arthur Probsthan.

Parpola, A., Koskenniemi, S., Parola, S., and Aalto, P. 1969. *Decipherment of the Proto-Dravidian inscriptions of the Indus Civilization : A first announcement.* Copenhagen

Parpola, A., Parpola, S., and Koskenniemi, S. 1973. *Materials for the study of the Indus Script : I : A Concordance to the Indus Inscriptions.* Helsinki : Suomalainen Tiedeakatemia.

Rao, S.R. 1973. *Lothal and the Indus Civilization.* Bombay : Asia Publishing House.

Ross, Alan S.C. 1939. The direction of the Mohenjo-daro Script. *New Indian Antiquary :* (1939-40)

Culture and Process

Gregory L. Possehl
University of Pennsylvania.

(Received on 20 July, 1980)

IN this paper I want to attempt a very brief exposition of a few concepts used to understand and interpret man's past. It will be in no way an exhaustive discussion since the topic has been covered rather fully in other places (see especially Binford and Binford 1968, Watson, LeBlanc and Redman 1971, and Sankalia 1977 for bibliography and discussion). There are, however, several issues, contrasting an anthropological approach to one which is more historical which may at this time deserve highlighting through readumbration.

The well known dictum that "American archaeology is anthropology or it is nothing" (Willey and Phillips 1958 : 2) has quite specific historical roots, and cannot be understood without some sensitivity to the context within which anthropology in North America emerged and prospered. The first, probably most important aspect of this context is that the early American anthropologists set as thier primary goal an historical reconstruction of the native American peoples, who were, by and large, non-literate. It was clear from the beginning that the completion of such a task, unaided by written documents, would require a multidimensional, many faceted approach. Thus, most of the early anthropologists were not narrow specialists within what have become the traditional branches of the discipline but were competent scholars who could investigate the human career using linguistics, ethnology, archaeology and the biological sciences as well. Franz Boas, A. L. Kroeber, Robert Lowie, C. Kluckhohn and Julian Steward, to name but a few of the more prominent personalities of this era, are examples of individuals who pursued their understanding of man within the holistic framework of anthropology.

Because of the special conditions pertaining to the American environment—a thin veneer of western culture overlying historically deep and rich indigenous traditions—the "direct historical approach" was defined by these scholars as the operative framework best suited to achieve their historical goals. This involved a careful documentation of the native Americans as they were known during the period of initial western contact and then by patiently working back in time, the reconstruction of various cultural traditions through the use of historical linguistics, human biological variation and archaeology. The concept of culture areas and the "age area hypothesis" were major tools used in most reconstructions of this ilk. In the latter hypothesis it was proposed that the historical depth of a cultural feature, or trait, could be determined through the spatial study of its distribution. By-and-large, the traits with the widest distribution were held to be the oldest. That this rather simple-minded hypothesis failed need not be more then mentioned, but it was also one of the reasons behind the ultimate demise of the entire culture area approach (see Steward 1956 for a more complete critical evalution of the concept). On the other hand, however, this approach bound archaeology in the Americas to anthropology, at least is so far as prehistory is concerned. Even with the specialization which the discipline underwent during the thirties, forties and fifties it held fast, and today most archaeologists in North America consider themselves anthropologists who approach the human career through the employment of a particular set of methodological tools. This point is further illustrated by the fact that : 1) the small scale non-western community remains in a normative sense the setting for investigation, 2) participant observation, excavation in the case of archaeology, is the predominant mode of investigation, 3) the reconstruction of traditional life ways remains an important objective and 4) the anthropological concern is centered on the cultural dimensions of human existence.

This final point, concerning the predominance of culturally oriented research, is one of particular interest since recent years have seen considerable revisions in the way American archaeologists have turned to using the concept. In its original form culture (or cultures specifically) was thought of as a finite set of features or traits, all distinctly human in character, which came to mankind via historical process. E. B. Tylor's definition of culture as all things learned, shared and socially transmitted is but one example of what is referred to here. Culture could thus be reduced to a trait list which in its most refined, sophisticated form was sufficient for perfect definition. Of course the link between the production of trait lists and the mapping process, as with culture areas, is obvious.

It is probably unfair to suggest that operational definitions of culture which stress content, which deal with what culture *is*, are inappropriate for archaeological use in all instances. This approach does however force those who employ them to address at least two more-or-less theoretical problems which often go neglected. The first of these issues deals with the proper definition, nature and weighting of tarits. What, from the host of cultural features, should be selected as a trait ? Are some of these traits more important than others; are they more heavily weighted ? How are traits to be compared ? For the archaeologist : What is the relationship between the physical objects found at a site and other cultural dimensions such as values, language or ethnicity ? Assuming these dimensions to be largely obscure in most prehistoric contexts, in spite of some methodological breakthroughs, how can the archaeologist arbitrarily select material remains (pots, house types, stone tools and the like) as the criteria by which cultures are defined ? The second point is that definitions of culture which are essentially trait lists largely ignore the relational aspects of cultural systems. In other words, by focusing on content such definitions tend to ignore the dynamic, or systemic qualities of culture : by illuminating what is present they tend to ignore what is going on. The final flaw in treating culture in this way is that there is a tendancy to begin to think of archaeological cultures as representing homogenous ethnic groups. Distinctive kinds of pottery, for example, suddenly become identified with particular peoples, without due recognition of the fact that there is no necessary relationship between the boundaries of any given body of material culture and notions of group affiliation; at least if the worldwide enthnographic record is an adequate guide.

It is for these reasons that anthropological archaeology has largely abandoned the notion of archaeological cultures. There is simply too wide a gap, given our current abilities to reconstruct the past, between the kind of culture with which an ethnographer works and that of the archaeologist. More-over, definitions of culture based on content have largely given way to more processually oriented conceptualizations which define culture not in terms of what it *is* but in terms of what it *does*. One of the most productive of these processual definitions has been to think of culture as the non-biological means man uses in adapting to both natural and social conditions. Needless to say such definitions are not mere trait lists.

If the shift is made in the study of culture from trait list to process the archaeologist is led to ask his questions in somewhat different ways, at times even to address entirely different problems. For example it is no longer of paramount importance to account for a given feature in terms of its place of origin. This kind of question may well be asked; however it becomes distinctly secondary to understanding the way in which culture as an holistic phenomenon integrates component subsystems in the "competitive," dynamic harmony of adaptation, be these features new and innovative or constituents of deep historical tradition. Thus, processual interpretation shifts attention away from an understanding of culture history in terms of *exterior* forces—diffusion, migration, invasion—to one which seeks and understanding based on the *internal* dynamics of total cultural systems in terms of a wide range of adaptive forces. This concern with process leads archaeologists to pay far greater attention to the construction of what I have called "interior cultural landscapes."

Some of these points deserve substantive examples. This can be provided by a brief consideration of the ways in which the megalithic phenemenon of India has been handled. One of the themes which has dominated the discussions of these monuments has been that of diffusion and a singlemindedness in attempting to account for the place(s) from which they "emanated." Without denying the legitimate nature of this theme I would suggest that it carries with it a set of assumptions concerning the nature of culture change. More to a point, however, is that archaeologists who feel most comfortable viewing culture as process are little concerned with accounting for the formal properties of these monuments—the trait list of port holes, hood stones, menhirs, secondary interment, iron, etc.—in terms of their place of origin. They are, however, profoundly concerned with the adaptive posture which "megalithism" represents in Central and Southern India for very nearly a millennium. What was the interior cultural landscape of the human groups who built these monuments and how might the remains recovered through reconnaissance and excavation best be viewed as harmonious, adaptive constituents of some larger whole? And this point serves to introduce a cautionary note to those who think in diffusionist terms. In a contact situation, where diffusion may have had an impact, the acceptance or rejection of a particular trait or trait complex is largely determined by the configuration of the interior cultural landscape, or organization, of a particular cultural system. In this sense culture is a screen, a selective system, through which only a few things may pass, and the determining factor which regulates this intercourse is system organization. Thus any appeal to diffusion as a causal factor in culture change which fails to investigate and understand the interior cultural landscape in these terms is incomplete and therefore flawed (see Steward 1958 for a particularly lucid discussion of this point).

That the anthropological approach should have taken the turn to process is quite understandable given the traditional concerns and approaches of the discipline. But there is another somewhat deeper and probably more important consequence of this perspective which deserves notice here as a final point. This centers on the very nature of process itself. I pretend not to have the final word, the bottom line as it were, on this matter; however it is possible to draw certain normative contrasts between the way in which this concept is employed by historians and anthropologists.

A. L. Kroeber, in his insightful little book *An Anthropologist looks of History*, made note of the fact that history, or historians, tend to see process as the force which causes events to cohere in time. Process is a conceptual binder, those factors of individual personality, charisma, particular political or economic alignments and "accidents" which can be used as tools to explain historical outcomes. The course of change in history proceeds by and large through a series of steps, events of special magnitude or importance. This concern with the particular, be it a battle or a personality, is of course a reflection of traditional history's place within the humanities, and it shares with its sister disciplines this common ground. The concern with events, or short periods of very rapid, profound change is reflected in archaeology through some of its terminology. Stages of cultutral development, as in the Three Age System, or shorter period within them, are exemples of what is referred to here. The stages or periods represent relatively long spans of time with, again, relatively changeless conditions or life ways. Stages and periods are set apart from one another by shorter term events, be they technological innovations (agriculture, bronze or iron) or shifts in dynasties. The box-like elements in our charts of time/space relationships are probably the most visual portrayal of this perspective on process.

Kroeber, in the same work noted above, contrasted the historians' view of process to one which he felt was more anthropological (see also Binford and Binford 1968, and Watson, LeBlanc and Redman 1971). Here process is not related to the understanding of particular events but is the abstraction employed to understand events generally. Process is the element common to all events within an historical tradition. In a sense. process for the anthropologist is the thread of continuity through time which is essential for an understanding of cultural traditions and explaining cultural change and development. It is probably an unfair reduction to state that process for the historian is particularizing and that for the anthropologist is generalizing, but it may serve the purpose of a catalyst in conveying some meaning.

Accepting this contrast in the way in which process is viewed, it is then clear that the anthropologist will tend to treat the archaeological record within a particular framework. For example, stages and periods recede into the background since process is that phenomenon which provides the continuity through the human career. Cultural traditions and phases within them are much more at harmony with anthropological conceptualization. The emphasis shifts from seeking an understanding of events themselves to investigating the multilinear, long term configuration of variably paced, continuous culture change. It is worth noting in closing that the tendency in anthropology to employ process as a generalizing, not particularizing, concept places the discipline within the fold of the social sciences, not the humanities.

Let it not be assumed that the contrasts I have drawn in this brief paper are intended to be critical of any style of archaelogical interpretation. It is probably unwise to be excessively doctrinaire when thinking of most of these issues. There are, however, some distinctively anthropological ways of looking at the past and it does no harm for these to be reiterated from time to time with the intention of bringing together more closely those who would seek an understanding of the human career. It is, after all, a truism that good archaeology is archaeolagy that makes sense.

REFERENCES

Binford, L. R. and S. Binford 1968 *New Perspsctives in Archaeology*. Chicago : Aldine.

Sankalia, H. D. 1977 *New Archaeology: Its scope and application to India*. Lucknow Ethnographic and Folk Culture Society.

Steward, J. 1958 *A Theory of Culture change*. Urbana: University of Illinois Press.

Watson, P. J., S. LeBlenc and C. Redman 1971 *Explanation in Archaeology*. New York : Columbia University Press.

Willey, G. and P. Phillips 1958 *Method and Theory in Archaeology*. Chicago: University of Chicago Press.

The Grey Ware Culture of Northern Pakistan Jammu & Kashmir and Panjab

T. N. Khazanchi

Indian Institute of Advanced Study, Simla

and

K. N. Dikshit

Archaeological Survey of India, New Delhi

(Received on 10 March 1978)

THE PROBLEM

SOME cultures have been reported in recent years from different Grey Ware horizons in northern Pakistan, Panjab and Jammu & Kashmir (Dani, 1967, Antonini and Stacul, 1972, 1977 and Mughal, 1972) (fig. 1). Hand made grey ware and burnished grey ware ranging from thick to fine fabric have also been found in the excavations at Burzahom, situated 16 km north-east of Srinagar in the Kashmir valley, (IAR 1960-61 to 1970-71). The recent excavations at Manda lying on the right bank of river Chenab in the foot-hills of Pir Panjal range, also revealed in the late Harappan complex a grey ware of the associated variety of Painted Grey Ware and also a thicker variety of burnished grey ware (Joshi, 1978). In this paper, an inter-relationship of these Grey Ware cultures which usually range from *c.* 1700—1000 B.C. and even earlier at Burzahom has been attempted. Co-relation of these cultures with those in West Asia, specially with the north-east Iran where a grey ware horizon (Dyson, 1967) was found overlaping with the terminal painted wares and then quickly developing characteristics of its own or showing an apparent change of cultural pattern and grey ware of northern and central China could be possible with more data as and when it is available. The problem of identifying one of these cultures with Aryans is beyond the scope of this paper. The following are the Grey Ware using cultures outlined here briefly.

NORTHERN PAKISTAN

Gandhara Grave Cultures

Giuseppe Tucci discovered grave-yards at different sites in Swat region between 1956 and 1960. The excavations at Butkara II, Katelai and Loebanr (Antonini and Stacul, 1972), revealed the general lay out of the graves, typology of the shapes and ornamental motifs on the vases and other objects that form part of the funerary furnishings. The material has been divided into three cultural periods ranging from *c.* 1400/1300 to 400 B.C. and compared to the periods V, VI and VII in Ghaligai sequence (Stacul, 1969).

The skeletons in these graves were placed in a crouching position with the legs and arms bent and hands placed near the head. The orientation of the skeleton was in accordance with the slope of the hill. In crematory graves, pots were generally found near the cinerary jar.

The grave pots are divided into wares ranging from grey thick-sided, red thick-sided, grey thin-sided,

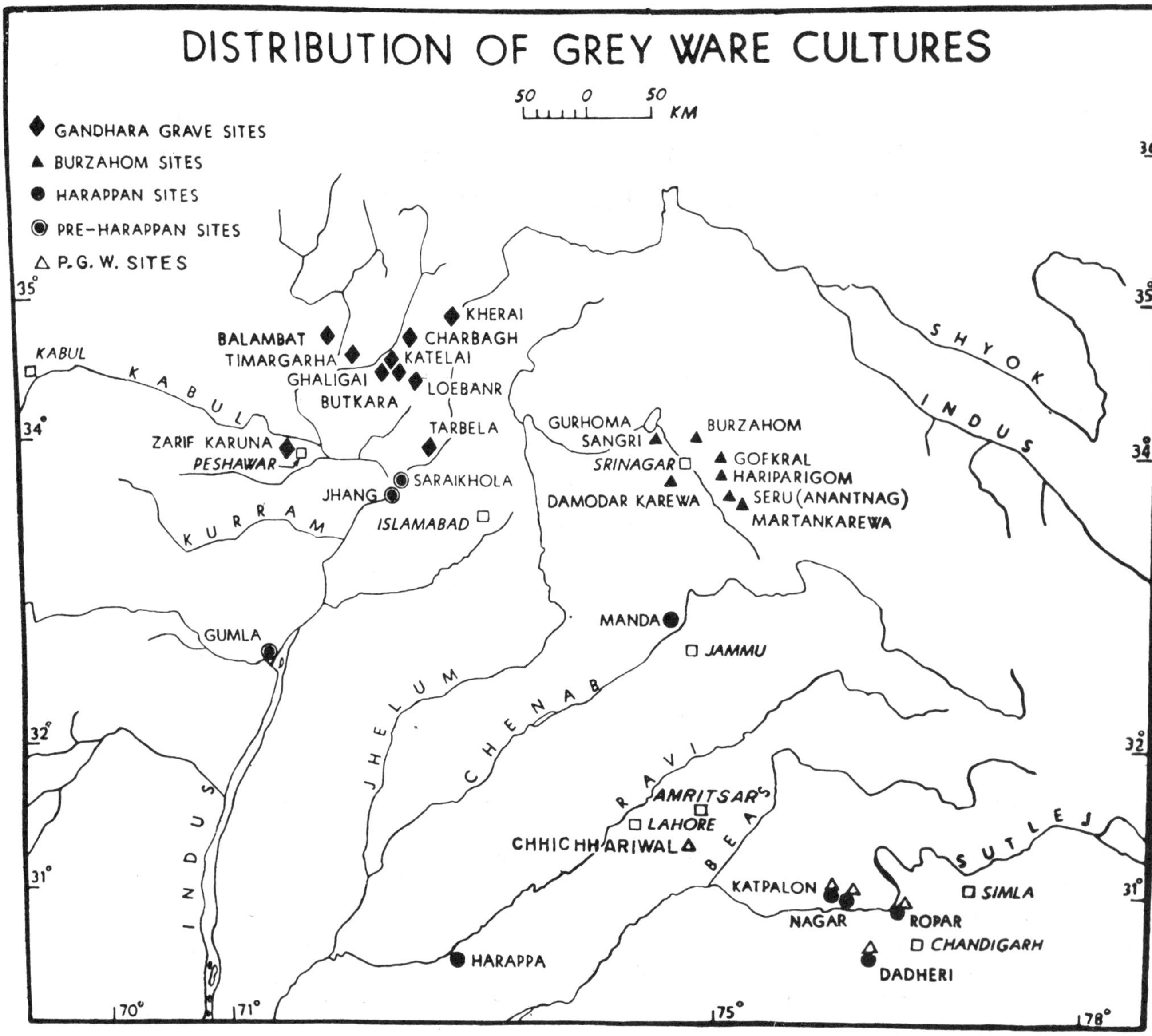

FIG. 1

red thin-sided, grey-brown ware with incised and applique decorations, large red vases and box-shaped urns. The shapes are bowls-on-stand, globular vessels with out-turned rims, small beakers, jugs, jars-lids; miniature vases and other miscellaneous types.

Besides pottery, the graves also revealed anthropomorphic and theriomorphic figurines, spindle whorls, needles, harpoons, mace-heads, arrow and spear heads, axes, rings, pins with disc-heads, beads and other objects.

In more recent years, excavations in the Swat valley seem to identify an earlier culture, the peculiar trait of which consists of black-grey burnished pottery. The settlement of Leobanr III, dated from *c.* 1700—1500 B.C. and related to Period IV in the Ghaligai sequence, provided the main evidences by this culture (Stacul, 1977). The graveyard of Kherai in the Gorband valley (Stacul, 1966), has been reported to belong to the same cultural complex,

The excavations of graves at Timargarha and at a habitational site at Balambat, just opposite the river, revealed three cultural periods dated respectively to *c.* 1600—1300 B.C., *c.* 1200—1000 B.C., and *c.* 900—600 B.C., (Dani, 1967). Period I is absent at Balambat. The pottery reported from here is grey as well as red in both the periods. In Period II, the grey ware continued with some new forms. A few shapes associated with the Painted Grey Ware could be also seen in this complex (Lal, 1977). The horse is also associated with this culture. Other cultural traits corresponds well with the material excavated by the

Italian mission in Swat valley. In any case the 'Gandhara Grave Culture' of Dani is contemporary with the cultural periods V, VI and VII in the Swat valley. It was also recognized in the deposits of of Period V at Gumla (Dani, 1970-71).

The excavations at Zarif Karuna, near Peshawar, a site akin to those in Swat and Dir and associated with Gandhara Grave cultures-revealed four types of burials. In addition to red and also grey pottery, terracotta female and bull figurines and personal ornaments in bone, silver, gold and stone were found (Mughal, 1972).

JAMMU & KASHMIR

Burzahom Culture

The excavations at Burzahom dating back to about *c.* 2500 B.C. revealed four cultural periods, the earliest periods I and II being the neolithic. Period I yielded polished stone-axes, bone tools and hand made steel grey ware. The habitational pattern is distinguished by dwelling pits, nearly circular in plan, wider at the base and narrower at the top. Besides, there were the rectangular or squarish semi-subterranean shelters cut about 0.50 m to 1.00 m into the natural soil, with post-holes, hearths, drains and landing steps. The side walls were plastered with *Karawa* mud. In neolithic Period II, although the habitational pattern had undergone a change, the earlier cultural traits continue, but some new cultural contacts are clearly indicated. Some new tool types are clearly in evidence, such as the harvestors in bone and stone, found for the first time in India. The double edged pick in stone also make its appearance. The incidence of tools in bone & stone is prolific. Human and animal burials have been found from neolithic Period II, but no burials have been found from neolithic Period I. The burials are either primary or secondary and within the settlement. In some cases red ochre has either been sprinkled or pasted. Ritual burial of animals, especially the practice of domestic dogs in the graves with their masters were also noticed (Khazanchi, 1977).

The pottery of Period I & II is a hand made grey ware of different shades. The early pottery with types *e.g.* bowls, vases and stems, is usually coarse both in fabric and finish. Period II yielded a great variety of fine pottery. The distinctive type is a high necked jar in grey or black burnished ware. On the lower part of the neck were incised oblique notches. Mat impressions formed exclusive designs on thin ware. Other shapes are bowls, globular pots, jars, stems and a funnel shapped vessel. Besides, a few red ware wheel turned sherds and a globular pot painted in black and wheel-turned, has been found from the earliest level of Period II.* A few copper barbed arrow-heads with the mid rib, ring bangle and pin have also been found from the earlier lsnsvels of neolithic Period II (pl. XII). As such intrusion from some contemporary culture or cultures from across the border with Harappan and pre-Harappan affinities is clearly indicated, A similar culture-interaction was also noticed at Sarai Khola near Islamabad. The Grey Ware also continued in restricted form in Period III at Burzahom which has predominantly red or gritty red ware.

The excavations at Manda in Jammu & Kashmir also revealed a Grey Ware from late Harappan horizon. The Grey ware, according to the excavator, belongs to the Painted Grey Ware assemblage of northern India. A thicker variety of burnished grey ware is also present. No Painted Grey Ware has been reported from any part of Jammu & Kashmir so far.

PUNJAB

Painted Grey Ware & Grey Ware Culture

The excavations at Ropar and at a number of ofher sites revealed a hiatus between Painted Grey Ware and the Harappan deposit. Recently, in excavations at Dadhari, Katpalon and Nagar, PGW has been reported from the late Harappan deposit. The black-and-red ware was also found in this level at Katpalon. (Joshi, 1978, Dikshit, 1967). The incidence of PGW is not prolific in these deposits, whereas in Haryana and Western Uttar Pradesh the position is different.

The village to village survey of Antiquarian Remains of Amritsar and Gurdaspur Districts revealed more than a dozen sites having grey ware, black-slipped and black-and-red wares all typologically belonging to the Northern Black Polished Ware period. Painted Grey Ware as such has been reported only from two sites of Tahsil Taran Taran, District Amritsar (IAR 65-66 and 66-67). The types are limited to dish and bowl, the fabric being fine to coarse. The associated red ware industry and

* Prof. H.D. Sankalia has published the drawing of this pot in *"Prehistory and Protohistory of India and Pakistan"*, 1974, Fig. 88K-E, but the same does not tally with the original. Shri S.S. Saar of Archaeological Survey of India, who has actually handled this pot has pointed out that the animal has no eyes in the painting, whereas Sankalia has shown them on the basis of Kot Diji example.

terracotta ghata-shaped bead correspond well with associated NBP Ware traits of northern India.

DISCUSSION

The flourishing of different Grey Ware cultures in this region poses a problem of inter-relationship and culture-contact. Dyson outlined a northern Grey Ware horizon in the north-east Iran along the Caspian and Hissar on the adjoining plateau which formed the major pattern of the second millennium B.C. (1967). Thapar also postulated a stage of plain grey ware in this region while discussing the archaeological remains of the Aryans in north western India in the second millennium B.C. (Thapar, 1977). The origin and meaning of this stage may be connected with folk movements of new peoples from the west in north western India in the centuries following *c.* 2000 B.C. The burnished grey ware of Swat Valley is significant when compared with a similar ceramic tradition having analogus shapes in Iran and other ports of Asia. As much the grey ware horizon of north western India becomes a part of a wider geographical area.

The period IV in the Swat Valley which precedes the 'Gandhara Grave Culture' of Dani and Burzahom II very nearly fall chronologically in the same time bracket. The Grey ware pots specially deep bowls or cups with splayed out rims or pedestalled or hemi-spherical bowls with a ring base, globular vases, copper pins, bone points, and crouched position of skeletons at Burzahom indicated some contact with Swat Valley. Stacul has also suggested a culture-interaction between Swat valley, Kashmir valley and China on the basis of underground pit-dwelling, jade beads and burnished grey ware. (Stacul, 1977). Burzahom has affinities with sites in the Shilka valley and some neolithic sites in Eastern Siberia in Russia; these relate to bone tools, harpoons, daggers, arrow-heads and pins. The neolithic cultures in Central and Northern China also have a bearing on the problem of affinities. (Khazanchi, 1977). Perforated harvestors of slate or jade is a fossil type of the Chinese neolithic culture of northern and central China. A Grey ware decorated with basket, toothed comb and cord impressions may also largely be seen in the north, through quite often present in central China. (Gupta, 1979). Besides, there is a geographical continuity between these two regions which cannot be ignored.

The position of Grey or black burnished grey ware of thicker and thinner variety found at Manda near Akhnoor needs further assessment since it has been reported from the late Harappan grey Ware nor does it bear any relationship with the Northern Black Polished ware reported along with black slipped and Black-and-red wares. The Black burnished Grey Ware of Period IV in the Swat Valley is just across the border in Pakistan and there is very liklihood that the deep in-curved bowls, flasks and shallow-lids of this culture which have a typological affinity at Manda, may be an intrusion in the late Harappan complex of north-west India. The presence of thicker variety of black burnished grey ware at Manda has also bearing on the problem and connects it with Swat and Kashmir valleys. (Dikshit, 1978). However, this work requires further confirmation by way of excavations and explorations.

Emergent Picture

The Culture of Period IV of Swat Valley and Burzahom II are the only Grey Ware related Cultures which are contemporary with late Harppans in Panjab (including Pakistan). The cultural instrusion has already been noticed in Burzahom II and so is the case in the cultural gemut of Swat valley. Other cultures Gandhara cultures of subsequent periods and Painted Grey Ware are chronologically much later for any possible co-relation with late Harppan cultures.

This new date of Grey Ware using cultures, however, require a detailed typological study of each and every item found in excavations and explorations. This work could be better handled, if the experts from India, Pakistan, Afghanistan also from Italy who have already done original work in Pakistan may have a joint Project under some International Agency such as UNESCO for taking up extensive explorations in the area and excavations of selected sites in the distributional zone of Gandhara Grave* Culture and sites which have a bearing Burzahom culture. Such Projects will also help in solving other much debated issues like the origin, end or survival of late Harappan cultures in Indo-Pak sub-contient.

REFERENCES

Dani, A.H. 1967 Timargarha and Gandhara Grave Culture, *Ancient Pakistan,* No. 3, Peshwar, 43-48.

* Dr. G. Stacul thinks, that 'Gandhara Grave Culture' may give rise to confusion and suggests its name as 'Gandhara Culture'. (Personal Communication from Dr. G. Stacul). However, we feel that in Indo-Pak sub-continent Gandhara Art is well known and a culture with 'Gandhara' will create more problems of cultural inter-relationship.

Dani, A.H. 1970-71—Excavations in the Gomal Valley, *Ancient Pakistan,* No. 5 Pashawar, 40.

Dikshit, K.N. 1978 The Late Harappan Cultures of India, *Essays in Indian Protohisory,* New Delhi.

——, 1967 Exploration along the right bank of river Sutlej in Punjab, *Journal of Indian History,* Vol. XLV, Part II, Trivendrum, 1561-68.

Dyscn, Robert H. 1967 Problems in Relative Chronology of Iran, 6000—2000 B.C., *Chronologies in Old World Archaeology,* (Ed. R.W. Ehrich), Chicago, 220.

Gupta, S.P. 1979 Archaeology of Soviet Central Asia and the Indian Borderland, Vol 2, Delhi, 302-305.

Indian Archaeology A Review 1966-67, 30 1965-66' 36 1961-62, 71-21 1960-61, 11.

Joshi, J.P. 1978 Interlocking of late Harappa culture and Painted Grey Ware Culture in the light of Recent Excavations, *Man and Environment,* Ahmedabad. 98-101.

Khazanchi, T.N. 1977 North-Western Neolithic Culture of India. News Letter 7&8, *Indian Institute of Advanced Study,* Simla, 24.

Lal, B.B. 1977 The Indo-Aryan Hypothesis vis-vis Indian Archaeology, *Indo-Soviet Symposium on Ethnic Problems of the Early History of the peoples of central Asia and India in the 2nd millennium B.C. Dushanbe,* USSR—(in the press).

Mughal, M.R. 1972 A Summary of Excavations and Explorations in Pakistan, Pakistan Archaeology No. 8. pp 114-158

Silvi Antonine C 1972 The Protohistoric Grave-yards & G. Stacnl of Swat, Pakistan, Rome, 2 Vols.

Stacul, G. 1977 Loebanr III (1700-1500 B.C. i.e. Period IV of Ghaligai) The Black Burnished Ware Period in Swat Valley, *Report on the Proceedings of the Fourth International Conference of South Asia Archaeology* Naples.

——, 1969 Excavation near Ghaligai (1968) and Chronological sequence of Protohistorical Cultures in the Swat Valley (West Pakistan), *East and West,* 19, 44-91.

——, 1966 Notes on the Discovery of a Necropolis near Kherai in the Groband Valley (Swat-West Pakistan), *East and West,* 16, 261-274.

Thapar, B.K. 1977 The Archaeological Remains of the Aryans in north western India; *Indo-Soviet Symposium on Ethnic Problems of the Early History of the Peoples of Central Asia and India in the 2nd millennuim B.C.* Dushanbe (USSR) (in the press).

The Economic Pattern of India during the Early Iron Age (1000 B.C.—100 A.D.) Gujarat

R. N. Mehta

M. S. University of Baroda, Baroda-2.

(Received on 10 Oct. 1978)

INTRODUCTION

THE economic pattern deals essentially with the activities of production of goods, their distribution and ultimate consumption by the producers or by other groups. In this basic life activity, various factors enter into the productive, distributive and consumptive activities. They are studied here on the basis of the archaeological data made available by explorations and excavations in Gujarat. Here it is not collated with literary data, but some known practices are cited for interpretation.

2. PRODUCTION

2.1. Due to the nature of the archaeological data, one finds that the production of the materials of clay, stone, bone and metals is represented on a much larger scale in comparision to the organic production of food-stuff or its acquistion, though in actual practice the situation might be different. Fortunately, however, still enough evidence of the materials of production are available, and they are treated here, to give an outline of the economic pattern prevalent in Gujarat.

3. FOOD-PRODUCTION

3.1 The basic pattern of food-production indicates at least three types of activities : (1) food production (2) animal husbandary (3) hunting and fishing. The available evidence indicates the existance of the production of rice and Kodra as recorded in the excavations at Nagara. The evidence is interesting. Nagara produces good rice even today. The land around it is fairy fertile. The rice production has two divergent lines. One is the cultivation of rice in the fields and its ripening period is sixty days. The other system is that of bunding the fields and transplating the saplings. This system is widely pravelent to-day. It requires some water reservoir to meet scarcity demand and use of low-lying land in which a type of terraced system is developed. Unfortunately the evidence of the field-system is nonexistant, but certain conclusions could be drawn on meagre evidence. This evidence is of two types. One of it is an indirect botanical evidence indicating the fertility and another is the human activity of bunding. The former evidence is given by "Lacromina Croix" seeds that were found at the base of the archaeological deposit at Nagara. Similar evidence was noted at Tripuri also. Lacromina Croix requires water and grows in swamp like fertile land which is admirably suited for rice cultivation. To-day also these seeds are found in similar situation and hence the evidence indicates that the land was suitable for rice cultivation. The other evidence is the existence of a bund. The earthen bunds for small agricultural tanks are essential for storing rain water and using it in the time of scarcity. At Nagara, a small section of the bund was exposed in the excavations, indicating that earthen bunds were used, but its exact nature could be better understood when the other bunds of early Historic period are studied as in the case of the study of Sudarsana lake at Junagadha and others in Sabarkantha. Some of the bunds are about a kilometre long, 100 meter broad at the base and 23 meters high. Such huge constructions cannot be undertaken by a village, but it requires much larger cooperative work undertaken after careful planning and supported by proper financing and organisational set-up. Such work, therefore, could be considered to the result of the state enterprise in different areas.

3.2. These two evidences along with the existence of charred rice-grains indicate the cultivation of rice and if these evidences are pulled to-gether, local irrigation of some nature could be envisaged. Along with rice, the evidence of *Kodra*, is also obtained and cultivated in the rice-growing districts, it is a quick growing type of grain requiring little less water and becomes staple when rice cultivation fails. A variety of legumes are grown in winter in fields where rice is cultivated at present. The evidence of legume is unfortunately non-existant in archaeological record and hence it is difficult to point out the presence of such a system. The proofs of existence of other crops could be collected by further work. The distribution of the settlements in the heavy soil area indicates that the capacity to dig, plough and cultivate, sufficiently heavy black soil known as regur was also developed. The agricultural activities might have led to deforestation of parts of our country.

4. ANIMAL HUSBANDARY

4.1. The existence of the bones of cattle, goat, sheep indicate the presence of animal husbandary. These are of domesticated variety but its sub-species cannot be identified for want of necessary evidence. The animal husbandary has two forms. One of them is the local one and the other is migratory. These forms cannot be identified as they do not leave enough evidence, hence archaeological data indicate the presence of domesticated animals and possibility of animal husbandary of local nature.

5. HUNTING AND FISHING

5.1 The existence of the bones of deer, sambar, neelgai, fish, turtle, along with those of domesticated animals indicate the presence of edible wild life. These animals are fast running agile ones which could be hunted by a group of persons, often supported by dogs. The animal could be taken by throwing sticks like boom rangs or arrows from sufficient proximity. This would become possible by organised efforts. The nature of this organisation is a moot-point in archaeological record from this region. Fish and turtle could be gathered by angling or by nets or traps.

6. VILLAGES AND TOWN

6.1 These activities require steady habitation at one place some amount of migration. The first requirement led to the growth of villages in the area. One finds that many small habitations like Nagara, Timbarva, sathod, Kamrej, Jokha, Dhatva, springing up on the western India litoral and the plants. These villages require house-building and the supporting metal industry, clay industry etc. for its growth.

6.2 The evidence from the early iron settlements indicate the presence of huts. Some times the impressions of stripes on clay indicate that the walls were of the type *Khaparda*, known and used to-day. Whether these houses were in rows as is the case decided for want of evidence. The area of these mounds indicate that these were small villages which grew to become commercial and administrative towns at a later date.

7. CERAMICS

7.1 In these villages and towns sufficient evidence of the manufacture of clay vessels exist. The Potters produced the Black and Red Ware, plain and burnished red ware and some amount of crude red ware. The first variety was more delicate and probably served as platters, bowls and water jars for eating and they were used in *antyesti* also. These are found from the megaliths from different parts of India.

7.2 Besides the manufacture of pottery, the terracotta figurines, beads, were also made by them. The Brick manufacture was also a noted activity.

7.3 The high degree of perfection noted in ceramics and brick work indicate a degree of proficiency of an expert. This would mean that potters profession was well established and might probably have been a full profession. But how his goods reached the users is unknown. If the practice of maintaining this professional as followed in the pre-British days be projected for this period, one can imagine the farmers supporting this important industry, in their own village. Compared to the local wares very few wares from other parts of world are available from some sites. These are the N.B.P. sherds known from Timbarva, Broach, Nagara, Jokha and Somnath and the Roman amphorae known from a few sites. Though their number is quite small, they point to the commercial contact either direct or indirect with the Gangetic valley on one side and the Roman world on the other.

8. STONE-WORK

8.1 Compared to these professions, those of a stone worker, though important enough is not a very essential local profession. The products of this work specially the querns, pestles are necessities but beads, earrings etc. are less in demand. The present day dying practice of these professionals migrating with their goods and selling them for demand be more prevalent, it could account for the small quantity of household goods like legged querns, pestles etc but the beads, ear rings and other objects could move through traders moving in fairs and bazars where the villagers could get these things. Here the stone workers had as producers to move to the mining districts, collect their semifinished or completely finished articals and move with them to the markets or the villages for sale. The mining centres as could be identified on the basis of the stones and some evidence of mining were within a range of 50 kilometers from the settlements. This led to the exploitation of local available material on one side, where as the other material is rare and show much larger area of movement. This profession, therefore, seem to be a more specialised one depending more movement. Whether it was an year round profession or a seasonal one have no evidence, but looking to the conditions of roads and heavy monsoon with its consequent floods, it seems that this might have been a seasonal profession in some of its aspects, i.e. mining and selling, but some aspects of its manufacture such as drilling, polishing of beads, earstuds etc. could continue even all the year round, as a part time economic activity. The fine stone objects moved over a large area and some decorative objects like cameo from Karvan moved from the western world.

9. METALS

9.1 It is interesting to find that the metallurgists of this period used iron, copper, lead, silver and gold. The evidence of iron fortunately is available in the form of slags, crucibles, tuyers and the raw materials from the site like Dhatva and the objects of iron from other sites.

9.2 The establishment of the metal industry at Dhatva depended on the supply of raw material from the surrounding area. The necessary lime, and water was also available in the area and hence the industry flourished. Batch production was the method used for extracting the metal. It was turned into useful objects specially, nails, hoe, sickles, chisels etct. The war materials are found in smaller quantity possibly because the search was made in the villages, where war material will not be stored nor used to the extent that could be found in military and administrative establishments. The sharp edge would have developed by hammering and case hardening, but repeated use of some of these tools would require reheating and resharpening. This would require the presence of a smith at a reasonable distance in a given area. This situation would be met by local smiths one side and migrating groups on other. It is possible that both these groups might be co-existing.

9.3 The silver gold and copper were probably traded in this area where their raw-material is scanty. Lead also might be in the same situation. The areas from which they might have been imported wouid mainly be Rajasthan and possibly south India or even the international trade as could be judged by the Roman bronze Handle from Akota.

10. BONES

10.1 The long bones and splinters of bone were utilised for making arrow-heads, pendants, points, and such objects of daily use. Their manufacture is comparatively simple and the industry might have been both local and sporadic.

11. DISTRIBUTION

11.1 The above discussion has given some indications of non-local material present in the early iron age villages. This includes stone imported from some distance; deluxe pottery such as N.B P. roman amphora etc. and all types of metal objects that are not avaialable locally. These objects could be distributed by travelling manufacturers-cum-salesmen or by businessmen purchasing the goods and distributing them or might have been brought by wandering people. These system might have been in existence along with organisation of overland transport, as well as marine and riverine transport. The pack animals, carts, could have been used for long distance transport by professional groups or small quantities could have been transported on the head of the workers as is practised in the villages. Boats and sea-going vessels would have used the ports of the river mouths. Such ports seem to be simple sit-uations where temporary wooden getty have been used to help the movement. In some places the ship would be kept at a distance and materials be transported in large. The large towns like Broach, Nagara, Kamrej, Somnath, Dwarka and other would have acted at entrepots at different times in this period. Some of these ports have been obsolete, but others still continue to function to a limited extent.

It could however be noted that manifold aspects of the distribution patterns are erased with the passage of time and they are to be reconstructed by distribution maps of certaln well-known commodities. On this basis a few roads could be inferred. One road moved from Broach to Timbarva, Sathod and in the Dabhoi region. While its another branch went past Karvan, Akota, Ajabpura and went to Panchmahals. From near Dohad it moved in the direction of Dhar and possibly reached Ujjain.

The other road moved from Negara, through Tarapur, Dahgam, to Shamlaji and Rajasthan on one side and from Tarapur, Kaira and towards the north Gujarat. The advancing research goes on filling up the gaps on these road patterns, of the early iron age.

12. MEDIUM OF EXCHANGE

12.1 The developing trade and commerce not only led to the growth of commercial centres, but also the medium of exchange in the form of stamped metal which ultimately form the basis of coinage. The punch marked die-struck, cast and regular coins developed very rapidly during the early iron age period.

13. CONSUMPTION

13.1 All the economic activites noted above supplied the basic needs of the consumers. The remains of the consumption as the worship offered to large hearths, discarded fragments of used pottery and the remains of animals after consumption, broken, deserted and buried residential structures and lost beads and other smaller itmes, ultimately were rescued by archaeological operations and these wastages of consumption give evidence of the other economic activities either ditectly or through reasonable inference, based on economic activities.

14. CONCLUSIONS

14.1 In the Early Iron age, the basic economic activity of production of food-stuffs and some local industries were well developed and established. New villages and towns were also being established or the deserted ones were reused. The economic activities show a large amount of local activities, and some amount of trade and commerce. The objects of far flung trade and commerce were very few when the totality of the objects is taken into consideration. Local trade supplied some basic tools and objects necessary for the village communities. The growth of larger commercial centres indicate the rising trade towards the close of this period. The main centres of international trade seem to be the western world. On the whole the economic activities indicate basic agricultural and animal raring groups living in small settlements, depending mostly on local exchange of materials and supplementing fashion goods from other areas.

The Timurid Mosque at Balkh in Afghanistan and Development of Mughal Domes in India

R. Sengupta

Archaeological Survey of India

(*Received on 9 Oct., 1978*)

THE style of art and architecture that flourished under the patronage of the house of Timur or Tamerlane (AD 1369-1405) is called 'Timurid'. The most important contribution of the Timurids to Islamic architecture is in the decoration of large surfaces with coloured encaustic tile-work. It was under Timur's youngest son Shah Rukh (AD 1405-1447) that Timurid art and architecture flowered, and was further nurtured to full bloom by Sultan Husain Bayqara (AD 1468-1506). Some of its finest examples can be seen at Samarkand in Soviet Central Asia and in Herat in Afghanistan. One such mosque is at Balkh, believed to have been built in memory of a distinguished theologian Khwaja Abu Nasr Parsa. Though Balkh was chosen by Timur to proclaim himself as supreme sovereign of Transoxiana and northern Afghanistan in AD 1379, only this mosque of Timurid style survives. The other building at Mazar-i-Sharif is believed to be the mausoleum of Hazrat Ali, the cousin and son-in-law of the Prophet Mohammad. Extensive restoration, however, has obliterated the orginal architecture.

The mosque is one of the finest among the existing monuments at Balkh. Its central location enhances its attractive features. The mosque, actually, is part of a *Hazira* with the grave placed outside the shrine according to the religious injections and usage, as to be seen elsewhere in Central Asia. The rooms flanking the main building appear to have been used as *Khanqah*. The mosque area has been converted into a circular park from which roads radiate in different direction to various parts of the town. Inside the park and in front of the mosque, a recently discovered grave is claimed to be that of the famous poetess Rabia Balkhi who was punished for falling in love with a Turkish slave.

It is a brick structure octagonal on plan with *peshtaks* (portals) on the front and back sides, of which the rear one is missing. It has an underground chamber. From the extant remains on the southern side, it appears that there were half domed arches on the four sides, with entrances on the front and north sides and two storeyed arched niches on the four corners. On the southern side, a passage leads to the underground chamber. The front and northern portions of the structure still retain their original form although much damaged.

Much has been made of the octagonal plan of the Islamic structures. Of the two important factors responsible for this particular shape, one appears to be an earlier tradition of the Buddhist rock cut shrines set up by still earlier mud-brick structures in the steppes of Central Asia. Where wood was available, the roof of a building could be made flat with wooden supports. But in the arid zone, wood being scarce, the entire building, including the roof, had to be made of mud-bricks. To do so, construction of vaults or domes had to be started from the corner, as in a squinch. In course of time, experience showed that it was convenient to make the building more durable if the roof was made to rest on a circular or near-circular base, instead of a rectangular or square one. Squarish and oblong buildings needed squinches at the four corners to convert the top to octagonal form for the base of the dome. If the

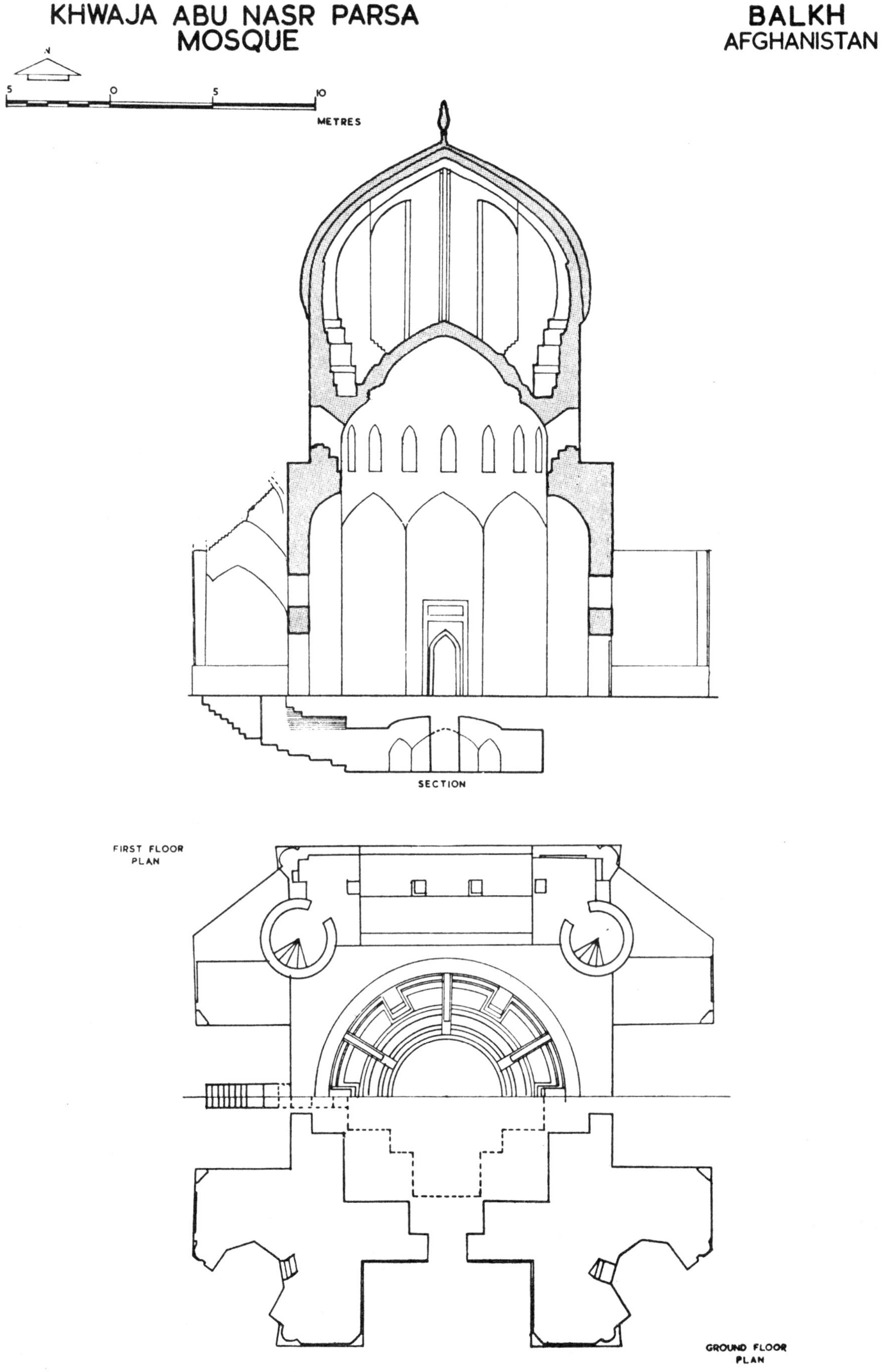
KHWAJA ABU NASR PARSA
MOSQUE
BALKH
AFGHANISTAN
N
5 0 5 10
METRES
SECTION
FIRST FLOOR
PLAN
GROUND FLOOR
PLAN

FIG. 1.

building itself was octagonal on plan, no extra effort was needed for preparing the base and a corbelled dome could easily be constructed on it. Such domes used for domestic purposes had an opening[1] at the top, to let out the smoke generated inside while cooking. The various forms in mud-brick served as models for the Buddhist rock-cut shrines in Afghanistan. Thousands of shrines were scooped out of rock and fashioned in stone after the prevailing types of mud-brick buildings having flat, trabeated and domed roof with or without squinches. Probably for the same reason, the earliest Islamic structural tomb of al-Muntasir, an Abbasid Khalif (AD 861), on the west bank of the Tigris at Samarra, was octagonal on plan (Creswell, 1958).

The entire outer surface of the mosque at Balkh was decorated with coloured enamelled tiles most of which have disappeared. A study of these tiles both in Iran and Afghanistan disproves the theory of Smith[3] (Smith, 1901) that the individual tiles were set on the wall as per the required pattern. In fact, the tiles were cast panelwise as a block (pl. XVI A), with the glazed face down on the ground and the backside plastered over; the size of a block depended on the design and was made to suit convenient handling by workers. The blocks of tiles were then fixed on wall with mortar.

The tiled decoration, on the Balkh mosque were not placed directly on the outer surface of walls as was the usual practice. On this mosque the blocks were fixed panelwise, on a made-up surface obtained by a sort of boxing arrangement with bricks projecting from the surface of wall. It was a construction of brick–on-edge both horizontally and vertically, thereby creating a net-work of squarish pockets which closed from the top provide a vacuum-like space as a layer of insulation between the wall and the veneering. This particular treatment of the outer surface of the mosque, presumably aimed at maintaining the internal heat within the structure in winter and to keep off the external freezing cold from coming into contact with the brick-wall.

The facade is flanked by two minarets which rise between the facade and dome; inside these minarets spiral staircases are provided. The two corner rooms at the top, to which one ascends, could have been used as *chilla* (retiring room). At the corners in front of the minarets, are two corkscrew turrets each rising from a bulbous vase. Behind the facade, a voluminous

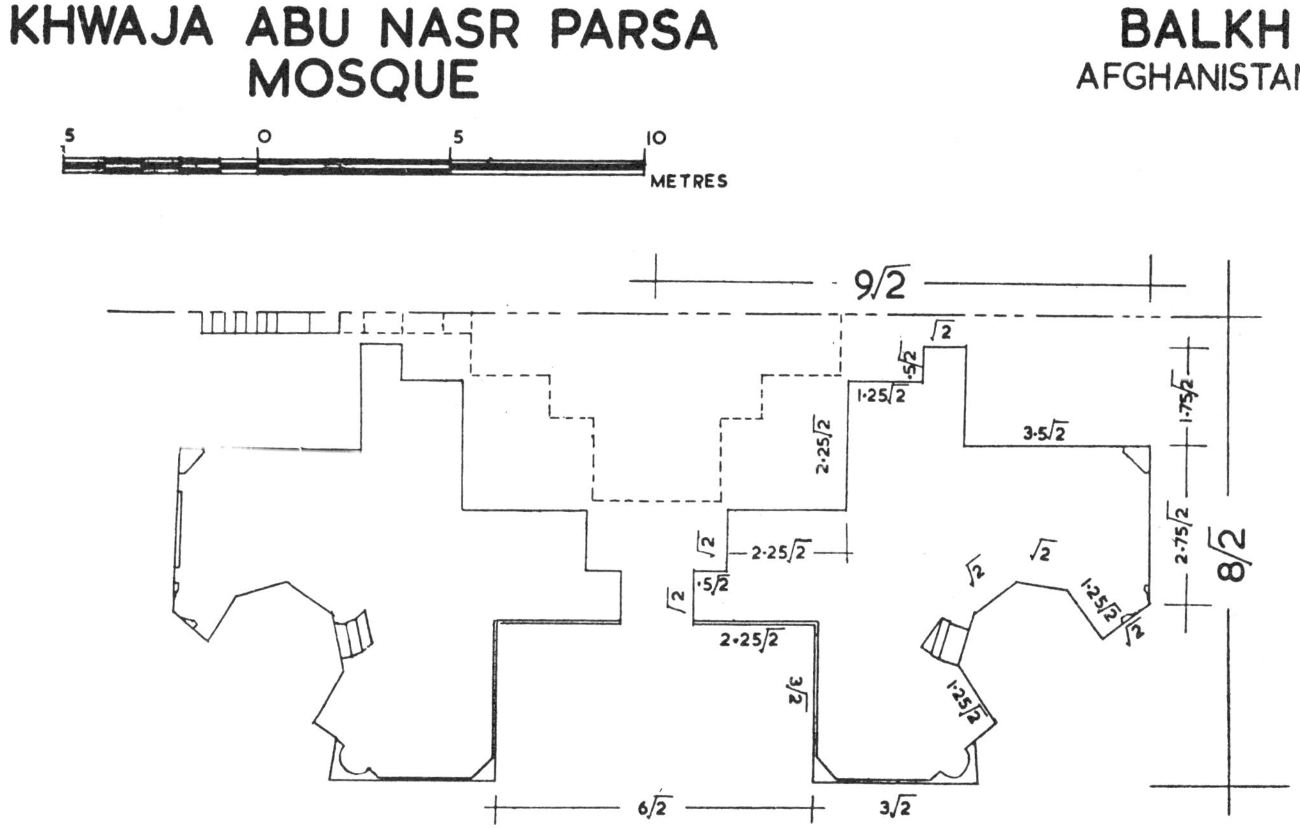

HALF PLAN.

FIG. 2

blue dome rises on a high cylindrical neck. The dome is in the shape of a cantaloup melon with bold convex flutes, on the extrados tapering and converging to the apex.

The crowing member of the mosque, the elegant dome (in spite of its earlier restoration) on a tall neck (XVI B) is of special interest to students of Indo-Islamic architecture. Although it has a decorative ribbed surface, as those of the domes on the mausoleums of Timur at Samarkand,[2] (Pugachinkova, 1976) and of Gauhar Shad (Mulk Raj Anand, 1970) at Herat and that at Koshan, its basic shape of a nomadic tent remains the same. This is the shape one sees in the dome on the tomb known as Sabz-Burj (Joshi, 1972) and its further development in the domes of Khan-i-Khanan's Tomb and Humayun's Tomb in Delhi and the Taj Mahal at Agra. The Mughals, though they retained the outer form of the dome resting on a high cylindrical neck, improved upon the constructional method of the dome as will be made clear later on.

In its simple form, as in the case of the Sabz-Burj near the Humaun's Tomb or the tomb at Koshan near Herat in Afghanistan, the dome has the shape of a traditional tent of nomads as will be evident from the subsequent discussions. This very shape of the tent, in course of time, was translated in the Timurid domes. The particular shape of the dome needed supports, especially, near the springing where the portion is under circumferential or hoop tension. The thin brick-shell of the dome was incapable of taking care of the tension,[3] hence a Timurid dome had to have as support, vertical walls resting on the inner dome and rising up to the crown near the apex along the intrados of the outer dome. Accordingly, the main dome of the Gauhar Shad is supported by twelve vertical walls, the tomb at Koshan has eight and the mosque at Balkh has six walls. There are other examples of this type of buildings in Bukhara and Samarkand. On plan, such a dome, near its base looks like a spoked wheel without the hub[4]. A study of these Timurid domes helps us in understanding the correct meaning and function of the eight vertical walls erected along the intrados of the upper dome of the Sabz Burj in Delhi.

The Timurid domes ware constructed from inside without any centering, as was the practice in Iran and Afghanistan. Along with the vertical supports which served as the framework, complete horizontal rings of brickwork were raised, each of the successive rings canting forward a little till the top was reached. Each ring of brickwork was under circumferential compression. The top-most ring worked as the connection between the opposite sides which was needed to develop the horizontal radial thrust that was also necessary for equilibrium. The brick shell, in effect, was like the membrane covering the wooden frame of nomads' tent. The domes on the tombs of Bade-Khan and Chhote-Khan (fifteenth century) suggest that arches were erected for supports, as was the ancient practice in Iran. The old tradition continues; even now they follow the same technique (Pl. XV B). In India there are numerous instances to show that even with out any support, domes were constructed using the corbelling system. The dome on the Chini-ka-Rouza at Agra and that on Darya Khan's mosque at Mandu depict clearly this technique which necessitated the plaster on the outer surface to be extra-ordinarily thick. to bring out the required curvature of the outer face.

Reverting to the Mughal innovation in the constuction of the outer dome ; to counter the hoop tension, the portion near the base of the dome was made strong and the thickness of shell wide. This treatment incidentally gave the dome of the Tej Mahal the *amaroodi* shape. as mentioned in the Badshahnama, Since the shell of the dome was designed to counter the hoop tension, no vertical wall along the intrados, as support, was needed in Mughal domes,

The Mughal innovation has an earlier parallel in Byzantine work. Many constructional features of the latter were imbibed by the Muslims and some of them were brought with them to India. For example, comparatively small sized, oblong and thin bricks were used by them, on a thick bed of a sort of concrecte-mortar which was made of lime, sand and crushed bricks, tiles or pottery-features also to be seen in Mughal buildings. To reduce the load of the roof, earthen pitchers were introduced in the brick shell of the dome of S. Vital (A.D. 526-47) at Ravenna in Italy. In the haunches of the half domed portal on the southern side of the Chini-ka-Rauze at Agra, in the saucer shaped dome at the entrance of Verinag in Kashmir and in the thickness of roof of the Deeg palaces in Bharatpur (Rajasthan) earthen pitchers were used. The early Byzantine domes had windows in the lower portion. At S. Sophia, Constantinopole (A.D. 532-7), to compensate the weakening effect of the window openings, the haunches were strengthened by a ring of small buttresses. The system of strengthening was improved by hoisting the windows on a high drum and made further effective by grouping of small domes or semidomes round the large central dome, to counter the outward thrust. It is not unlikely that the Byzantine high drum and shape of the dome which led to the development of the bulbous or onion shaped domes on the church of S. Sophia at Novogorod (A.D. 1052) might have also influenced in shaping the Timurid domes.

Regarding the origin of Timurid domes, Creswell (Creswell, 1915) propounded a theory in 1915 that the Umayyad Mosque at Damascus, in AD 705-13, which was burnt and re-constructed with a double dome of wood and covered by lead, was seen by Timur in January, AD 1400 and he was so impressed by the shape of it that he took some workmen from Damascus to Samarkand to erect buildings.[5] To support his theory he could not produce any argument to convince that the shape of the dome was bulbous. But he insists on the point that the workmen from Damscus (he also mentions of Timur's admiring the Juma Masjid and the Qutab Minar and of his carrying off some workmen from Delhi) constructed in brick the domes of Gur Amir and Bibi Khanum at Samarkand. His main points of argument are : the diameter of the dome at Damascus and that of Bibi Khanum is almost the same and that the dome on Gur Amir has sixty-four brick convolutions (as on that of S. Theodore, Constantinopole, c. 1100) against forty-eight wooden ribs of that at Damascus.

According to the writer's view, the shape of the Timurid dome was copied from the shape of an *Ooy* or Uzbek tent used in that area which agrees with that of the former. An *Ooy* can be carried on domestic animals and so is used by the Uzbek-and Turkoman-nomads of the steppes of Central Asia. The simple cylindrical wall on the ground and its broadly conical roof could be put up easily with a bundle of wooden scantlings. The top is covered with either leather or blanket of wool provided by the domestic cattle they maintain. The wooden ribs converging to a circle at the apex lend the roof the shape of a squattish cone.[6] The arrangement can very well be studied in the *Yurt* (*Khedgah* in Dari) adopted and improvised tastefully by the Afghan Tourism Department. In support of the assumption, several examples of tents before and after, the date of Timur may be cited. To begin with, the specimen of a tent used by nomads may be seen (Kislyakova *et al.* 1957) where felt has been used and the tent has the rudimentary shape of a Timurid dome with a low rise. The next example comes from a painting (Ettinghausen, 1962) depicting encampment of al-Hariri (*c.* 1225-1235), at Baghdad from Maqamat Manuscript in Oriental Institute, Leningrad. In this painting two shapes of tents are shown, one with a conical roof and the other to the right side, near the bottom, depicts the squattish hemispherical top. And the third example also is supplied by a painting (*c.* 1310) (Blochet, 1929)[14] which depicts Chengiz Khan sitting on his throne in a tent, proclaims himself emperor, after his victory over Turkey. The painting is from Tabriz and is now in the Bibliotheque Nationale, Paris. The shape of the tent is different from the earlier forms cited so far, as it shows a prominent bulging at the springing and the top, instead of conical, and is rounded off at a higher level. another painting (Blochet, 1929)[9] of the same date (*c.* 1310) depicting the Mongol Army under Oroghotu Noyan, having taken Baghdad comes to besiege Irbil, there is a tent, the dome of which looks very much the same as that of a Timurid one. But the tents in the painting (Stchonkine 1929) of Akbar's time, depicting the story of the unfaithful wife (Bodleian Library, Oxford), very faithfully copied the Timurid dome, including the swelling above the springing. Thus it will be seen that in paintings the shape of the contemporary tent has faithfully been copied since the 13th century. The practice of translating the domestic architecture through durable materials into secular and religious buildings has been commented upon. It is a well-known fact that in India also rock-cut architecture was copied from earlier wooden prototypes. Later, *Kutas* and *salas* which are but rural huts, were used by the Pallavas and their successors on *dravida* temples. Jahangir introduced the common Bengal hut, with a thatched roof, on Mughal palaces for decoration. And again the Vishnupur temples, (Percy Brown) famous for their terracotta decorations, are also huts in brickwork. It was, therefore, no wonder if Timur with his strong bias for native things would use the shape of the nomads' tent on his buildings. The amount of interest he took in the construction of the buildings would be borne out by the report that he used to supervise the works himself and get demolished the portions which he did not like, to be redone. So, one cannot agree with Creswell's theory that the construction of Gur Amir and Bibi Khanum was left to the workmen of Damascus.

The main defects in the Balkh mosque were that at the junctions and corners of walls no bonding was established and the use of poor quality of mortar, already referred to above in respect of the Bibi Khanum mosque. Besides the constructional defects, the mosque also suffered from earth-quake shocks to counter which wooden logs were introduced in these buildings at various levels. The dome of the mosque had developed several radial cracks due to tension, even though there were vertical supports along the intrados. In brick-work, the potential tensile resistance of the individual units could be developed by frictional forces induced by a strong mortar at the horizontal bed-joints. This was achieved in respect of the brick-shell of the Mughal domes where extra supports were discarded. The bricks used in the Mughal domes were not of the same size nor the mortar was similar to that, as used in the Timurid buildings, even though the Timurid architectural style was followed

The form of the dome called 'Timurid' was already in use in Turkestan and Samarkand in the late 14th century. His house naturally adopted it on the Timurid buildings, be at Samarkand or Bukhara or Herat. In India the shape as produced in the dome of the Sabz Burj was introduced probably during the time of Babur who was a descendant of Timur and a staunch Uzbak. His strong attachment to Samarkand as also his distaste for 'Hindustani' buildings were well known. Besides, the sloped wall of the high neck of the dome again betray the earlier Tughlaque trait which continued in Lodi buildings as well. In the true Timurid or early Mughal buildings this slope in the high drum was not used.

The other point which may be taken into consideration in dating the Sabz Burj is the size of bricks used. In Afghanistan, in Timurid monuments bricks of the size of $24 \times 24 \times 6$ cm. size have been used. The superstructure of the Sabz Burj is of rubble masonry but the dome and the drum are partially made of bricks ; in the drum bricks with an average $24 \times 24 \times 4$ cm. size have been used. In the dome which has a rubble covering, small bricks of the size of $22 \times 13 \times 4$ cm. have been used at the bottom, and at the top still smaller sized bricks 15 x 9 x 4 cm. have been used. It appears that taking advantage of the vertical walls as supports, small sized bricks were used at the same time making room for the rubble veneering.

In reducing the size of the bricks no previously known size seems to have been in their view, the main consideration evidently was to reduce the width for the brick to be placed horizontally to form a ring. It was made rectangular unlike its earlier form, to establish a better bonding in the brick-work. The big rectangular size, however, agrees generally with that used (21 x 14 x 4) in the Ram Bagh at Agra, a garden layed by Babur. The size of bricks used in the portions added or repaired subsequently is small. In Delhi at Palam a mosque, on which the inscription says that it was erected during the time of Babur has the bricks of the sizes of 28 x 22 x 5 cm. and 28 x 19 x 5 cm. In this connetion it is worthwhile to note that in the earliest Islamic brick dome in India on the Tomb of Iltutmish (*c.* AD 1235) the bricks used are 27 x 22 x 5 cm. and 22 x 18 x 4.5 cm. In the Lal Kot similar sized bricks were used. The brick sizes used in the Palam mosque agree in general with the sizes used locally by the Tomars and Chauhans. In the mosque with an inscription of Hamayun's time at Kachpura in Agra, bricks of the same size as was used at Ram Bagh are to be found. Against this background, it may be deduced that in the constructions put up by different people or with the introduction of a new dynastic rule, wholesale changes in the use of materials and methods should not be expected ; the part played by age-old usage and traditions should also be considered. In the case of the smaller rectangular brick used on the Sabz Burj also a comparison is no less interesting. The size does not tally with any of those used in the buildings in the neighbourhood. It may only be compared with one of 15 x 9 x 3 cm. size in the Zafar Mahal, the abode of the last Mughal King Bahadur Shah Zafar. But in Mughal buildings the thickness of bricks shrunk from 4 cm. to 3 cm. or even less.

No square brick was used on the Nila Gumbad, Humayun's tomb or Khan-i-Khanan's tomb where the domes were made of bricks with a rubble covering. In the Nila Gumbad the bricks are of 19 x 11 x 3 cm. size and in Khan-i-Khanan's tomb the size is 17 x 11 x 3 cm. ; whereas in Humayun's tomb the bricks are of 12 x 8 x 3 cm. size.

A study of drawings of the Balkh mosque has unravelled interesting statistics in respect of the proportions and relationship between the different parts of the building and the unit used as the key to measurements of the parts. The total width of the building, if divided into four equal parts of $4.5\sqrt{2}$ m. each, a side works out to two parts which is $9\sqrt{2}$ m.; The ends of four sides when connected make the octagon. The width of the building also makes the total height of the mosque, upto the apex of the dome. The width of the facade is equal to the inner height of the building—from the floor upto the crown of the inner dome. So, from that point upto the apex of the outer dome the height is equal to two parts $9\sqrt{2}$ m. or the width of the facade. The same is the total width of the drum of the dome. The height of the superstructure is about $8\sqrt{2}$ m. and that of the drum of the dome is $4.5\sqrt{2}$ m. These measurements and proportions give out general framework of the building.

The basic unit for working out the plan of the mosque works out to be $\sqrt{2}$ m. But to which unit of measurement $\sqrt{2}$ m. corresponds — Turkish[7] or otherwise—has to be found out. The various measurements worked out on the basis of the unit are shown on a quarter portion of the plan (fig. 2)of the mosque at Balkh.

The writer gratefully remembers his deceased colleague N.J. Thirunavukarasu who started preparing the drawing of the mosque while engaged in the conservation work at the monument and died there. Thanks are also due to the late S. G. Korde, Sarvashri Balbir Singh, V. Ramasubramaniyam and Rama Rao for preparing the drawings at various stages. Shri Ganesh Rao assisted in working out the measurements to whom the writer is beholden.

COMMENTS

1. Following the tradition, the outer dome on the tomb of Khan-i-Khanan was provided with such an opening without any functional value.
2. See Prof. Pugachinkova—splenders of Samarkand Architecture' in *Marg*, Vol. XXXIX, No. 2, (March 1976), pp. 36-41, Fig. 59. For a section of the building showing the constructional features of the outer dome, see page 83 in Living Architecture, Islamic Indian (1970), Andress Voluashen (Pl. VI). Twelve vertical walls again are fixed horizontally with wooden tiebeams which practice was repeated in trying the supports in the dome at Koshan. In Balkh mosque the vertical walls are tied to the shell of the dome.
3. The mosque erected by Timur in five years (A.D. 1399-1404) is locally known as Bibi-Khanum, erroneously associating Timurs wife, Sarai-Mulk-Hakim, who actually got a Madrasa built up in that complex. According to Prof. Pugachinkova 'The principles on which the pavilion was built are geometrical. The grandeur of the mosque of Timur has been obtained by its proven architectural values, rising above the building technique of that time. Contemporary writers write not of the initial years of the construction of the building, but when bricks from the top were falling on the heads of the people offering prayers..... The brickwork was commented by a solution that could be broken even by a light stroke of the pick' Ibid, p. 35. The mortar used in the Balkh mosque was gypsum and sand, probably the same type of mortar was used in all Timurid monuments in that region, including those in Bukhara and Samarkand.
4. On plan some Buddhist stupas are in the shape of a spoked wheel, so that the thrust of the back-filling is divided into many parts and the impact is lessened. It cannot be said with any certainty if in the construction of the outer dome, the Timurids followed the above mentioned Buddhist practice. According to Blochet the Mongols tried to bring about a revival of Buddhism but it did not work. Nonetheless, Mongols under the orders of the Chiefs of the house of Chingiz Khan, got Tibetan Buddhist books translated, when they had attained to the sovereignty of the Chinese Empire, (Musulman Painting, pp. 69 & 71).
5. Chingiz Khan and his Mongols had no metropolis, but wandered in the steppes ;......... The princes of the Mongols when they have conquered Persia, the Turks of Tamerlane when they had quitted the deserts of Central Asia to come and reign in Iran, did not inhabit the Persian towns... like true descendants of those nomads who, in ancient times, prowled by the side of the Great Wall, they pitched their tents in the country under the ramparts of their cities......' (Blochet, Ibid, p. 66).
6. For a full discussion on the subject see 'The White House of Khurasan : The felt Tents of the Iranian Yomut and Goklen' by P.A. Andrews in Iran, Vol. XI, 1973 pp. 93-110. There were also tents with conical roof (Fig. 1b) which were translated in structural representations.
7. According to a Turkish linear unit qari, the length may vary from 24 inches to 36 inches. If the maximum value of the unit is taken then $\sqrt{2}$ m. will be about 1.3 qari (A S. Beveridge-Baburnama, Vol. 1 pp. 630 and 631 f.n. 1.).

REFERENCES

Anand, Mulk Raj, 1970, 'The Development of Islamic Architecture in Afghanistan', in *Marg*, Vol. XXIV, No. 1, pp. 39-40.

Blochet, E., 1929, *Musalman Painting*, pl. LX, Fig. 1(c), pl. LXII, Fig. 1(d).

Brown, Percy, 1956, *Indian Architecture* (Hindu and Buddhist), pl. CXXXIII.

Creswall, K A.C., 1915, 'The history and evolution of dome in Persia' in the *Indian Antiquary*, Vol. XIV, pp. 133-159.

——, 1958, *'Early Muslim Architecture'* pp. 287-88 ; fig. 59.

Ettinghausen, Richard, 1962, *'Arab Painting'*, p. 112 ; Fig. 1(b).

Joshi, M.C., 1972-73, 'Sabz-Burj' : An early Mughal Tomb' in *Puratattva*, No. 6, pp, 87-89.

Kislyakova, N.A., and Pershitsa, A.I. Ed., (in Russian), 1957, 'People of former Asia,' figure on p. 113 ; Fig. 1(a).

Smith, E.W., 1901, *'Moghal Colour decoration of Agra'*, pp. 6-11,

Stchonkine, Iuan, 1929, *'La Peinture Indienne,'* pl. X ; Fig. 1(e).

Did the Painted Grey Ware continue up to the Mauryan Times ?

1. INTRODUCTORY

TWENTYFIVE years ago, in my report on the excavations at Hastinapura, I suggested that Periods II and III of the site, characterized respectively by the Painted Grey Ware (PGW) and the Northern Black Polished Ware (NBPW) may be dated to *circa* 1100-800 B.C. and *circa* early sixth-early third century B.C. (Lal 1954-55). It was further stipulated that though there was no overlap at Hastinapura between these two wares, the same could have taken place elsewhere, and that the overlap phase would be assignable to the time-gap between the two Periods. In so far as the PGW was concerned, the implication was that the ware was unlikely to have continued later than the sixth century B.C.

At that time the radiocarbon method of dating was not available and thus the above-mentioned dates were suggested on the basis of comparative stratigraphy. Since then the ^{14}C method has come into use and has been applied to a large number of sites (including Hastinapura where a small, partly excavated portion was further dug up to obtain the samples). The dates initially proposed by me have either been supported or challenged by scholars, one of whom, at a seminar held in 1972, under the auspices of the Tata Institute of Fundamental Research (TIFR), Bombay, put forward the thesis that (i) the Painted Gray Ware continued without any change up to the Mauryan times and (ii) its antiquity could not go back prior to 800 B.C. (Dikshit 1973). The radiocarbon experts of TIFR lent a 'scientific' support to such a thesis, by assigning to the PGW a time-bracket of *circa* 800-400 B.C. in the first instance (Agrawal *et al.* 1974) and later on pushing the upper limit of the bracket to 300 B.C. (Agrawal *et al.* 1978). To put the issue in a historical perspective, these authors would like us to believe that if we were living during the reign of Chandragupta Maurya we would have taken our meals in the PGW dishes and bowls. In fact, Dikshit would like to place such an event during the reign of Asoka or even his successors, for in the course of his excavations at Allahapur in District Meerut, Uttar Pradesh, he found 'a terracota sealing inscribed in the *late* Mauryan characters' from sub-period IB in which 'the PGW fabric continued to remain fine and did not show degeneration in the technique of manufacture and painted designs as happened at other PGW sites'. (Dikshit 1973).

The purpose of the present article is to examine if the PGW did really continue into the Mauryan times and whether there is no case for its having begun before 800 B.C. In doing so, the evidence from all the sites which have yielded the PGW and for which ^{14}C dates are available in respect of either the PGW itself or the succeeding NBPW, will be examined, for thus alone can a general picture of the chronology of this ware be expected to emerge. If, in the course of the study, it is found that certain sites give erratic evidence, an attempt will be made to understand the reason for the aberration. This kind of site-wise and detailed analysis seems to be called for, since a tendency is growing to overemphasize the evidence from one or two sites ignoring the evidence from the bulk of the other sites—in other words, the view of the wood as a whole is being lost for the sake of an isolated tree here or there !

The main regions of the occurrence of the PGW in India are : Panjab, Haryana, northern and eastern Rajasthan, and western Uttar Pradesh. In small quantities and in a somewhat latish form the ware has been found to occur up to southern Madhya Pradesh (e.g. Kayatha) and eastern Uttar Pradesh (e.g. Kausambi). In Pakistan it has been noted to occur at Harappa in Panjab (Allchins 1968, p. 210) and even further to the south-west, at Lakhiyo Pir in Sind. Recently, Rafique Mughal has explored many sites containing this ware, in the erstwhile Bahawalpur State.

As stated earlier, we shall take up only those sites in the present discussion, for which ^{14}C dates are available. In this context, however, it may also be stated the ^{14}C *dates are not calender dates* and, therefore, it is necessary to 'calibrate' them if we are indeed looking for a proper chronological horizon in terms of years before Christ. Thus, in this paper, for each ^{14}C

date two calibrated dates are given, one according to E.K. Ralph (*et al.* 1973) and the other according to R.M. Clark (1975). Since there is some minor variation between these calibrations, the reader may make his own choice.

2. ANALYSIS OF THE DATA

WE shall begin with sites in Panjab and proceed eastwards. It may, incidentally, be added that no ^{14}C dates are available for the PGW sites in Pakistan.

The only site in Panjab which has yielded the PGW and for which ^{14}C dates are available is Ropar. However, the ^{14}C dates relate to the NBPW strata and not to those of the preceding PGW. The following is the relevant extract from 'Tata Institute Radiocarbon Date List IV', published in *Radiocarbon*, Vol. 8, 1966, p. 450 :

"Ropar series, Punjab

Ropar (30° 58′ N Lat, 76° 32′ E Long), Dist. Ambala, has given a sequence from the Harappan to late historical times. Site was excavated by Y.D. Sharma in 1953. Samples subm. by A. Ghosh.

TF-213. N.B.P. ware deposits 2275±100
325 B C.

Charred wood from Trench RPR-1, Locus o-VIII, Layer 26, depth not given, Field No. RPR-1-1710.

TF-209. N.B.P. ware deposits 2365±100
415 B.C.

Charred wood from Trench RPR-2, Locus X′-XI′, Layer 30, depth 11 m, Field No. RPR-2-3094."

Since the above dates are based on the radiocarbon half-life value of 5568 years, these have first to be recalculated on the basis of the half-life value of 5730 years, and then their calibration done. The results are given in a tabulated form below :

Laboratory number	Cultural horizon	Value in B.C. based on 5730 half-life	Calibrated date in B.C. according to Ralph	Calibrated date in B.C. according to Clark
TF-213	Middle (?) NBPW	390±105	420±105	410±105
TF-209	Early NBPW	485±100	470±100	465±100

Since the report on Ropar has not yet been published, it is difficult to say if sample TF-209 comes from the earliest layer of the NBPW period or there were a few more layers below it. Nevertheless from the foregoing date it would be clear that beginning of the NBPW at Ropar cannot be placed later than the first half of the fifth century B. C. In these layers no PGW as found, which essentially preceded the NBPW. *Thus, by no strech of Imagination can it be said that at Ropar the PGW continued after c. 500 B C.* Since no ^{14}C dates are available for the PGW itself, it would be futile to assess the beginning of this ware at Ropar.

For the PGW sites in Haryana no ^{14}C dates are available. Hence we pass on to sites in Rajasthan. Of these, only two viz. Noh and Jodhpura, have been dated by this method. Two laboratories have given ^{14}C dates in respect of Noh. The following is an extract from the UCLA Date list published in *Radiocarbon*, Vol. 7, 1965.

"Painted Gray Ware series, India

A joint expedition by Univ. of Rajasthan, India, and UCLA excavated in January 1964 a site at Noh near Bharatpur, Rajasathan, about 30 miles from Agra (27°10′ N Lat, 78°00′ E Long). Charcoal samples listed here originated in a stratified layer at bottom of a hill associated with painted gray ware under 6 ft of earth cover. This pottery type is generally considered to date from 600-1000 B. C., although more recent theories suggest 600-800 B.C. Coll., subm. and comments by J.L. Davidson, UCLA.

UCLA-703 A. Noh, India 2480±250
530 B.C.

Sample H. Tr. A XXII-XXIV. This date and the following support the newer theory and will be useful in placing the painted Gray Ware Culture within a specific time limit.

UCLA-703 B. Noh. India 2690±220
740 B.C.

Sample E, Tr. A XXII–XXIV. See Comments for UCLA-703 A."

In addition, the TIFR Date List of August 1971 has the following data to offer.

"Noh, Rajasthan, India

Samples submitted by the Director, Arch, & Museums, Rajasthan, Jaipur.

TF-993. P.G. Ware Culture 2600±145 (2675±150)

Charcoal from Tr. G., Layer 20. Depth 6.9 m.

TF-994. N.B.P. Ware Culture 2560±100 (2635±105)
Charcoal from Tr. G., Layer 14, Depth 4.7 m.

TF-1144.P.G. Ware Culture 2370±85 (2440±90)
Charcoal sample from "a stratified level"."

On piecing the evidence together, the following picture emerges in respect of Noh :

Laboratory number	Cultural horizon	Value in B.C. based on 5730 half-life	Calibrated date in B.C. according to Ralph	Calibrated date in B C according to Clark
TF-994	Early NBP	685±105	795±105	810±100
TF-1144	Late PGW	490±90	470±90	470±90
UCLA-703A	Mid PGW	605±260	745±260	735±260
TF-993	Mid PGW	725±150	805±150	840±150
UCLA-703B	Mid PGW	820±225	900±225	915±225

Of these, the dates for the middle sub-period of the PGW are consistent. There is, however, an inconsistency between TF-1144 and TF-994, belonging respectively to the late PGW and early NBPW sub-periods. In this context, it may be added that in a recent communication the excavators of Noh have stated that these TF samples belong to 'disturbed layers' and 'therefore cannot be much relied upon.' However, whichever way we look at the issue, *the end of the PGW at Noh cannot be placed later than about the middle of the first millennium B.C;* in the general context of the other dates, it may well have occurred even in the sixth century B.C.

Unlike Ropar, Noh provides good circumstantial evidence for dating the beginnig of the PGW. Since the middle subperiod would range between 900 B C. and 745 B.C. according to Ralph's calibration, or between 915 B.C. and 735 B.C.according to Clark's and since the early sub-period may go back by another 150–200 years, *the beginning of the PGW occupation at Noh may safely be placed some time in the eleventh century B.C.—at any rate before 1000 B.C.*

We may now pass on to the other site in Rajasthan, viz Jodhpura. The folowing is an extract from PRL ^{14}C Date List 1/1976.

"Jodhpura series, Rajasthan,

Jodhpura (27°31'N, 76°5'E), District Jaipur, collected by Vijai Kumar, submitted by Director, Archaeology and Museums Rajasthan, Jaipur.

PRL-212. BRW and PGW deposits 2270±100 (2330±100)

Charcoal, Locus Trench D, Layer 9, depth 2.6 m. Rootlets removed.

PRL-213. PGW deposits 2210±110 (2270±110)

Charcoal, Locus Trench E, Layer 7, depth 3.5 m"

To this may be added the relevant extract from PRL ^{14}C Date List 1/1977.

Jodhpura series, Rajasthan

"Jodhpura (27°31' N, 76°5[1] E), District Jaipur, submitted by the Director, Archaeology and Museums, Jaipur.

PRL-272. PGW deposit 2670±150 (2750±150)

Charcoal Trench D, Layer 12, Depth 1.97 m. Sender's sample No. JRA 3/7/75. NaoH pretreatment given.

PRL-273. PGW deposit 2310±140 (2370±150)

Charcoal, Trench E, Layer 8, Depth 2.5 m. Sender's sample No. JRA 4/75. NaoH pretreatment given.

PRL-274. PGW deposit 2250±110 (2320±110)

Charcoal, Trench D, Layer 12, Depth 2.9 m. Sender's sample No. JRA 5/75. NaoH pretreatment given.

PRL–275. BRW deposit (?) 4360±160 (4480±160)

Charcoal, Trench D, Layer 13, Depth 2.87 m. Sender's sample No. JRA 6/75. NaoH pretreatment given.

PRL-277. OCP deposit (?) 2610±110 (2690±110)

Charcoal, Trench D, Layer 14, Depth 1.94 m. Sender's sample No. JRA 9/75. NaoH pretreatment given.

PRL-278. OCP deposit 460±170 (4180±180

Chacrcol, Trench D, Layer sealed by 14, depth 3 m. Sender's sample No. 12/75. NaoH pretreatment given."

(Note: In the above extract the ^{14}C dates are B.P. i.e. Before present; the one within brackets is based on 5730 half-life, while the other is on 5568 half-life.)

The site of Jodhpura has yielded the remains of three cultural periods. From bottom upwards, these are : Ochre colour pottery (OCP) period, the Black and Red ware (BRW) period and painted Grey ware (PGW) period. Further, while there was a break of occupation after the OCP period, there was no such occupational break between the other two.

After re-arranging these dates in our usual tabular form we have the following :

Laboratory number	Cultural horizon	Value in B.C. based on 5730 half-life	Calibrated date in B.C. according to Ralph	Calibrated date in B.C. according to Clark
PRL-212	PGW and BRW (Trench D, Layar 9, depth 2.6 m)	380±100	410±100	415±100
PRL-272	PGW (Trench D, layer 12, depth 1 97 m)	800±150	900-880±150	900±150
PRL-274	PGW (Trench D, layer, 12, depth 2.9 m.)	370±110	410±110	400±110
PRL-213	PGW (Trench E, layer 7, depth 3.5 m.)	320±110	400±110	380±110
PRL-273	PGW (Trench E, layer 8, depth 2.5 m)	420±150	430±150	435±150
PRL-275	BRW (Trench D, layer 13, depth 2.8 m.)	2530±160	3150±160	3105±160
PRL-277	OCP (Trench D, layer 14, depth 1.94 m)	740±110	810±110	850±110
PRL-278	OCP (Trench D, layer sealed by layer 14, depth 3 m)	2230±180	2800-2690 ±180	2680±180

A look at the above dates would show that most of them are self-contradictory. For example, samples PRL–272 and PRL-274, though *coming from the same layer of the same trench, viz. layer 12 of Trench D, give such varying dates as 900-880±150 B.C. and 410±110 B.C. could a single layer subsist for as many as 470 years ?* Since we have no information about the stratigraphical relationship between Trenches D and E we cannot offer any comments on samples PRL-213 and PRL-273. However, it may be observed that although the former comes from *the lowest depth* as compared to any other sample in the entire list, yet it gives the *latest date.*

We may now have a look at samples PRL 277 and PRL-278. *Both the samples come from almost the same deposit, yet they give such divergent dates as 2800—2690±180 B.C. and 810±110 B.C. Where do we stand ?*

Again, it is well known that the *BRW was far removed from the OCP and was nearer to the PGW, yet sample PRL-275 gives a date of 3150±160 B.C. In fact, this is even earlier than the earliest date for the OCP, represented by PRL-278. If we were to accept the date for PRL-275, we would have to accept that BRW preceded even the pre-Harappan Culture of Kalibangan* !

There also seems to be something wrong about the cultural association of sample PRL-212 : while layer 9 is said to have yielded both the BRW and PGW, a much earlier layer, 12, has yielded only PGW.

From the foregoing analysis it becomes absolutely clear that there is something wrong somewhere. Was the site highly disturbed, resulting in the contamination of the samples ? Where exactly the trouble lies, it is for the excavators or the laboratory experts to determine.* As assessors of the chronology, we have, I believe, no right to pick and choose.

In spite of the foregoing, should one insist on our accepting the dating of the PGW at Jodhpura, let it be recalled that sample PRL-272 gives a date of 900-880±150 B.C. Finally, *even the late dates of Jodhpura do not cross the upper limit of 400 B.C. and thus do not support the thesis that the PGW continued up to the Mauryan times.*

To take up the sites in Uttar Pradesh, we may begin with the westernmost one, namely, Mathura, and then proceed gradually eastwards where the Painted Grey Ware occurs in a very limited quantity and in a devolved form.

The following is an extract from PRL ^{14}C Date List I/1977 :

"Mathura series, Uttar Pradesh

Mathura (27° 28′ N, 77° 42′ E), District Mathura, Sample submitted by the Director General, Archaeological Survey of India, New Delhi.

PRL-333. NBP & PGW overlap 2490±140 (2560±150)

Charcoal, Trench MTR-8, Locus BI-Qd. 2, Pit 3 sealed by Layer 5, Depth 3.18 m. Sender's sample No. 1 NaOH pretreatment given.

PRL-334. NBP & PGW overlap 2600±150 (2680±150)

Charcoal, Trench MTR-10, Locus AI-Qd. 4, Layar 9, Depth 1.45 m. Sender's sample No. 3. NaOH pretreatment given.

PRL-336. NBP & PGW overlap 2540±90 (2610±100)

Charcoal, Trench MTR-8, Locus BI-Qd 2, Layer 6, Depth 3 m. Sender's sample No. 5. NaOH pretreatment given.

PRL-337. NBP deposit 2340±100 (2410±100)

Charcoal, Trench MTR-11, Locus Trial Trench, Pit 5 sealed by Layer 20, Depth 5.45 m. Sender's sample No. 6. NaOh pretreatment given.

PRL-338. NBP deposit 2280±100 (2350±110)

Charcoal, Trench MTR-11, Locus T T. Layer 18, Depth 4.7 m. Sender's sample No. 7. NaOH Pretreatment given.

PRL-339. NBP deposit 2380±100 (2450±100)

Charcoal, Trench MTR-8, Locus BI-Qd. 3, Pit 2, sealed by Layer 3. Sender's sample No. 8 NaOH Pretreatment given. Rootlets removed.

PRL-340. NBP deposit 2390±150 (2460±150)

Charcoal, Trench MTR-8, Locus AI-Qd. 4, Layer 11, Depth 4.2 m. Sender's sample No. 9. NaOH pretreatment given. Rootlets removed.

PRL-342. NBP deposit 2180±160 (2250±160)

Charcoal, Trench MTR-8, Locus BI-Qd. 2, Pit 8 sealed by Layer 8, Depth 3.65 m. Sender's sample No. 11. NaOH pretreament given.

PRL-343. NBP deposit 2150±100 (2220±100)

Charcoal, Trench MTR-11, Locus T.T., Layer 18, Depth 4.2 m. Sender's sample No. 12. NaOH pretreatment given. Rootlets removed."

*Professor D. P. Agrawal has since told me that the site was full of large-sized rat-holes and thus the samples may have been greatly disturbed.

According to the above Date List, samples PRL-333, PRL-334 and PRL-336 belong to the phase of overlap between the PGW and the NBPW, and the rest to the NBPW alone. The calibrated dates for the three samples relating to the overlap phase are as follows ;

Laboratory number	Value in B.C. based on 5730 half-life	Calibrated date in B C. according to Ralph	Calibrated date in B.C. according to Clark
PRL-333	610±150	750±150	745±150
PRL-336	660±100	790±100	790±100
PRL-334	730±150	810±150	840±150

This places the overlap phase between 840 B.C. and 745 B.C. (Clark) or between 810 B.C. and 750 B.C. (Ralph). *The implication would be that at Mathura the PGW did not persist later than the middle of the eighth century B.C.* As to it beginning, nothing can be said, since there are no ^{14}C dates for the pure PGW deposits.

However, in a recent article Agrawal *et al.* have assigned all the samples from Mathura to the NBPW levels. (Agrawal *et al.* 1978.) Thus, according to Agrawal's own assessment the NBPW at Mathura would commence around 810 B.C. (Ralph's calibration) or 840 B.C. (Clark's calibration). In that case, *the PGW would have ceased before 800 B.C., or even earlier.*

When the excavator of Mathura, Shri M.C. Joshi, was contacted to clarify the position, he came out with still another ascription. According to him, the *inter se* position of the samples now is as follows (quoted from a personal letter) :

Laboratory number	Cultural horizon	Value in B.C. based on 5730 half-life	Calibrated date in B.C. according to Ralph	Calibrated date in B.C. according to Clark
PRL-339	Post NBPW	500±100	480±100	470±100
PRL-343	Late NBPW	270±100	380-230±100	205±100
PRL-338	Late NBPW	400±110	420±110	415±110
PRL-333	Late NBPW	610±150	750±150	745±150
PRL-337	Mid NBPW	460±100	440±100	440±100
PRL-336	Mid NBPW	660±100	790±100	790±100
PRL-342	Early NBPW	300±160	390-270±160	250±160
PRL-334	Early NBPW	730±150	810±150	840±150
PRL-340	PGW and NBPW overlap	510±150	490±150	480±150

While most of these dates present a coherent picture, some do not. Let us then analyse which ones are to be accepted and which ones not, any why. To begin from top downwards, it may reasonably by argued that the post NBP phase cannot be as early as 480 B.C. (Ralph's calibration for PRL-339), since the Late NBPW phase, represented by PRL-343 and PRL-338, ranges between 420 B.C. and 230 B.C. Thus, sample PRL-339 will have to be rejected.

Likewise, sample PRL-333, giving the value of 750 B.C. for the late phase of the NBPW, will also have to be ignored, in view of the fact that sample PRL-337, coming from a middle phase of the NBPW, gives the value of 440 B.C.

Samples PRL-336 and PRL-334 are quite consistent, giving the values of 790 B.C. and 810 B.C. (Ralph) or 790 B.C. and 840 B.C. (Clark), respectively for the middle (lowest limit) and early phases of the NBPW. This would show that the NBPW at Mathura commenced around 800 B.C.

In view of the foregoing, sample PRL-342, giving a date of 390-270 B.C. for the early NBPW, will have to be rejected outright. Even otherwise, by no strech of imagination can the beginning of the NBPW at Mathura be ascribed to *circa* 390-270 B.C., since even the latest date for the late NBPW gives the value of 380-230 B.C. (PRL-343).

To come to PRL-340, which purports to date the phase of overlap between the PGW and NBPW. In view of tho dates for the early, middle and late NBPW levels discussed above, PRL-340 will also have to be rejected.

To recall, for the reasons given above, we have rejected samples PRL-339, PRL-333 PRL-342, and PRL 340. After this deletion, the follwing consistent picture emerges :

Laboratory number	Cultural horizon	Value in B.C. based on 5730 half-life	Calibrated date in B.C. according to Ralph	Calibrated date in B.C. according to Clark
PRL-343	Late NBPW	270±100	380-230±100	205±100
PRL-338	Late NBPW	400±110	420±110	415±110
PRL-337	Mid NBPW	460±100	440±100	440±100
PRL-336	Mid NBPW	660±100	790±100	790±100
PRL-334	Early NBPW	730±150	810±150	840±150

In view of the foregoing,, the end of the PGW at Mathura would ante-date circa 800 B.C. As to its beginning, nothing definite can be said in the absence of ^{14}C dates from the actual PGW levles. However, *it would be reasonable to assume that it preceded 1000 B.C.*

we may now pass on to Hastinapura. The following is the relevant extract from, 'Tata Institute Radiocarbon Date List II', published in *Radiocarbon,* Vol. 6, 1964, pp. 227-28.

"Hastinapur Series, Uttar pradesh

Hastinapur (29°9' N Lat, 78°3' E Long) is located on the left bank of Ganga River in meerut District. The site was excaveated by B.B. Lal, Director, School of Archaeol., in 1950-52 and 1962. The samples presented in this paper belong to periods II and III, characterized by the occurrence of painted Grey Ware and Northen Black polished ware, respectively, in the site. The excavator has suggested an association of Aryans with the P.G. Ware industry of Period II. Samples subm. by A. Ghosh.

The eight dates presented here have an internal consistency borne out by the stratigraphic sequence of the site. The C^{14} measurements suggest the spread of period III between ca. 400 and ca. 100. B.C. (on the basis of $T\frac{1}{2}=5730$ yr)., There also does not appear to be much of a gap between the end Period II and the beginnig of Period III. It is highly desirable to obtain more C^{14} measurements for these crucial periods in Indian archaeology in order to define the chronlogies of N.B.P. and P.G. Wares.

TF-80, 82. Period III — 1940±110 A.D. 10

A composite of two samples of charcoal (mixed with soil) from Trench HST-1/1962 (northern extension). Locus G-H, Layer 23, Field Nos. HST/62/C/1& 4, depth 3.9 m below surface. *Visible rootlets were hand-picked* Comment: samples derived from identical depths and layers. They are believed to be associated with the end of period III, which marks the culmination of N.B.P. ware.

TF-81. period III — 2015±95 65 B.C.

Charcoal sample (Mixed with earth) from Trench HST-1/1962, Locus XC-XCIV, Layer 18, depth 5.1 m below surface. Field No. HST/62/C/2. *Visible rootlets were hand-picked.* NaoH pretreatment was also given. CO_2 was evolved by wet combustion method. Comment : sample derives from the uppermost layer of period III, marking the end of N.B.P. Ware. Compare with TF-80, 82, 1940 ± 110

TF-88. Period III — 2225±110 275 B.C.

Charcoal sample (mixed with earth) from Trench HST-1/1962, Locus XCIV-XCVII, Layer 25, Field No. HST/62/C/15, depth 6.45 m below surface. *Visible rootlets were hand-picked.* Comment: sample is from the lowest layer of Period III which marks the beginning of N.B.P. Ware.

TF-83. Period II — 2220±110 270 B.C.

Charcoal Sample (mixed with earth) from Trench HST-1/1962, Locus XCIV-XCVII, Layer 26, and pit Y sealed by Layer 25, Field No. HST/62/C 6, depth 6.75m below surface. *Visible rootlets were hand-picked.* Comment: sample derives from the uppermost layer of period II marking the end of P. G. Ware.

TF-112. period II — 2260±95 310 B.C.

Bone Sample (coated with earth) from Trench HST 1/1962, Locus XC'-XCVII', Layer 26 and pit Y sealed by Layer 25, depth 6.8 m below surface, Field No. HST/62/C/7. Comment : sample derives from the latest layer of Period II and will date the flooding of the site which led to its desertion by P.G. Ware-using people.

TF-90. period II — 2270±110 320 B C.

Charcoal (mixed with earth) from Trench HST-1/1962, Locus XCIV-XCVII, Layer 26, Field No. HST/62/C/17, depth 6.6 m below surface. Comment : sample is from the same layer as TF-83.

TF-85. period II — 2385±125 435 B.C.

Charcoal (mixed with earth) from Trench HST-1/1962, Locus XC-XCIV, Layer 28 and pit Z which is sealed by Layer 27, field No. HST/62/C/10. depth 7.25 m to 7.45 m below surface. *Visible rootlets were hand-picked.* Comment : sample belongs to the late levels of period II

TF-91. period II — 2450±120 500 B.C.

Charcoal sample (mixed with earth) from Trench HST-1/1962. Locus XCIV-XCIIV, Layer 27, depth 6.9 m below surface, Field No. HST/62/C/18. *Visible rootlets were hand picked.* Comment: sample derives from late levels of period II.

By arranging these samples in the usual style, we get the following ;

Laboratory number	Cultural horizon	Value in B.C. based on 5730 half-life	Calibrated date in B.C. according to Ralph	Calibrated date in B.C. according to Clark
TF-80,82*	uppermost NBPW	50±115	AD 50±115	AD 70±115
TF-81*	uppermost NBPW	125±100	80-05±100	60±100
TF-88*	Lowest NBPW	340±115	400±115	385±115
TF-83*	uppermost PGW	335±115	400±115	390±115
TF-112	uppermost PGW	375±100	410±100	410±100
TF-90	From same layer as TF-83	390±115	420±115	415±115
TF-85*	Late PGW	550±130	485±130	475±130
TF-91*	Late PGW	570±125	720—660±125	600±125

It would be seen from the laboratory report (quoted above from the *Radiocarbon*) that "visible rootlets were hand-picked" from as many as six (marked with asteriks) out of the eight samples examined. Since the site is full of trees, their rootlets must have been penetrating into these samples as and when the site remained abandoned : it remained so each time after the end of the PGW, NBPW, Sunga-kushan and mediaeval periods. some of the more ancient rootlets must have also been so carbonized in the course of time as to have become indistinguishable from the charcoal which, in many cases being of bamboo, was itself fibrous. In any case, the contamination must have been going on through the ages and as such all the samples are bound to give younger values. It is in this context that the ^{14}C dates from Hastinapura have to be viewed.

There is another point which has to be borne in mind. Merely on the ^{14}C dates, Agrawal et al. have pronounced the judgement that 'there does not appear to be much of a gap between the end of period II (PGW) and the beginning of period III (NBPW) (cf. above). In fact, this is a good example which tells us that blind reliance on ^{14}C dates in a manner like this can be very misleading, we know that period II at Hastinapura had full-fledged PGW but no NBPW, no burnt-brick structures and no coinage, whereas in period III there was no PGW, good NBPW, many burnt-brick structures and a system of coinage. Thus, there is good reason to suppose that there was substantial time-lag between the end of period II and the beginning of period III, for *such a marked evolution in material cultural does take time to come about.* (The postulation of such a time-lag would not have been necessary had a different cultural group come from elsewhere and occupied the site.) It is in this time-gap that we have the phase of overlap between the PGW and NBPW, which would approximate to one to two centuries. This shows that value of TF-88 viz 400 B.C., for the beginning of the NBPW Period and that of TF-83, viz. 400 B.C., for the end of the PGW period are mutually incompatible. we have two other dates for the Late PGW levels, viz. 485 B.C. and 720-660 B.C. (Ralph's calibration), which are more in keeping with the gap in the cultural reality.

The value of the middle and early PGW levels at Hastinapura is anybody's guess, for there are no ^{14}C dates for these sub-periods.

However, if, in spite of the foregoing objections in respect of the Hastinapura ^{14}C dates' one presses for their acceptance, it would be observed that even at Hastinapura the PGW did not cotinue up to the Mauryan times.

The following is the extract from 'PRL 14 C Date List-July 1974', in regard to Allahapur :

"Allahapur, District Meerut

Samples submitted by K. N. Dikshit' Archaeological Survey of India.

PRL-81, P.G. Ware 2270±90 (2335±95)

Charcoal from Trench AI, Qd. 1, layer 11, depth 2.30 m; Field No. ALP 2/70-71.

PRL-83, P.G. Ware-N.B.P. Ware 2160±105 (2225±110)

Wood from Trench AI, Qd.4, layer 5, depth 1.10m; Field No. ALP/4/70-71. NaoH pretreatment given ; *rootlets present.*"

On rearranging the above data in the system adopted in this paper, we have following :

Laboratory number	Cultural horizon	Value in B.C. based on 5730 half-life	Calibrated date in B.C. according to Ralph	Calibarted date in B.C. according to Clark
PRL-83*	PGW-NBPW	275±110	380-240±100	215±110
PRL-81	PGW	385±95	415±95	410±95

As mentioned in the laboratory report, rootlets were present in sample PRL-83. Therefore, there is every possibility of the date having been much older than what it is.

But the more important point is that of the cultural equipment of the sub-period (IB, as called by the excavator) from which sample PRL-83 is derived. This has yielded not merely the PGW and the NBPW (or NBPW-associated red wares) but also burnt-brick structures and a seal in late Mauryan characters. *If we look round all over India, we cannot find a single site other than Allahapur where the PGW co-occurs with burnt-brick structures and any kind of writing, much less a late Mauryan seal.* Burnt-brick structures and seals in Mauryan characters have been found to occur usually in middle NBPW phase by which time the PGW had *completely* disappeared, for example in Period III of Ropar (Sharma, Y. D. 1953, p. 123). Such a situation should have in fact set the excavator thinking about what may have happend at the site. As for my self, I can only recall my recent experience at Ayodhya. Over there, in one of the trenches near Asharfi Bhavan, I started getting plentiful of the NBPW in levels which otherwise contained material ascribable to the second century A.D This set me wondering, and after about two weeks I discovered that the NBPW had come out from the much lower strata through which a deep and wide refuse-pit had been dug in the second century A.D. The dug-out earth had been spread all over the area to provide a flooring, while the pit itself had been lined with bricks. This brought home to me the need to be alert all the time and not to run to hasty conclusions.

A similar experience was had in a trench in the Janma-Bhumi area, where a good deal of the NBPW was found along with the medieval glazed ware.

Since sub-period IB at Allahapur yielded burnt-brick structures, the NBPW and a Mauryan seal, it would no doubt be reasonable to ascrible it to *circa* fourth-third centuries B.C. However, for laying out the floors and/or constructing the houses, earth may have been dug and brought up from earlier deposits. This might explain how in sub-period IB 'the PGW fabric continued to remain fine and did not show degeneration in the technique of manufacture and painted designs as happened at other PGW sites.' (Dikshit 1973, p. 150). I have, however, no intention of imposing my explanation on the excavator of Allahapur. He has to find out his own answer to the problem.

In the same Meerut District of Uttar Pradesh is located Alamgirpur which has given another erractic date for the PGW.

"TF-51. Alamgirpur, India 1060±95
A.D. 890

A composite of three bone samples believed to have been derived from the Painted Grey Ware deposit of the site, Alamgirpur (30° 45′ N Lat, 75° 50′ E Long), District Meerut, U.P. Subm. by A. Ghosh. Comment : date obtained is at considerable variance with the archaeological estimate. Because such a large contamination is unlikely and because from the sections the samples appear to belong to disturbed strata, the possibility of a wrong identification of the levels cannot be ruled out."

The above is an extract from 'Tata Institute Radiocarbon Date List II', published in *Radiocarbon*, Vol. 6, 1964, p. 227.

It is just a chance that the ^{14}C date for this sample from the PGW level comes to A.D. 860 (based on 5730 half-life). No body would thus touch it with the longest tongs. However, had the amount of contamination in the sample been much less and thus had the date been say around 200 B.C., it would have surely been quoted as a supporting evidence for the PGW to have continued into 'late Mauryan' times. (The excavator recorded that the samples had been collected from the PGW levels.)

We may now pass on to Atranjikhera, another site in the Ganga-Yamuna *doab*. In regard to it we have the evidence of a total of ten samples, examined variously by the TIFR, British Museum, and Washington State University. The TIFR dates are published in three parts. In 'Tata Institute Radiocarbon Date List III', published in *Radiocarbon* Vol. 7, 1965, the following occurs on p. 291.

"TF-191. Atranjikhera, India, P.G. Ware doposit 2890±105
940 B C.

Charcoal sample from Atranjikhera (27°42′ N Lat,

78° 44′ E Long), Dist. Etah, Trench ARJ4-D1, top of SW corner, Layer 6, depth 3.20 m. Subm. by Nurul Hasan, Aligrah Univ., Aligarh. Comment : sample belongs to P.G. Ware level."

The following is available in the 'Tata Institute Radiocarbon Date List IV', appearing in *Radiocarbon*, Vol. 8, 1966, p. 444

"Atranjikhera series, Uttar pradesh

Atranjikhera (27°42 N. Lat.; 78°44 E. Long), Dist. Etah, is very important site for protohistory of Doab, as a distinct pre-P.G. Ware black-and-red ware horizon has been established there. Site is being excavated by R.C. Gaur, Aligarh, Univ., Aligarh, who subm. the samples.

TF-283. N.B.P. ware deposits 2150±105 200 B.C.

Charcoal from Trench ARJ 4, Locus A1 (NW), Layer 27, depth 4.85 m, Field No. ARJ4/64-1.

TF-284. N.B.P. ware deposits 2180±95 230 B.C

Charcoal from Trench ARJ 4, Locus A1 (SW), Layer 29, depth 5.0 m. Field No. ARJ4/64-2. NaoH pretreatment was also given.

TF-194. Period III 2410±85 460 B.C.

Charcoal from Trench ARJ4, Locus A1 (NW), Laver 16, depth 3.10 m, Field Na. ARJ4-AI (NW)

TF-287. P.G. ware deposits (?) 1605±95 A. D. 345

Charcoal from Trench ARJ4, Locus E2 (NW), Layer IY, depth 1.34 m. Field No. ARJ 4/64-5. *Visible rootlets were hand-picked. :* Comment : *Site is disturbed by later floods* : sample seems to be a later intrusion.

TF-291. P.G. Ware deposits 2415±100 465 B.C.

Charcoal from Trench ARJ4, Locus DI (SE), Layer 6 depth 2.50 m. Field No. ARJ 4/64-9. Comment : Sample belongs to late levles.

TF-289. Black-and-red ware deposits 2550±105 600 B.C.

Charcoal (coated with mud) from Trench ARJ4, Locus EI (SW), layer 4, depth 0.95 m, Field No. ARJ4/64-7. NaOH pretreatment was also given."

In *Radiocarbon*, Vol. 10, 1968, on p. 132, one more sample from Atranjikhera is given, as follows :

TF-195. Atranjikhera, India Period IV 1845±95 A.D. 105

Charcoal from Atranjikhera (27°42′N Lat, 78°44′ E Long), Dist. Etah, Trench ARJ-4, Locus AI NW, Layer 14, depth 2.15 m, Field No. ARJ 4 (AI NW). NaOH pretreatment was also given. Subm. by Nurul Hasan, Aligarh Univ., Aligarh "

In addition to the above, we have two dates from the British Museum and one from Washington State University, I do not have the published references, but information in respect of these dates has been communicated to me in a letter by professor R.C. Gaur who excavated Atranjikhera. In that letter, he has also given further clarificaton about the cultural horizons of the samples.

On arranging the entire date, the following picture emerges :

Laboratory number	Cultural horizon	Value in B.C. based on 5730 half-life	Calibrated date in B C. according to Ralph	Calibrated date in B.C. according to Clark
TF-195	Post NBPW	AD 50±100	AD 110-130±100	AD 180±100
TF-194	Post NBPW	530±85	640-500±85	500±85
TF-283	NBPW	260±105	380-210±105	205±105
TF-284	NBPW	295±100	390-270±100	350±100
BM-193	PGW-NBPW	150±150	110-70±150	85±150
BM194	PGW-NBPW	540±150	660-510±150	505±150
WSU	PGW-NBPW	530±150	640-500±150	500±150
TF-291	Late NBPW	535±100	650-505±100	505±100
TF-287	PGW	AD 300±100	AD 390±100	AD 395±100
TF-191	lowest layer of Mid PGW	1025±110	1155±110	1165±110

While TF-195 seems to be in order, TF-194 does not seem to be so, since from all known facts a post-NBPW deposit cannot be dated to the sixth century B.C.

The two dates for the NBPW represented by TF-283 and TF-284 are all right. With these also go well BM-194 and WSU, which represent the phase of overlap between the PGW and NBPW. According to the excavator, BM-193 comes from a disturbed stratum and thus has to be discounted. (If the disturbed nature of the stratum had not been noted, this would have been perhaps a ready case to say that the PGW continued into the Sunga period :

BM-194 and WSU clearly show that at Atranjikhera the PGW overlapped with the NBPW in the seventh-sixth centuries B.C. and, since there is a continuous occupation of the site, *there is no likelihood whatsoever of the PGW having continued after circa 500 B.C.*

In view of samples TF-191 and TF-291, samples TF-287 has to be discarded. The laboratory report also says that visible rootlets were 'hand-picked' from the sample and that the stratum too might have been disturbed.

Sample TF-191 comes from the lowest layer of the middle sub-period of the PGW, which may thus be ascribed to *circa* twelfth century B.C. *However, even if the margin of error, viz. 110 years, is deducted from the date the figure would still be earlier than 1000 B.C. the lowermost sub-period of the PGW may have indeed begun much earlier.*

Moving to the east of the upper *doab*, we come to Ahichchhatra in District Bareilly. The following is an extract from 'Tata Institute Radiocarbon Date List', appearing in *Radiocarbon*, Vol. 8, 1966, pp. 443-444.

Ahichchhatra series, Uttar Pradesh

Ahichchhatra (28°22′ N Lat, 79°7′ E Long), Dist. Bareilly, is site of ancient capital of North Panchal. Excavations are being directed by N. R. Banerji. Samples subm. by A. Ghosh, Director General of Archaeol; New Delhi–11.

TF-301. Defences 2255±105
305 B.C.

Charcoal from Locus CXIII-CXIV, Layer 1, depth 0.8 m, Field No.2 (Defences). *Visible rootlets were handpicked.* NaOH pretreatment was also given. Comment : sample was found in debris just above mud-filling belonging to Phase II of defences.

TF-310. N.B.P. ware deposits 2050±90
100 B.C.

Charcoal from highmound, Locus XI, XII, Pit No. 4 sealed by Layer 8A, depth 0.5 m, Field No. 177 (H.M.) Comment : red ware of N.B.P. ware association was found in these deposits.

TF-311. N.B.P. ware deposits 2360±105
410 B.C.

Charcoal from highmound, Loous IX′-X′, Pit No.5 sealed by Layer 14, depth 3.8 m, Field No. 196 (H.M.). Comment : these deposits also yield P.G. ware.

TF-317. Late P.G. ware deposits (?) 2155±100
205 B.C.

Charcoal from highmound, Loous X-XI, Layer 15, depth 3.4 m, Field No. 214 (H.M.). Comment : *sample belongs to disturbed strata.*"

On rearranging the above dates, we get the following :

Laboratory number	Cultural horizon	Value in B.C. based on 5730 half-life	Calibrated date in B.C. according to Ralph	Calibrated date in B.C. according to Clark
TF-301	Defences, Phase II	370±105	410±105	405±105
TF-310	Red Ware of NBPW association	160±95	120-70±95	95±95
TF-311	NBPW	475±105	470-440±105	460±105
TF-317	Late PGW(?)	270±105	380-230±100	210±105

While TF-311 is all right for the NBPW period, we do not know from which sub-period of the NBPW it comes. The laboratory report, however, mentions that the deposits which yielded this sample also contained some PGW sherds. One would then think that this sample comes from the early sub-period of NBPW.

Samples TF-301, being incompatible with TF-310, has to be ignored. In this context, however, one point deserves to be mentioned. It has been stated in the report that sample TF-310 came from deposits which contained "red ware of NBP Ware-association" It is thus clear that no NBPW as such was found in these deposits. Since there does occur plenty of the NBPW at Ahichchatra—sample TF-311 actually comes from such a deposit-It would appear that by the middle of the second century B.C. the NBPW had actually gone into disuse. irrespective of the fact that the red ware that once co-existed with it continued for some time more.

As reggrds TF-317, it has to be written off in view of the evidence given by TF-311. Furthermore, the laboratory itself has questioned its association with the PGW, saying that the 'sample belongs to disturbed strata.'

The evidence thus indicates that the *PGW at Ahichchhatra was in the main earlier than the middle of the first milliennium B.C.*

In Agra District of Uttar Pradesh, ^{14}C dates are available for two sites, namely Khalaua and Bateshwar,

There are three dates for Khalaua. *Radiocarbon*, Vol. 17, No. 2, 1975, P. 220. gives the following information about one of these dates :

2420±95

"TF-1228 Khalaua, India. P.G. Ware level 470 B.C.

Charcoal from Khalaua, (27°6′ N, 77°52′ E). Dist. Agra, Loc Khl-L, II-IV (a), Layer 9. depth 2.6m to 2.75 m. Subm. by Dir. Gen., Archaeol., New Delhi."

The other two dates occur in 'PRL ^{14}C Date List II/1974 ; Khalaua series, Uttar Paradesh

Khalaua (27°6′ N Lat., 77°52′ E Long.), Dist. Agra, Subm. by D.G.A.

PRL-67. PGW and BRW deposits 2450±155 (2520±160)

Charcoal Loc. KHL-I, II and IV, Layer-7, depth 2.15 m. Rootlets removed.

PRL-68. PGW and BRW deposits 2370±170 (2435±170)

Charcoal, Loc. KAL-I, II to IV, Layer 8, depth 2.35 to 2.48 m."

On putting together the date, we get the following :

Laboratory number	Cultural horizon	Value in B.C. based on 5730 half-life	Calibrated date in B.C. according to Ralph	Calibrated date in B.C. according to Clark
PRL-68	PGW	485±170	470±170	470±170
TF-1228	PGW	545±100	660-510±100	510±100
PRL-67	PGW	570±160	720-660±160	600±160

Although in the above laboratory reports samples PRL-67 and PRL-68 have been mentioned as coming from 'PGW and BRW deposits' and sample TF-1228 from merely 'PGW level', the fact is that all these samples come from the same cultural complex in which both PGW and BRW co-occur. (Cf. *Indian Archaeology 1965-66-A Review, PP 41-42*).

While it is not clear from the published reports if these samples come from early, middle or late levels of the PGW deposit, all that can be said is that at Khalaua this ware was in use at least between *circa* 700 B.C. and *circa* 500 B.C. *In any case, there is no indication of the ware having run into the third century B.C*

We have five date in respect of Bateshwar. The concerned extract from 'PRL ^{14}C Dete List III/1975' is as follows :

"Bateshwar series, Uttar Pradesh

Bateshwar, District Agra, submitted by J. S. Nigam, Archaeological Survey of India, Agra. Some dates show considerable scatter.

PRL-197. Period II deposits 2410±100 (2480±110)

Charcoal, Locus BTR 1, A-1 Qd1, Layer 14, depth 4.70 m, Field No. BTR 1/3.

PRL-198. Period I deposit 2490±90 (2570±90)

Charcoal, Locus BTR 1, A-2 Qd3, Layer 19, depth 6.65 m, Field No. BTR 1/5.

PRL-199. Pre-Mauryan or Mauryan Period (?) 590±130 (610±130)

Charcoal, Locus BTR 2, A-2 Qd4, Layer 7A, depth 3.10 m, Field No. BTR 2/6.

PRL-200. Transitional phase from BRW, PGW to Mauryan Period (?) 5130±240 (5280±240)

Charcoal, Locus CTR 2, A–W Qd4, Layer 8, depth 3.15 m, Field No. BTR 2/7.

PRL-201. Period II deposits 2520±160 (2590±160)

Charcoal, Locus BTR 1, A-2 Qd 1, Layer 11, depth 4.2 m, Field No. BTR 1/2."

In a personal communication, Shri J. S. Nigam, excavator of Bateshwar, has given the cultural horizons of the samples. On re-arranging them in a sequence, the position is as follows :

Laboratory number	Cultural horizon	Value in B.C. based on 5730 half-life	Calibrated date in B.C. according to Ralph	Calibrated date in B.C. according to Clark
PRL-199	'Pre-Mauryan or Mauryan	AD 1340±130	AD 1350±130	AD 1385±130
PRL-200	Transition from BRW, PGW to Mauryan	3330±240	3940±240	3970±240
PRL-201	Late NBPW	640±160	780±160	770±160
PRL-197	Mid NBPW	530±110	640-500±110	500±110
PRL-198	Late PGW	620±90	760±90	445±90

Prima facie the dates for PRL-199 and PRL-200 are unacceptable, the former being far too young and the latter far too old. The date for PRL-201 also seems to be on the high side. *The remaining two samples, however, clearly show that the PGW did not continue at Bateshwar after the seventh century B.C.*

Going down along the Yamuna we come to Kausambi in Allahabad District. Although there are no dates for the PGW deposits, we have as many as eight dates for the NBPW.

In *Radiocarbon*, Vol. 6, 1964, pp. 230-231 we have the following one date :

"Kausmbi series, Uttar Pradesh

Kausambi (25° 20′ N Lat, 81° 23′ E Long), modern Kosam, is situated on the northern bank of Yamuna. According to the Puranas, the capital of the Pandavas was shifted from Hastinapur to Kausambi at the time of Nichaksu, fifth in descent from Parikshita, the grandson of Arjuna. The measured samples cover Periods III and IV of the Site (Sharma, 1960). Site excavated every year during the past decade by Allahabad Univ. under direction of G. R. Sharma who subm. these samples.

TF-100. Period III 2160±95 210 B.C.

Charcoal (mixed with earth) from Trench KSB-G/R-YZ 2, Locus 1-2, Pit A sealed by Layer 18 A, BK, depth 2.15 m. below surface, Field No. KSB/63/GR-103. Visible rootlets were hand-picked. Comment : sample derives from the last phase of N.B.P. Ware from Ghositarama area."

Three dates are available in *Radiocarbon*, Vol. 7, 1965 pp. 293-94.

"Kausambi series, Uttar Pradesh

Kausambi (25° 20′ N Lat, 81° 23′ E Long), now known as Kosam, Dist. Allahabad, is located on N bank of Yamuna. Site is being excavated (Sharma, 1960) by Inst. of Archaeol., Allahabad Univ., under direction of G. R. Sharma, who Subm. these samples.

TF-103. Period III 2295±105 345 B.C.

Charcoal from Trench KSB-GR, Locus YZ 2, 2-3 Pit C sealed by Layer 18 A BK, depth 3 m, Field No. KSB/63/GR-106. Visible rootlets were hand-picked. NaOH pretreatment was also given.

TF-104. Period III 2150±105 200 B.C.

Charcoal from Trench KSB/GR, Locus YZ 2, 2-3, layer 22 BK, depth 2.4 m, Field No. KSB/63/GR-107. Visible rootlets were hand-picked.

TF-105. Period III 2220±110 270 B.C.

Charcoal from trench KSB/GR, Locus YZ 2, 1-2, Pit A sealed by Layer 21 BK, depth 2.4 m, Field No. KSB/63/GR-108. Visible rootlets were hand-picked. NaOH pretreatment was also given."

On p. 449 of Volume 8, 1966, of *Radiocarbon*, the following four dates occur :

"Kausambi series, Uttar Pradesh

Kausambi (25° 20′ N Lat, 81° 23′ E Long), now known as Kosam, Dist. Allahabad, is located on N bank of Yamuna. It is known as capital of later Pandavas. Site is being excavated by G. R. Sharma, who subm. these samples.

TF-226. Rampart II 2110±95 160 B.C.

Charcoal from Trench KSB-GR, Locus YZ 3, 1-2, Layer 12, depth 1.8 m, Field No. KSB/63/GR-138. Comment : excavator's archaeological date bracket for sample is ca. 535-185 B.C.

TF-225. N.B.P.W. Ware deposits 2285±105 335 B.C.

Charcoal from Trench KSB-GR, Locus YZ 3, 1-2, Layer 11, depth 1.6 m, Field No. KSB/63/GR-136.

TF-219. N.B.P. ware deposits 2325±100 375 B.C.

Charcoal from Trench KSBI-III-RD, Locus 2-7, Road I, depth 3 m, Field No. KSB/63/AP-9.

TF-221. N.B.P. ware deposits 2385±100 435 B.C.

Charcoal from Trench KSB-I-III-RD, Locus 5-7, Pit B sealed by Layer 12, depth 4.3 m, Field No. KSB/63/AP-15. Comment : excavator's date on archaeological considerations is ca. 400 B.C."

On arranging these dates in their proper sequence we get the following :

Laboratory number	Cultural horizon	Value in B.C. based on 5730 half-life	Calibrated date in B.C. according to Ralph	Calibrated date in B.C. according to Clark
TF-100	Mid level of Late Phase of NBPW	275±100	380-240±100	215±100
TF-103	Mid level of Late Phase of NBPW	410±110	420±110	420±110
TF-226*	Late level of Mid Phase of NBPW	220±100	200–170±100	170±100
TF-104	Late level of Mid Phase of NBPW	270±110	380-230±110	205±110
TF-105	Late level of Mid Phase of NBPW	335±115	400+115	390±115
TF-225	Mid level of Mid Phase of as NBPW	400±110	420±110	410±110
TF-219	Mid level of Mid Phase of NBPW	440±100	430±100	440±100
TF-221	Early level of Mid Phase of NBPW	500±105	480±105	475±105

The above dates show that the middle phase of the NBPW began around 500 B.C. Since the middle as well as the late phase of the NBPW seem to have a life ranging from 150 to 200 years, the beginning of the NBPW at Kausambi may well go back to the seventh century B.C.

The report on Kausambi (Sharma, G.R., 1960, pl. 4) states that the PGW preceded the NBPW. *Hence in no case is the former likely to have continued at Kausambi after the sixth century B.C.*

For Ganwaria in District Basti, Uttar Pradesh, we an uncalibrated date of 2790±110 B.C. (based on 5730 half-life) in respect of the PGW deposit. (PRL ^{14}C Date List II/1979). obviously, it cannot be accepted.

We may now have a look at what happens in the outlying area of Madhya Pradesh. At Kayatha, the following two dates are available for the NBPW period (Agrawal *et al*., 1974, p. 136) :

Laboratory number	Cultural horizon	Value in B.C. based on 5730 half-life	Calibrated date in B.C. according to Ralph	Calibrated date in B.C according to Clark
TF-674	NBPW	470±100	460-440±100	450±100
TF-394	NBPW	495±100	475±100	470±100

Below the NBPW level occurs at Kayatha a thin deposit containing some sherds of the PGW. On this *this outlying site the PGW cannot be said to have continued later than circa 500 B.C.*

3. SUMMARY AND CONCLUSIONS

IN the foregoing pages we have made an assessment of the data in respects of sites in Panjab, Rajasthan, Uttar Pradesh and Madhya Pradesh, which have yielded the PGW and for which ^{14}C dates are also available. No PGW site in Haryana or Pakistan has so far been dated by the ^{14}C method.

It may be recalled that we set out to answer the question : Did the Painted Grey Ware continue up to the Mauryan times ? That it did so was the thesis propounded by Dikshit (1973) and recently indirectly supported by Agrawal *et al*. (1978). The evidence obtained from each of the sites discussed above may briefly be summarized as follows.

At Ropar in Panjab the PGW came to an end before the middle of the first millennium B. C. Noh, in Rajasthan, has a similar picture to offer. However, the other site in Rajasthan, viz. Jodhpura, has given some dates which take the end of the PGW up to *circa* 400 B.C. But, as already shown above most of the ^{14}C dates from this site are topsyturvy and have, therefore, to be taken with a grain of salt.

In respect of Mathura in Uttar Pradesh there is some confusion. If the 'PRL ^{14}C Date List I/1977' is to be relied upon, the overlap between the PGW and NBPW took place between 840 B.C. and 745 B.C. (Clark) or between 810 B.C. and 750 B.C. (Ralph), showing that the PGW did not continue after the middle of the eight century B.C. Agrawal *et al*. (1978) have, however, assigned all the Mathura ^{14}C dates to the NBPW levels. Since the three lower most of these dates range between 810 B.C. and 750 B.C. (Ralph), or between 840 B.C. and 745 B.C. (Clark), according to Agrawal's own estimate the Painted Grey Ware at Mathura would have ceased before 800 B.C.

M. C. Joshi, however, has advanced a somewhat different cultural association of these samples. But in spite of this shift in position, the PGW at Mathura would antedate 800 B.C.

The samples from Hastinapura had been found mixed up with rootlets of which 'the visible' ones 'were hand-picked'. Because of this contamination, which must have been going on at the site for ages, the samples have given younger dates. However, even these younger dates do not support the view that the PGW continued up to the Mauryan times

Allahapur is the only site where a 'late Mauryan seal' was found in deposits which also contained the PGW. These deposits were also associated with burnt-brick structures a feature peculiar only to Allahapur and not supported by the evidence from any other site discussed above, for example, Ropar, Noh, Mathura, Hastinapura, etc. Thus, as stated earlier, something has gone wrong somewhere and the excavator himself would be the right person to sort things out.

The date from Alamgirpur falling the tenth century A.D., has to be discounted for obvious reasons.

The evidence from Atranjikhera shows that the PGW came to end about the middle of the first millennium B. C. Ahichchhatra and Khalaua also support such a view. The ^{14}C dates from Bateshwar, on the other hand, demonstrate that the PGW did not continue after the seventh century B.C.

Although no ^{14}C dates are available for the PGW levels at Kausambi, yet on the basis of the dates for the middle phase of the succeeding NBPW deposits, it can very well be said that at this site the PGW is unlikely to have continued after the sixth century B.C.

The date from Ganwaria, falling in the first quarter of the third millennium B.C. has no doubt to be ignored.

As seen above even at an outlying site like Kayatha, where a late survival of the PGW would have normally been expected the ware did not persist after about the middle of the first millennium B.C.

To put it succinctly, Allahapur stands out in sheer isolation when it says that the PGW continued up to the 'late Mauryan' times. The overwhelming evidence from all other sites is that this ware ceased to exist by about the Middle of the first millennium B.C.

As to the beginning of the Painted Grey Ware, we have so far not a single date from its : lowest level at any site. In view of this, all that can be done is a sort of computation, proceeding from the known to the unknown. we have ^{14}C dates for the middle PGW levels from sites only, namely Noh and Atranji Khera. At the fromer site the dates are :

Laboratory number	Cultural horizon	Value in B.C. based on 5730 half-life	Calibrated date in B.C. according to Ralph	Calibarted date in B.C. according to Clark
UCLA-703A	Mid PGW	605±260	745±260	735±260
TF-993	Mid PGW	725±150	805±150	840±150
UCLA-703B	Mid PGW	820±225	900±225	915±225

From the foregoing it would be clear that the PGW may have appeared at Noh well before 1000 B.C.

The date (TF-191) for the middle levels of the PGW or Atranjikhera has been taken by some scholars as erratic. But in view of the evidence from Noh, there should be nothing surprising about it. Its value is as follows :

Laboratory number	Cultural horizon	Value in B.C. based on 5730 half-life	Calibrated date in B.C. according to Ralph	Calibrated date in B.C. according to Clark
TF-191	Lowest layer of Mid PGW	1025±110	1155±110	1165±110

This would indicate the PGW at AtranjiKhera may have begun in the twelfth century B.C.

From the foregoing it would be amply clear that the beginning of the sites discussed above cannot be later than circa 100 B.C. and may well go back even earlier.

In this connection, one may recall the recent discoveries by J.P. Joshi at Bhagwanpura, Kathpalon, Nagar, Dadheri, etc. (Joshi 1978, P.P. 98-101). At these sites he has found the interlocking of the PGW with a late amalgam derived from Harappan and pre-Harappan strains. While no ^{14}C date is yet available for these overlapping strata, a very significant fact is that iron is conspicuous by its absence at Joshi's sites. *Since the PGW sites discussed in this paper are all associated with iron, Joshi's sites seem to make out a case for a pre-iron and thus still earlier phase of the painted Grey Ware. We may, however, await more corroborative evidence in this regard.*

REFERECNES

Agrawal, D.P. and Sheela Kusumgar. 1974. *Prehistoristoric Chronology and Radiocarbon Dating in India* (New Delhi).

Agrawal, D.P., R.V. Krishnamurthy, Sheela Kusumgar and R.K. Pant. 1978. Chronology of Indian Prehistory from the Mesolithic Period to the Iron Age, *Journ. of Human Evolution*, No.7, pp. 37-44.

Allchin, Bridget and Raymond. 1968. *The Birth of Indian Civilization*, (Penguin Books, Harmondsworth, England)

Clark, R.M. 1975. A Calibration curve for Radiocarbon Dates, *Antiquity*, XLIX. pp. 251-66.

Dikshit, K,N. 1973. The Allahapur Evidence and the Painted Grey Ware Chronology, in *Radiocarbon and Indian Archaeology*, ed. by D.P. Agrawal and A. Ghosh. pp. 148-53 (Bombay).

Joshi, J.P. 1978. Interlocking of Late Harappa Culture and Painted Grey Ware Culture in the light of recent excavations, *Man and Environment*, Volume II, pp. 98-101.

Lal, B.B. 1954-55. Excavations at Hastinapura and other Explorations, 1950-52, *Ancient India*, Nos. 10 and 11, pp.4-151.

Mandal, D. 1972 *Radiocarbon Dates and Indian Archaeology*, (Allahadad).

Ralph, E.K., H.N. Michael and M.C. Han. 1973. Radio-Dates and Reality, *Masca News letter, Vol. 9 No. 1, pp. 1-20*.

Shrama, G.R. 1960. *The Excavations at Kausambi (1957-59)* (Allahabad).

Sharma, Y.D. 1953. Exploration of Historical sites, *Ancient India*, No. 9, pp. 116ff.

Tripathi, Vibha. 1976. *The Painted Grey ware ;-an Iron Age Culture of Northern India* (Delhi).

4. ACKNOWLEDGEMENTS

The author would like to place on record his grateful thanks to Shri S.K. Srivastava for the help given in the preparation of this paper, particularly in the calibration of the ^{14}C dates. His thanks are also due to Shri K. Rahman and Shrimati Promilla Jassal for taking great pains in making the type-script press-ready.

Shrimati Kusum Lal, as usual, has been most helpful in sorting out several complex issues relating to his much vexed topic. She has been discussing with me the various aspects of the Panited Grey Ware Culture ever since we started our work at Hastinapura.

Director
Indian Institute of
Advanced Study
Simla.

B. B. Lal

COMMENTS

The Painted Grey Ware (hereafter PGW) deposit at Hastinapur was initially dated from c. 1100—800 B.C. (Lal, 1954-55). However, Ghosh, Gordon and Wheeler did not accept this antiquity and assigned the emergence of PGW to c. 800 or even later (Ghosh, 1952, Gorden, 1958, Wheeler, 1959). At Allahapur for this culture a time bracket between c. 800—300 B.C. was proposed. (Dikshit, 1973). ^{14}C dates also supported this bracket (Agarwal and Kusumgar, 1974). Recently this ware was found inter-locked with late Harappan in Haryana and Panjab (Joshi, 1977).

RECENT DATA

The excavations at Atranjikhera, Etah District (Gaur, 1969) while confirming the Hastinapur sequence to a large extent added a new factor in so far as it demonstrated the occurrence of the black-and-red and black-slipped wares together with copper between the painted Grey Ware and Ochre-coloured ware deposits, This sequence was also confirmed at Noh, Bharatpur District and Jodhpura, Jaipur District, but at both these sites iron was found associated with black-and-red ware (Agarwal and Vijay Kumar, 1976).

At Allahapur, Meerut District, in Period IA a preponderence of black-and-red and black slipped wares was noticed over the Painted Grey Ware in the lowest most layers 13 and 14. From layer 12, the PGW pots outnumbered the black-and red ware pots. The black slipped ware is very restricted in quantity. No structure was encountered. Hearths closed and opened mouthed, successive mud-floors with post-holes, patches of ash and traces of burnt reed impressed mud plaster were duly found. These early layers, in fact, provide, an important link with the separate phase of black-and-red ware noticed at Atranjikhera, Noh and Jodhpura. In Period IB, the PGW overlapped with NBPW associated miscellany such as associated red ware, bone points, terracotta discs, antimony rod, profussion of iron implements and a seal in late Mauryan character. (Dikshit, 1973). No sherd of NBPW was found at Allahapur. A bone point inserted with an iron rod is of particular interest. Amongst the very few remains of indeterminate structures, was a circular mud wall containing some well-preserved hearths, burnt-floors, post-holes, and burnt-bricks. In the early stage of this phase, people were found contented with mud structures, but in late stage use of burnt-bricks of varying sizes with finger marks ($33 \times 16 \times 5{\cdot}5$ or $39 \times 19.5 \times 5$ cms) and rice husk as degraissant was also noticed. This evidence corresponds weel with other north Indian sites where burnt-brick came into vogue in the late phase of NBPW.

Khalaua, Agra District, also confirmed the evidence of Allahapur and Alamgirpur II where black-and-red ware was found overlapping in the earliest levels with PGW. (Sharma, Pers. Comm).

A new evidence has also come to light from excavations at Jakhera, Etah District. The Period I is characterised by black-and-red, black-slipped, burnished, grey and red wares, whereas Period II is divided into two phases. Phase A revealed painted pottery mostly black on various shades of red, along-with a few pieces of PGW. Important antiquities of this phase are copper-bangles, iron slags, stone ball, arrow-heads and bone points. Phase B is a full fledged PGW period. The settlement is encircled by a low mud embarkment. For the first time human terracotta figurines were also reported from this level. The Period III represents an overlap stage of PGW and NBPW. (Sahi, 1978).

At Mathura, PGW has been found only at *Ambarish Tila*. In phase IA which has an occupational thickness of about 0.80 m (including thickness of platform-0.65 m), no NBPW was found in PGW levels. It had a few variants of red ware types of the mid and late levels of Period II and even of early levels of Period III at Hastinapur. The upper limit of Period I (including Phase IB) which has overlapped with NBPW assemblage appears to be somewhere slightly before the Mauryan Period. (Joshi and Agarwal, 1978). The excavations from Sonkh also support Mathura evidence.

DISCUSSION

In northern Rajasthan, Harappan occupation started at Tarkhanwala Dera on a natural sand-deposit, but at Chak 86 which is just across the road, PGW was found over two flood deposits superimposed on natural sand, thereby suggesting no direct connection of these two cultures in this region (Ghosh, 1952).

The excavations at Atranjikhera, Noh, Jodhpura, Allahapur and Takhera provided new evidence for the reassessment of the PGW cultural traits and chronology in western Uttar Pradesh and eastern Rajasthan, whereas excavations at Bhagwanpura, Dadheri, Katpalon and Nagar revealed for the first time the interlocking of late Harappans with PGW users in Haryana and Punjab. The late Harappan phase has tentatively dated to c. 1600 — 1000 B.C. in this region. The overlap phase revealed three structural phases at Bhagwanpura and Dadheri starting from round or semi-circular huts, houses of mud-walls and ultimately houses of baked-bricks. As no iron object was found from these levels a case for a pre-iron PGW phase has been made out. At Bhagwanpura IB, plain Grey ware precedes in two layers to PGW occuring along with late Harappan wares (Joshi, 1979). This new proposition can be aceepted only by regional studies of material, as it is almost opposite of earlier profounded views of Joshi. Moreover, geographically Bhagwanpura is not lying in a direct receiving zone of Harappans, but is in an area of diluted influence.

The overlap phase of black-and-red PGW noticed in western U.P may be contemporary with the overlap phase of Harappa PGW in Haryana and Panjab, as no indipendent phase of black-and-red ware has been noticed in Haryana and Panjab so far.

The upper limit of the PGW period at Hastinapur was assigned on the basis of the NBPW sherds found in the pre-Aledandrian levels at Taxila, whereas the evidence of Ahichchhatra, where PGW continued with NBPW without any cultural break was not at that time thoroughly considered. The NBPW pottery types ef Hastinapur III compare closely with Ahichchhatra stratum VIII (c. 300 — 200 B.C.). The PGW associated red ware of Hastinapur occurs along with the NBPW assemblage at Sravasti, Rajgir ane Vaisali. In Bikaner, the PGW towards its end appears to have touched the historical cultures of the Mauryan and post-Mauryan times. (Ghosh. 1952).

The NBPW phase at Kausambi having nine sub-periods also support a late date of PGW. The earlier five-periods are pre-structural while remaining structural ones could be dated by coins and sealings. As there is no PGW at Kausambi, the NBPW phase could be safely placed between c. 500 — 200 B.C. ^{14}C dates of this phase which are quite consistant also confirm this time-bracket. It is now confirmed beyond doubt that PGW has a western epicentre whereas, NBP has an eastern epicentre and diffusion in a very wide area.

Lal has questioned the time-bracket of Allahapur. He thinks that for laying out the floors and/or constructing the houses, earth may have been brought up from earlier deposits in sub-period IB, which yielded burnt-brick structures, the NBPW and a Mauryan seal. In support of his contention, an evidence of above nature from Ayodhya was quoted. (Lal, 1979). However, at Allahapur as more than 10 squares were taken up and if any such mistake was there, it was bound to be detccted in other trenches.

^{14}C AND DENDRO-DATES

Recently, Ralph, Stuvier, Suess, Wendland and Donley have suggested some minor variations in Radiocarbon dates. But these corrected dentro-dates at the moment are difficult to apply. According to this correction end of Mohenjodaro becomes earlier than the historically dated beginning. For historical period In India more firm datable material such as coins and inscriptions are available which are quite consistant with ^{14}C dates. Significant descripancies noticed between the results of the same tree-ring samples from Arizone and La Jolla thereby suggest that the method has not provided so far unambigous evidence to calibrate the present ^{14}C dates. (Agarwal, 1974).

Lal has not accepted this position but celibrated PGW dates, ^{14}C one according to E.K Ralph et al and the other according to R.M. Clark. According to him PGW cannot be later than circa 1000 B.C. and must have ceased to exist by about the middle of the first millenium B.C. (Lal, 1979).

IN THE SEQUEL

The amalgam of late Harppa culture lingered in Haryana, Panjab and wastern Uttar Pradesh but only in certain pockets. It was not a regular phenomenon because the excavation at Ropar, Daulatpur, Alamgirpur and Hulas never presented any such picture and as such the stage of late Harrappa-PGW overlap has only raised upper limits of late Harappan amalgam at certain places than pushing back the antiquity of PGW. The excavations at Jakera, Atranjikhera, Noh and Jodhpura no doubt revealed a pre-PGW stage which can certainly be dated earlier than c. 800 B C. How much it would be early is a matter of conjecture ? Keeping in view the thickness of independent deposit of black-and- red ware a time-bracket somewhere between c. 900—800 B C may be correct for the emergence of black-and-red ware in the region.

The upper limits of this ware could be placed between c. 400 and 300 B.C. The NBPW. Complex

(Period III) which is deviod of PGW and occurs after a break at Hastinapur appears to be much later than Allahapur IB, as it has burnt-brick structures right from the beginning of the period. Allahapur is also marked by the absence of punch-marked coins. The end of Allahapur seems to be coevial with the beginnig of Period III at Hastinapur. The mean ^{14}C dates for NBPW deposits at Hastinapur ranging from c. 310 to 50 B.C. also support this fact. At Allahapur and Kausambi (Sharma, 1960, burnt bricks were noticed after the introduction of NBPW complex and not from the beginning.

Archaeological Survey of India K.N. Dikshit
New Delhi

REFERENCES

1. Agarwal, D.P. 1974 On the Calibration of ^{14}C dates, *Puratattva*, No. 7, New Delhi

2. Agarwal, D. P. & Shela Kusumgar 1974 *Prehistoric Chronology and Radiocarbon dating in India*, New Delhi.

3. Agarwal, R. C. & Vijay Kumar 1976 *Mahabharata Myth and Reality*, New Delhi.

4. Dikshit, K N. 1973 The Allahapur Evidence & the Painted Grey Ware Chronology, *Radio-Carbon and Indian Archaeology*, Bombay.

5. Gaur, R.C. 1969 Painted Grey Ware at Atranjikhera — an assessment, *Potteries in Ancient India*, Patna.

6. Ghosh, A. 1952 The Rajaputana Desert—Its Archaeological Aspect — Proceedings of the Symposium on the Rajaputana Desert, *Bulletin of the National Institute of Sciences of India*, Vol. No. 1, Calcutta, 37-42.

7. Gordon, D.N. 1958 The Prehistoric Background of Indian Culture, Bombay.

8. Joshi, J. Pr & Madhu Bala 1979 Manda— A Harappan Site in Jammu & Kashmir *Seminar on Harappan Civilization*, Srinagar (in the press)

9. Joshi, M.C. & R.C. Agarwal 1978 The Painted Grey Ware in Mathura (in the press).

10. Lal, B.B. 1979 Did the painted Grey Ware continue upto the Mauryan Times ? *Puratattva No. 9* (in the press).

—1954-55 Excavations at Hastinapur and other Explorations in the Upper Ganga and Sutlej Basins 1950-52, *Ancient India*, No. 10-11.

11. Sahi, M.D.N. 1978 New light on the life of Painted Grey Ware People as revealed from Excavations at Jakhera (Distt. Etah), *Man and Environment*, Vol. II, Ahmedabad.

12. Sharma, G.R. 1960 The Excavations at Kausambi (1957-59), Allahabad

13. Sharma, V.D. 1978 Personal Communication.

14. Wheeler, R.H.M. 1958 *Early India and Pakistan*, London.

Notes and News

The Early Harappan Cultural Phase : A Reply

NOWHERE in my thesis (Mughal, 1970 ; Fig. 16) I have staed that impluses from northern Baluchistan came directly to Kot Diji and then spread towards Taxila. It seems that Dani (1970-71 : 167-8) has misinterpreted my delineation of cultural interaction sphere existing during the Early Harappan period i.e. early third millennium B.C. As the distributional pattern of ceramic evidence reveals such an interaction sphere consisted of parts of eastern Iranian plateau, southern Afghanistan, southern Tnrkmenia, northern Baluchistan and the Greater Indus valley. An obvious inference is that prehistoric populations in this region had already established contacts through exchange/ trade or otherwise by the early third millennium B.C. It is the same period during which we find archaeological evidence of inter-connection among the sites of south-western Asia (Iran and Persian Gulf and Western Asia sometimes called a period of 'international' trade. The extent of overland contacts during early third millennium B.C. contradicts widely-ropogated belief that it was only during the mature phase of the Indus Civilization beginning around 2400 B.C. that contacts with outside regions were established or maintained is another example of the traditional view (Romila Thapar, 1975). Within this large interaction sphere, northern Baluchistan did assume a central place for transmitting cultural impulses from and to the Indus valley. Close links among the sites of Indus valley and northern Baluchistan specially those rocated in the Zhob, Loralai and Quetta valleys on the one hand and northern Baluchistan, north-eastern Iran, and southern Afghnistan on the other, are well established and further confirmed as a result of an intensive exploration of northern Baluchistan in 1972. (Mughal, 1972 & 1974). It was for this reason also that northern Baluchistan forms an integral part of the discussion on the development of early third millennium B.C. cultural phenomenon in the Greater Indus valley.

On the basis of my extensive survey in Pakistan it would have been illogical to emphasise the evidence found only at the type site, Kot Diji. I have discussed 'Kot Dijian Culture' implying, all those assemblages of the Indus valley which are comparable and contemporary with those found from the lower Kot Dijian levels of Kot Diji. I never thought of Kot Diji as *the* only central place of the Kot Dijian (Early Hrappan) culture, just as it would be illogical to regard Harappa as *the* place/centre of the Hrappan civilization. As I said five years ago and shall repeat again, I regard Bahawalpur region (central Indus valley) probably the centre of Kot Dijian culture. (Mughal, 1970; 98-100 & 102-105).

It is to be regretted that Dani's comment on Jalilpur excavation was premature. It was printed at a time when he had not seen the entire body of material. In actual fact, the evidence from Jalilpur (and also Sarai Khola) further substantiated and confirmed our argument in favour of the Early Harappan phase culturally linked with the mature Harappan phase. There is no evidence of mature Harappan occupation at Jalilpur (and also at Sarai Khola) but Harappan—like pottery forms and decorative designs and other objects occur both at Jalilpur and Sarai Khola, as they occur at the type-site Kot Diji in the Kot Dijian levels and elsewhere in the Indus valley. Dani claimed 'new excavation at Jalilpur completely falsifies such an assumption (of the existence of Early Harappan phase) as also do the geographical factors' but has not shown what and how the new evidence from Jalilpur 'falsifies' my contention to regard Jalilpur II as belonging to the early Harappan period contemporary with Kot Diji, Kalibangan I, and Sarai Khola II. Also, Dani has not specified or demonstrated those 'geographic factors' the Indus valley which do not support my framework and how ? Supportive evidence to my contention gathered recently from northern Baluchistan, entire evidence from Jalilpur, and Sarai Khola excavations was not *seen* by him.

In a recent article Dani (1975) enunciates his view on the 'geographic' aspects concerning the Bronze Age cultural growth in the Indus valley (Dani, 1975). The Gomal valley does have significance due to its location on one of the lines of communication but this factor cannot be overplayed without sufficient evidence and without regard to other relevant topographical features the northern Indus valley. He has emphasised the Gomal and Kurrum passes to the exclusion of other routes of ancient movement. In additional to a heavy bias towards an area where Dani worked, such statements reflect disregard for the total physical environment of that area. The Kurrum pass has *never* been as important in prehistoric days as the Gomal and other passes through the Sulaiman range. Furthermore, the Gomal pass was an important connecting link but it was *not* the only link existing between Baluchistan and the Indus valley. Another important, direct and easy link, according to my studies was the Sakhi Sarwar—Sangar Pass near Fort Munro which linked Kandahar through Loralai valley with Dera Ghazi Khan, Mulan, Bahawalpur and Kalibangan (Muhal, 1970 ; 195-203). From West, access to the central part of the Indus valley where greatest concentration of the Harappan sites exists, the Gomal Pass would have been long and difficult. Alternately, the easiest route was and is available through the Loralai valley. This route to Kandahar has been used even during the Mughal period. My survey of this area in 1972 has demonstrated that the ceramics characteristic of the Quetta valley spread northwards to the Zhob and then spilled over the Gomal valley (Mughal, 1972 & 1974). The geographic factors do not allow us to consider *direct* links existing between the Gomal valley and southern Afghanistan and even further west as intensively as advoacated by Dani. The Quetta Painted wares which occur so frequently at Mundigak, Said Qila Tepe, Deh Morasi Ghundai, Shahr-i Sokhta (Biscione, 1973; Tosi, 1968 & 1969) and the Quetta valley do not occur at all in the Zhob and the Gomal valleys. The archaeological evidence contradicts Dani's contentlon to consider the Gomal Pass as *the* important link with regions on West.

Unfortunately, the stratigraphical sequence of Gumla on Which Dani's conclusions are bassed, if itself questionable. When We try to relate the contents of various 'periods' as proposed by Dani at Gumla with the occupational sequences of Sarai Khola and Jalilpur, the discrepancies in the proposed divisions into 'periods' of Gumla become apparent. In the first place, the distinction between Gumla periods II and III does not appear to be real. Also, there is no discontinuity between III & IV. I have already pointed out this discrepancy in Dani's report (Mughal, 1972 : 121-22, footnote). One major correction in Dani's proposed sequence of Gumla must be pointed out right now. Gumla II is *not* earlier than Kot Dijian occupation at the type-site. In fact, Gumla II is contemporary with the Kot Dijian occupation at Kot Diji, Sarai Khola II, Jalilpur II (Mughal, 1972 ; 1972B & 1974a) and Kalibangan I. The levels grouped into Gumla III by Dani have not produced significantly different materials from those of Gamla-II. Thus, Gumla II and III *together* belong to the early third millennium. B.C. or to the Early Harappan Cultural Phase. The ^{14}C date (P-1812) from the earliest layer (11) of Gumla II (lying above the non-pottery period I) is 2248$\pm$74 B.C. (on new half life) or 2798 B C. with MASCA corrections. Though it is only one date so far available from Gumla, yet it appears to correspond to the middle levels of Kot Dijian occupation at the type-site.

On the basis of a thorough re-study of the entire evidence from Kot Diji, it is difficult for me to attach any 'cultural' significance to the 'burnt' level at Kot Diji, though the original excavator has streessed this point in the preliminary report (Khan, 1965). The reanalysis of all categories of small finds recovered by Dr. Khan at the citadel mound of Kot Diji demonstrates that nearly 50% of the total ceramic types of the (Early Harappan) Kot Dijian levels also occur in the mature Harappan period at Kot Diji. Similarly over 80% of the total number of small finds of the Kot Dijian levels persist into the mature Harappan levels. At Gumla, the alleged 'burnt' level, if at all existing, is not as pronounced as at Kot Diji. According to Dani, Gumla IV represents (mature) Harappan occupation at that site but ironically, difference between the material culture or Gumla III and IV is not as well marked as to justify such an assertion. Some perforated wares do emerge in Gumla IV but we all Know that occurence of only one pottery type or so, does not justify conclusions such as 'invasions', 'cultural 'break' or 'destruction'.

With the exception of expressing my immediate reaction to the stratigraphical sequence of Gukla and its division as suggested by Dani further comments would have been premature because field works were in progress at the early Harappan sites of Sarai Khola, Jhan, Jalilpur and in northern areas of Baluchistan located to the Gomla valley. Also, I intended to study the ecological situation on the Hakra river near Bahawalpur in the Cantral Indus valley relevant to human adaptation to that environment and cultural growth. These studies are still in progress but whatever evidence has been gathered so far, allows me to assert that during the last four years, additional and substantial evidence has been discovered which fully *confirms* the ideas already expressed in my thesis concerning the Early Harappan phenomenon of the early third millennium B.C. Our recent field investigations have further elaborated on the early Harappan developmental phase of the Harappan civilization, relevant to the question of the origins of civilization in the Greater Indus Valley. Most recently, 90 sites representing the early, mature and late stages of the Harappan culture have been recorded within only 100 miles long strip along the Hakra river bed. Among these sites, 35 belong to the Early Harappan (Kot Dijian) culture, 31 sites represent mature Harappan stage, and 24 are assignable to the late Harappan cemtery-H culture). In view of such an overwhelming mass of information. it is difficult to accept Dani's criticism on the Eerly Harappan phenomenon existing before the maturity of the Harappan civilization which I proposed in 1970 after detailed analysis and was reconstructed by demonstrable evidence. To that evidence, much more has been added now through excavations on a succession of early third millennium B.C. sites and extensive surveys carried out under my direction.

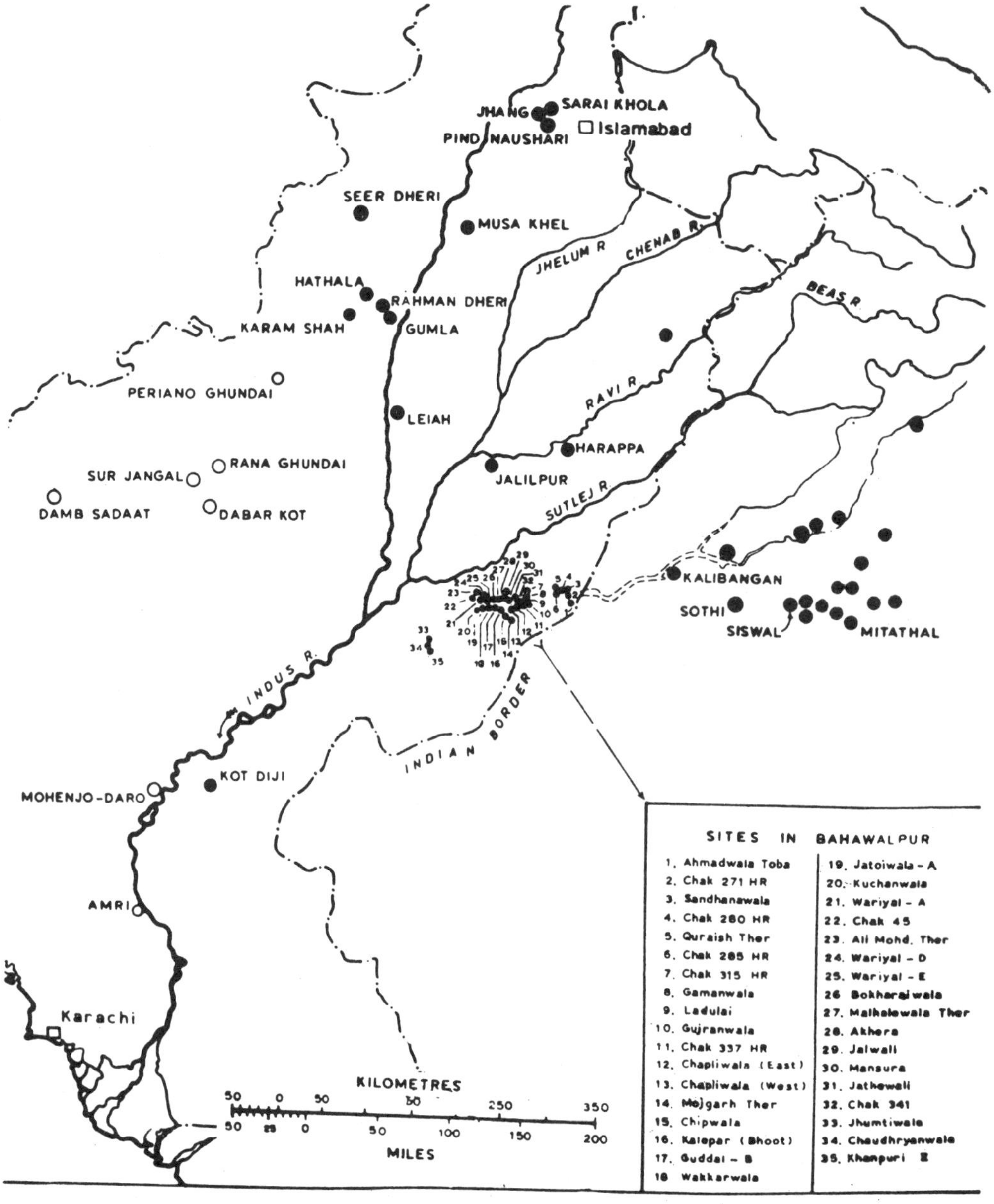

EARLY HARAPPAN SETTLEMENTS IN THE INDUS VALLEY

KOT DIJIAN SITES .... ●

The views of Thapar & Gupta (1972; & 1972-73) on the early Harappan phenomenon do not allow me to agree with them. The arguments should not be lost of bogged down in mere discussion on terminologies and also should not reflect my political, regional or academic bias. Instead, our collective efforts should be direected towards understanding the cultural and chronological significance of the early cultural growth before full urbanization in the Greater Indus valley in order to reconstruct early formative and developmental stage of the Indus Civilization. It is needless to repeat that II material from Kot Diji-related sites namely, Gumla, Sarai Khola, Jhang, Jalilpur, Kalibangan. I, Siswal A, Mitathal and 35 contemporary sites in Bahawalpur, are chronologically earlier than the mature phase of the Indus civilization. Among the material assemblages if we take out much repeated Kot Dijian short-necked, globular and flanged vessels and few peculiarities in figurines, most of the materials persisted into the next mature phase. In addition to the cultural as well as chronological priority of the Kot Dijian related cultural phenomenon, its distributional pattern within the Greater Indus valley is also most important factor indicating maximum possible human adaptation to the environment (Mughal, 1973 & 1974). So far, 54 sites have been definitely identified as Kot Dijian. This number does not include 22 Amri-related sites in southwestern Sind and 15 more in east Panjab mapped by Suraj Bhan (1973; 253). In view of this, is it still reasonable to regard Kot Diji-related cultural phenomenon as pre-Harappan, implying chronological priority over the mature Harappan, phase but not cultural ? If so, some of us are perhaps expecting to find *the* site such as Mohenjodaro, which should give us an evolutionary sequence on unilinear scale from the early to mature and late Harappan cultural phases. This brings up the vital and fundamental question of civilizational processes operative in the Indus valley which led to urbanization gradually. Can we expect to find *all* changes in the socio-political, economic and religious instituions, and even in the material culture represented through time on a single site ? I wish to ask further that if the Indus Civilization represnts, as it does, the fully developed, matured and urbanized stage of human endeavour, then, where are its early stages which immediately preceded it ? Do we have any evidence of the Kot Diji-related or mature Harappan cultural stages outside the Indus Valley ? I shall appreciate valid and logical comments, criticisms and questions from my colleagues in the interest of research. Be it repeated that Kot Diji is only a part of that cultural phenomenon which was most extensive in the Indus valley proper, contained many mature Harappan-like cultural traits in it, was chronologically and at some sites stratigraphically earlier than the mature Harappan phase. Therefore, Kot Diji—related cultural assemblages and other traits collectively constitute an *early Harappan* stage of cultural developmet in South Asia.

Department of Archaeology
Government of Pakistan
Karachi

Rafique Mughal

BIBLIOGRAPHY

Agrawal, D. P, 1972-73 Genesis of Harappa culture, *Puratattva* (New Delhi), No. 6, pp. 37-47.

1975 Radiocarbon chronology of the Harappa culture. *In* Lal, B. B. and Gupta, S. P. (Edt.) *Fifty years of Harappan Discovery* (in press).

Bhan, Suraj 1973 The sequence and spread of prehistoric cultures in the upper Saraswati basin. *In*, Agrawal, D. P. and Ghosh, A. (edt) *Radiocarbon and Indian Archaeology* (Bombay), pp. 252-263.

Biscione, R. 1973 Dynamics of an early South Asian urbanization ; the first period of Shahr-i-Sokhta *Jn*, and its connections with Southern Turkmenia. *In* Hammond, N. (edt). *South Indian Archaeology* (London), pp. 105-118.

Casal, Jean-Marie : 1961 *Fouilles De Mundigak* Memoires de lo Delegation Archaeologique Francaise en Afghanistan, Tome XVII), 2 Vols. (Paris),

Dales, George F. 1973 Archaeological and Radiocarbon chronology for protohistoric South Asia, *In* Hammond, N. (edt). *South Asian Archaeology* (London), pp. 157-169.

Dani, Ahmad Hassn 1970-71 Excavation in Gomal valley, *Ancient Pakistan* (Peshawar), No. 5.

1975, Origins of the Bronze Age cultures in the Indus basin—a geographic prespective, *Expendition* (Philadelphia), Vol. 15 (2), pp. 12-18.

Dupree, L. 1963 Deh Morasi Ghundai : A chalcolithic site in South-central Afghanistan. *Anthro. Pap. of the Am. of Nat. Hist.* Vol. 50, Part 2 (New York).

Gupta, S.P. 1972 The dichotomy of Harappan and pre-Harppan cultures. *In*, Manchanda, O., *A study of the Harppan pottery (Delhi)*, Appendix, pp. 395-405.

1972-73 A model for understanding the first urbanization in India, *Putatattva*, No. 6 (New Delhi), pp. 42-50.

Khan, F.A. 1965 Excavations at Kot Diji. *Pakistan Archaeology* No. 2 (Karachi), pp. 11-85.

Mughal, Mohammad Rafique 1970 *The Early Harappan Period in the Greater Indua Vallsy and Northern Baluchistan (C. 3000-2400 B.C.)* Ph. D. Dissertation in Anthropology, University of Pennsylvania. Philadelphia.

1972 Explorations at Jalilpur, *Pakistan Aachaeology* No. 8 Karachi, pp. 117-124.

1972a Excavation in Northern Baluchistan, *Pakistan Archaeology, No. 8* Karachi), pp. 117-124.

1972b Introduction to the pottery of Periods I and II of Sarai Khola. *In*, Halim, M.A., "Excava tions at Sarai Khola, Part II", *Pakistan Archaeo logy*, No. 8, (Karachi), pp. 34-40.

1973 *Present State of Reseerch on the Indus Valley Civilization.* International Symposium on Moenjodaro, February 1973, (Karachi)

Maghal Mohemmad Rafique

1974 Expiorations in Northern Baluchistan, 1972 : 1974 Explorations in Northern Baluchistan, 1972: New evidence and fresh interpretation, *Proceeding of the IInd Annual Symposium on Archaeological Research in Iran*, (Tehran), pp. 276-286.

1974a New Evidence of the Early Harappan Culture from Jalilpur, Pakistan, *Archaeology* (New York), Vol. 27 (2), pp. 89-127.

Shaffer, Jim G. 1971 Preliminary Field Report on Excavations at Said Qala Tepe, *Afghanistan* (Kabul), Vol. XXIV, (2-3), pp. 89-127.

1974 The Prehistory of Baluchistan ; Some interpretative problems, *Arctic Anthropology* (Madison, Wisconsin), Vol. XI, Supplement, pp. 224-235.

Thaper, B.K. 1973 New traits of the Indus Civilivation at Kalibangam : an appraisal. *In* Hammond, N. (edt), *Sauth Asian Archaeology* (Duckworth, London), pp. 85-104.

1973a Synthesis of the multiple data as obtained from Kalibangan. *In*. Agrawal, D.P. and Ghosh, A. (edt), Radiocarbon and Indian Archaeology Bombay, pp. 264-271.

Thaper, Romila 1975 A possible identification of Meluhha, Dilmun and Makan, *Jour. of the Economic and Social History of the Orient*, (London), Vol. XVIII, Part I, pp. 1-42.

Tosi, Maurizio 1968 Excavatlons at Shahr-i-Sokhta, a Chalcolithic Settlement in the Iranian Sistan : Preliminary Report on the First Campaign, October-December, 1967, *East and West* (Rome), Vol. 18 (1-2), pp. 9-66.

1969 Excavations at Shahr-i Sokhta, Preliminary Report on the Second Campaign, September-December 1968, *East and West* (Rome), Vol. 19 (3-4), pp. 283-386.

Locating the Graves at Kalibangan

Kalibangan[1] (Lon. 29°, 25'N, Lat. 74° 05'E) is an important Harappan site situated on the left bank of the Ghaggar (ancient Saraswati) in Ganganagar district of Rajasthan. The site which was excavated by the Archaeological Survey of India from 1960, has brought to light several new features hitherto unknown in the Harappan context. The Harappan cemetery at Kalibangan[2] is situated about 300 m. west-south-west of the habitation area. It is located on the present flood plain of the Ghaggar and usually gets submerged by the flood waters of the river during rainy seasons.

1. Indian Archaeology—1962-63, A Review, (New Delhi, 1965) P. 20.
2. Indian Archaeology—1963-64, A Review, (New Delhi, 1967), P. 38.
3. I.A.R.—1963-64, op. cit.

Three seasons of systematic dig in the cemetery area at Kalibangan has enriched our knowledge in the direction of locating ancient graves, particularly where the climatic and geographical conditions similar to Kalibangan prevail. As it has already been written earlier else-where[3] that it was the salt action that played a major role in locating the Harappan graves at Kalibangan, there were other factors too which contributed towards this end. Each point is being described here in detail :-

1. SALT ACTION :-(Plate XIII A)

Numerous white patches were noticed on the hard flat ground on the present flood plain of the river, nearly 300 m away from the citadel mound in the west-south-west direction. These patches consisting of loose earth, are caused due to the action of salt-petre. When water enters the pit through the loose

earth, it dissolves salt-petre present in the soil. The salt solution rises upward by the capillary action of the loose earth and reaches the top. As the solution is exposed to the arid atmosphere of the area, after reaching the surface of the pit, salts get crystallised forming a thin sheet of whitish patch in the pit area only. Such salt actions are more viggorous after a brisk shower or after a misty night.

2. PATCHES OF LOOSE SOIL :

Presence of numerous patches of loose earth is another indication of graves in the cemetery area. Loose earth is formed due to the salt action. It is a well known fact that salt in solid state increases in volume. In the process of crystalisation, tiny crystals of salt that are formed, exert tremendous pressure on the soil, due to increase in their volume. It is this pressure that makes the soil loose, thus forming a honey-comb like structure. This phenomenon is generally observed only in the pits and disturbed areas, because salt action will be more viggorous in such areas only.

3. DIFFERENCE IN THE FILLING OF THE PIT :- (Pl. XIII-B)

The graves at Kalibangan have generally not been filled with self same earth. The virgin soil in the cemetery area in this site consists of greenish loose sand. The grave pits have been generally filled either with (a) local greenish sandy soil mixed with whitish speckled clay or (b) with brown compact clay brought from elsewhere. When a particular area in the cemetery where the presence of a grave suspected on the basis of salt action, is scraped clean, a close examination of the area (in favourable light) marks out the difference in colour composition of the pit area from that of the virgin soil. This difference in colour and composition is due to the presence of foreign soil in the pits. Brown compact clay is available a little distance away on the banks of the river. Even 4000 years have not been able to merge the pit filling with the natural soil of the area. By careful observation the area of the graves can be clearly demarcated.

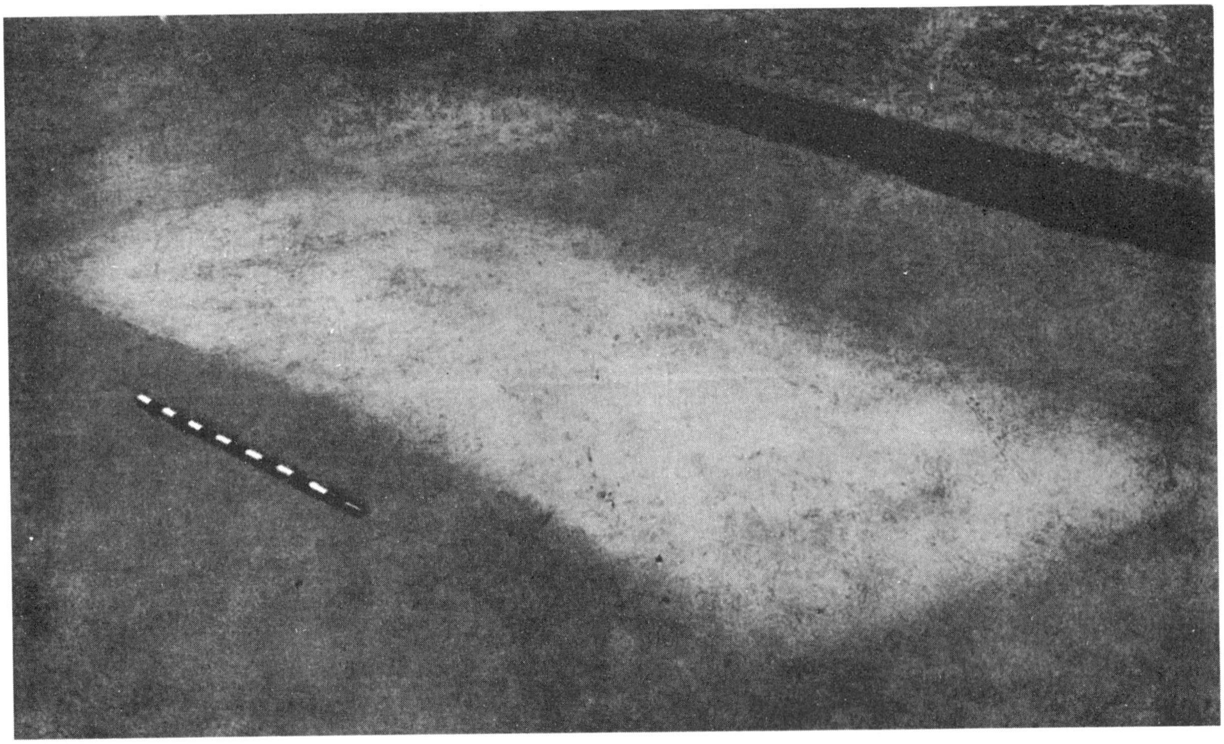

4. SOUNDS :

On thumping, sound emitted by disturbed and undisturbed areas differ. Walking up and down the cemetery gives two distinctly different sounds. At certain places the sound suddenly changes from high to low pitch. It becomes dull, heavy and hollow. This happens in the disturbed areas only. Natural, undisturbed area gives a uniform sound, but the sound becomes dull due to the loose nature of the soil in pit areas. By carefully tapping, the outline of the graves can be roughly demarcated.

5. ANT ACTION : (Pl. III).

Many a time cluster of ants can be seen at different places in the cemetery area. Presence of graves can be suspected at such places. In the pit area due to the loose nature of the soil and dampness, ants prefer to burrow holes. In the process they bring soil from the lower level to the top. This generally contains small grains of whitish clay (from the pit filling), terracotta particles (probably pieces eroded from the pottery buried below). In the process of burrowing holes they make the soil further loose. Digging on the basis of this indication has generally yielded good results.

6. NEGATIVE CROP-MARKS :

At Kalibangan in the fields adjacent to the known cemetery area, certain patches devoid of any vegetation, were observed. Size and orientation of such patches gave a temptation to dig one of these. Surprisingly, it turned out to be a rectangular type pot burial. Some more such patches were tried and they also came true to the expectations. It appears that the presence of harmful salts and its crystallisation in the pit area generally prevents the growth of vegetation in this area.

All these factors combined together help a lot in locating the graves. Generally one factor acts as a substitute to the other. In case none of these methods prove fruitful, the usual method of search by laying out squares in the suspected area and direction is to be tried. Using these factors nearly 130 Harappan burials were located in the cemetery area. (Pl. 4)

The methods enumerated above may not hold good every where. As it has already been said that under the similar climatic and geographical conditions these methods individually or collectively may be of some help to the future excavators. In other conditions also they can be tried.

Archaeological Survey of India — A.K. Sharma
Nagpur.

Depiction of Cattle Motifs on Amri Pottery

(A comparative study with Baluchistan)*

Cattle motifs on the painted pottery is one of the commonest motifs occurring on the pottery in the contiguous regions of Iran, Afghanistan, Baluchistan and Sind from 4th millennium B.C. to 2nd millennium B.C. A comparative study of this particular motifs offers scope for examining the possible link between contemporary cultures oi the regions. Accordingly we have selected for a detailed comparative study the Cattle Motif on the pottery from Amri. The site of Amri has been selected in view of its importance as a focal point through which early pre-Harappan traits have found their way into the Harappa Culture of the Indus Valley.

Amri in Sind (Pakistan) is an important site because of the presence of both Harappan and pre-Harappan levels. Its importance was first brought to light by Majumdar (1929), subsequently, the site was selected for a detailed excavation by Casal (1959).

Casal in his excavation has divided the habitation into five periods. Peried—I, which is pre-Harappan, has been named as 'Amri' civilization. This period has four subphases. Almost in all the phases, both handmade and wheelmade wares occur. Period—II is Intermediate period where typical 'Amri' ware occurs with the Harappan pottery with a noteciable increase of the cattle in the upper levels. Period—III has four phases. In period III A we get all the characteristics of the Harappan occupation. Period III-B is Transitional period, Period III–C is closely parallel with the upper levels of 'Mohenjodaro' and Period III-D is linked with 'Jhukar Type' pottery. Period—IV is of 'Jhangar' period, and this is found on mound A. Period—V is of Muslim occupation, with which we are not concerned here.

Briefly, one sees a gradual development in the decoration and technique of pottery. The animal motifs represented on pre-Harappan 'Amri' pottery consist of cattle, snake, birds and ibex.

The total number of cattle figurines found on Amri pottery are seven in number. These are distributed as follows :- In period I-D four cattle motifs are found. In period II, the number of cattle motifs decreases so we found only two cattle motifs, and in Period III-C single cattle motif is found. The whole figurine of cattle is painted with red colour and no attempt was made to give details of facial features.

Now we shall enumerate the features of each of the seven representations.

'AMRI' PERIOD I-D

Below the horizontal bands is the representation of cattle. First the outline was drawn and then it was filled with colour. Only the head and a part of the body of the animal have been drawn. It has long and pointed horns, which are very roughly drawn. The hump is prominent. The ears of rhe animal are relatively small. This drawing thus dipicts a crudely painted cattle. (Fig. 1:1)

On another pottery a complete figure of cattle is found (fig. 1:2). The horns of the animal are drawn carefully and smoothly. The hump is broad and prominent. In relation to the body, the tail of the animal is small and thin. The legs are pointed at the end and the feet are not drawn. The ears of the cattle are in the side of the horns. It seems that the painter has tried to decorate the animal by drawing curved lines on its body.

In figure 1:3 only face and neck of the animal have been drawn. The whole figure of animal is painted with colour. This figure resembles the previous one except that the curved lines on the body of the animal are not drawn.

On another sherd (Fig. 1:4) a part of the body is seen with both the forelegs of the cattle. Instead of filling the body of the animal, it shows strips. This representation recalls to mind the 'Kulli Style'.

The use of cattle as a motif is found in period II, but only a few examples are found. This cattle motif is not found in period II-A potteries but is used as a decorative motif in period II B.

PERIOD II-B :—

A cattle, with a prominent hump, horn and a part of

* This paper has been prepared under the general guidance of my supervisor, Prof. K.K. Sinha.

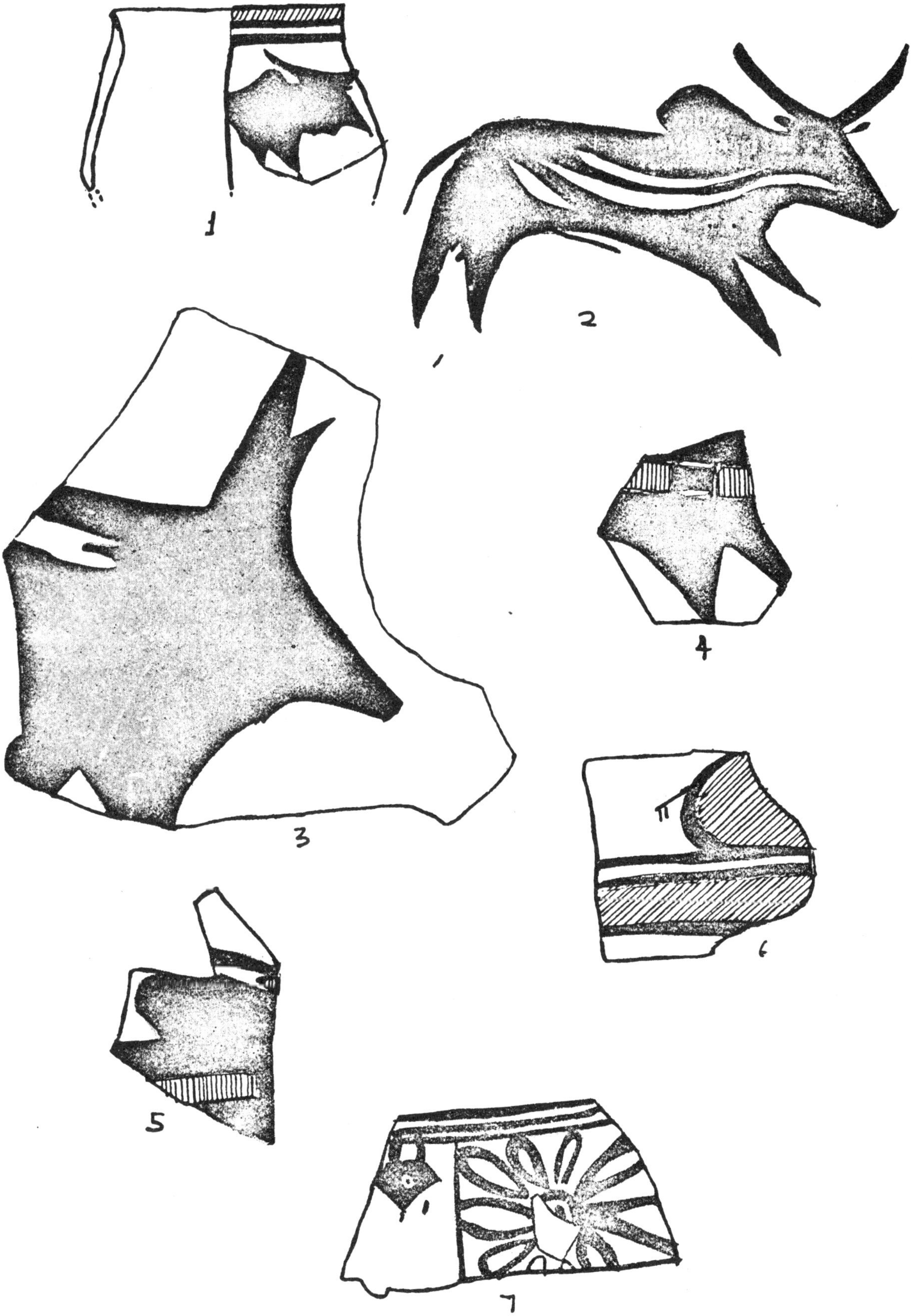

Fig. 1

body is found on a sherd. (Fig. 1:5) The body of the cattle bears strips. There is some resemblance between this and the animal of period I-A (Described above, Fig. 1:4)

In the second example (*Fig.* 1:6) the body of the cattle is delineated with black colour and is hatched with thin lines in red colour. The bull is shown in sitting posture and only the back of the body is visible on the sherd. It has a small tail which is divided at the end.

PERIOD III :—

In this example only the face and the neck portion are to be seen. The cattle's horns are drawn in its natural way. This is the only sherd found from Amri, wherein the eyes of the animal are drawn in the form of a black dot enclosed within a white circle (Fig. 1:7)

Thus, we find a gradual development in the cattle motifs as drawn on the potteries. Although the number of specimen is limited, it is possible to group cattle motifs in four stages.

STAGE A :—

Here the whole body of the cattle has been coloured (Fig 1:1, 3)

STAGE B :—

The body of the cattle is decorated and striped (Fig. 1:2, 4, 5,)

STAGE C :—

The body of the cattle is delineated with black colour and is hatched with red lines. (Fig. 1:6)

STAGE D :—

This is the developed stage and here the eyes of the cattle have also been drawn in a realistic manner. (Fig. 1:7)

Some terracotta cattle figurines are also found at Amri, also the hump of bull is prominent and these figurines are crudely made. Some time these terracotta figurines are decorated by drawing few lines on its body. But in some cases hump is not present.

Casal has reported the occurrence of bones of cattle. The 'Amri' people were agriculturalists and urban dwellers and it is likely, that cattle was an important element in the agriculture for ploughing. Thus the depiction of the cattle motifs on pottery could be taken as natural consequence.

Cattle are also used on Baluchistan potteries as decorative motifs. But in Baluchistan the cattles are more decorated and some-time stylized. The main sites of Baluchistan where cattle motifs are found are discussed below.

QUETTA VALLEY

Fairservis in his excavation has found two main sites, Kile Gul Mohammad (KGM) and Damb Sadaat. A new type pottery named 'Kechi Beg' is found in Period III of Kile Gul Mohammad and continues in the upper level of Kile Gul Mohammad and lower level of Damb Sadaat. Cattle motifs are found in the second phase of Damb Sadaat which is parallel to Amri II. The pottery surface is strewn with the black on buff pottery, known as 'Quetta Ware'.

On one sherd two cattle motifs are drawn together (Fig. 2:1). The hump of animals are shown on the head and the horns are emerging from the forehead. The legs of the animals are smaller in comparison to its longish body and has a long tail, which is plump at the end. There is continuous inclined hatching on the body of the animal.

In another example the hump of the cattle is made with criss-cross pattern (Fig. 2:2). The bull is stylized and has more resemblance to goat in appearance. It seems that the potter was first trying to draw a goat, but later on he changed his idea and, thus made hump on the body of the animal.

Sometime the cattle body is decorated by drawing wavylines, spots, and vertical lines. (Fig. 2:3, 4, 5)

RANA GHUNDAI :—

Rana Ghundai is situated less than 20 miles from Sur Jangar, in Loralai District of North Baluchistan. The decoration of the pottery is usually in black on red.

The depiction of Rana Ghundai cattles as totally different from all the other mentioned sites. The body of the cattle is extremely elongated and stylized (Fig. 2:6a, 6b). The legs are long and thin. The body is small and some time it gives an impression of a thick line only, hump is also small. The cattle's tail is long.

NAL :—

Nal is situated in South Baluchistan and is parallel to Amri I-D. Few cattle motifs occurs on Nal pottery. One is very simple and another motif is decorated and more clear. First cattle is in walking position and has longish body. The whole body is filled with colour. Another example of cattle painted on pottery is in its mature stage and the facial part of cattle is drawn carefully. The hump is prominent and body of the animal is drawn by lines.

KULLI-MEHI :—

Mehi is located forty miles far from Nal in South Baluchistan. Some cattle motifs are drawn on Kulli and Mehi pottery. The main characteristics of Mehi and Kulli cattle are that it has 'bug-face' and big eyes which looks like a black disc encircled by white. Sometime this animal is supported by small animals like 'ibex' (Fig. 2:7). A pipal tree or 'spiky' tree is drawn between two cattles. The cattle is usually tied with some unidentify thing but according to V.S. Agrawal this unidentified thing is a 'pillar' and he believes, that this is the origin of the 'pillar'. Some

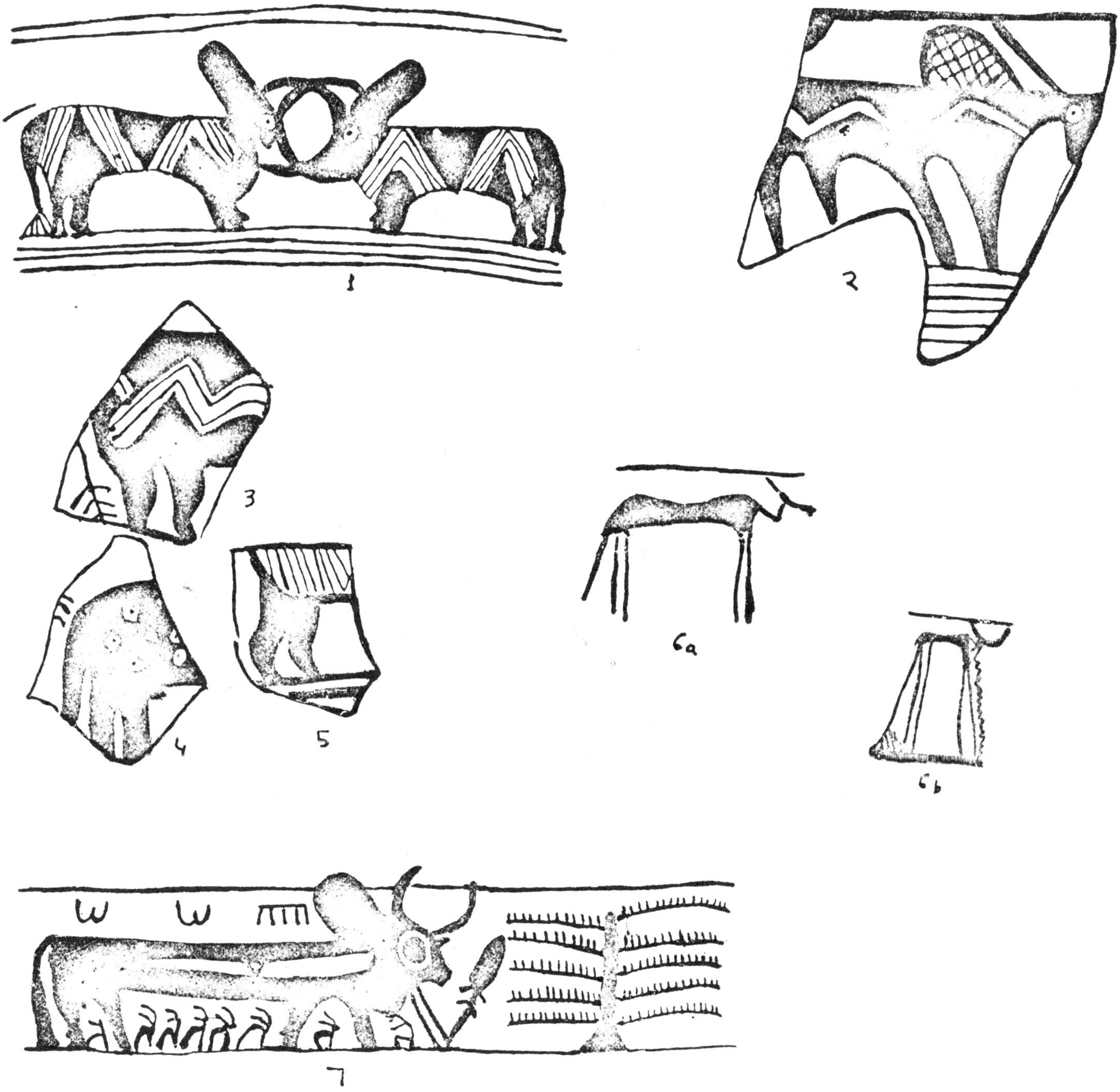

Fig. 2

time a comb shape motif or 'W' shaped motif is also drawn. Piggott thinks that this 'W' shaped motif is a bird. On the whole, this painting gives an impression of mythological scene and is usually in landscape painting.

COMPARISON AND CONCLUSION :

Amri and Quetta Valley :-

Though on Amri pottery also the painter had tried to decorate the bull but has never changed the exact figure of the animal. On Amri the hump of the bull is always on its place, but on one example of Quetta Valley, the hump is on the head of the bull. Tail of Quetta Valley bull is long and plumpy but Amri bull's tail is small and thin. There is a single example of Quetta in which the bull is stylized, Amri bull is decorated but not stylized.

Amri and Kulli :-

Amri cattle is drawn in its proportion, but the body of Kulli cattle is lengthened The Kulli cattle is usually supported by small animals, like goat or ibex, but Amri cattle has no supporting animal. Amri cattle is always left free and is not tied to anything but Kulli cattle is usually tied to some unidentified thing.

There is some similarity also. The Amri cattle is also some time striped in Kulli manner as it is seen in Fig. 1:4, 5. The eyes of the Kulli bulls looks like a black disc encircled by white but Amri bull's eye has a black dot in white circle.

Amri and Rana Ghundai :-

There is not a single similarity between Amri and Rana Ghundai. Rana Ghundai cattle is highly stylized and entirely changed from Amri cattle.

Banaras Hindu University
Varanasi

Poonam Chitkara

REFERENCES

Agrawala, V.S. 1972 *Bhartiya Kala* (in Hindi) Varanasi.

Casal, J.M. 1964 a. "Fresh Digging at Amri" *Pakistan Archaeology* No. 1 1964.

1964 b. *Fouilies D' Amri*, Vol. 1, 1964.

Fairservis Jr. W.A. 1956 "Excavation at Quetta Valley, West Pakistan" Anthropological Papers of American Museum of Natural History. Vol. 45, No. 2 1956.

1971 *The Roots of Ancient India* 1971, New York.

Majumdar, N.G. 1934 "Exploration in Sind" Memoirs of Archaeological Survey of India, Calcutta, No. 48, 1934.

Piggott, S. 1950 *Prehistoric India*

Stein, A. 1925 "An Archaeological Tour in Northern Baluchistan and Waziristan" Memoirs of Archaeological Survey of India, Calcutta, No. 37 1925.

1931 "An Archaeological Tour in Gedroasia" Memoirs of Archaeological Survey of India, Calcutta, No. 43, 1931.

"Copper Hoards" from West Bengal

DATA

In 1883 C.W. Anderson listed a copper shouldered celt from Tamajuri in Midnapur district. In 1966 the Directorate of Archaeology, Government of West Bengal, reported a similar shouldered celt from Chatla in the same district. Although Tamajuri and Chatla belong to the same district, their physiographic environments are different. While the region around Tamajuri at the foot of the hill-range beyond Sildah lies on the eastern fringe of the Chotanagpur plateau, Chatla on the Midnapur-Balasore (West Bengal-Orissa) border is in the lower, alluvial reaches of the Suvarnarekha. It was hypothesized in 1968 that this distribution in widely separate areas suggested the possibility of more finds within this zone. The third discovery comprising three shouldered celts and one pick-like object (still not properly published) was made in 1963 at Kulghera (Police Station : Hura) in Purulia district. This discovery was made during the re-excavation of a tank in a Test Relief operation and the finds are now with the Directorate of Archaeology, Government of West Bengal. The length and breadth of the three Kulghera celts vary from 20 to 21.5 cm, and 15 to 18.5 cm. respectively. Their thickness varies from 1 to 1.5 cm. Their weight is apparently uniform : 2.5 Kg. The pick-like object is 45.5 cm. long, 5.25 cm. broad and 3 cm. thick. This weighs 2.7 Kg.

Three more sites have been recently added to this list : Bhaktabandh (Police Station : Gangajalhati) in Bankura district, Aguibani (Police Station : Garbeta) in Midnapur district and Parihati (Police Station : Jhargram) in Midnapur district. The finds from Bhaktabandh and Aguibani are with the Directorate of Archaeology, Government of West Bengal, while the objects from Parihati are with the Department of Archaeology, Calcutta University. The discoveries were made by local people in all cases.

(1) Bhaktabandh (Pl. XIV-B) : 2 shouldered celts and 1 picklike object. One of the shouldered celts is 24.8 cm. long, 22.9 cm. broad and 1.5 cm. thick and weighs 4.24 Kg. The second one is 19 cm. long, 15 cm. broad and 1.5 cm. thick. Its weight is 2.485 Kg. The fragmentary pick-like object is 1.5 cm. thick.

(2) Aguibani : 2 shouldered celts (one of them is broken), 11 rings (of usual "copper hoard" type), and a few discoidal lumps of metal. One celt is 18.7 cm. long, 16.4 cm broad and 1.5 cm. thick. It weighs 2.16 kg. The broken specimen is 12 cm. long, 10 cm. broad and 1 cm. thick, weighing in its present broken condition 565 gm.

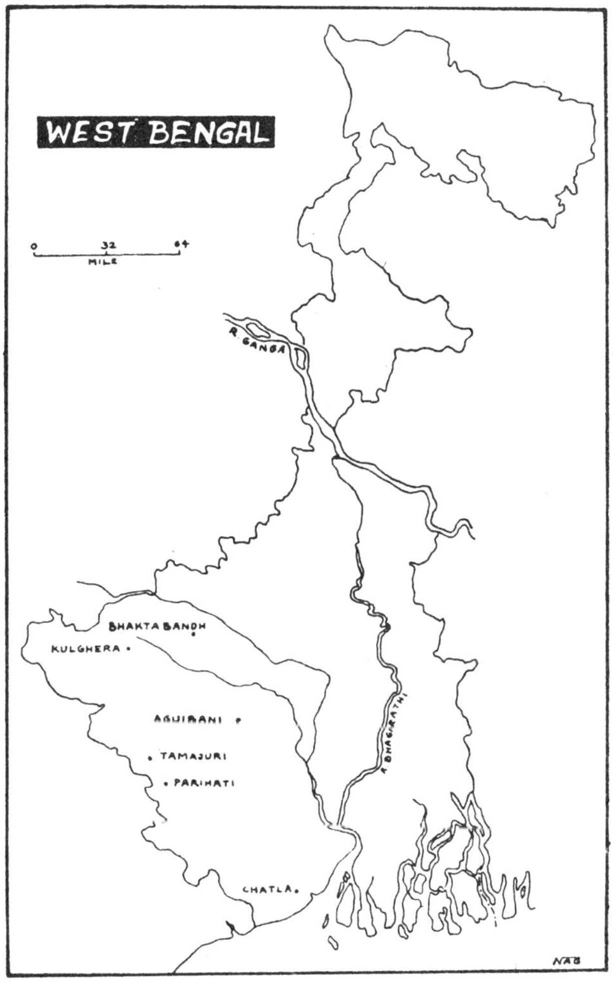

(3) Parihati (Pl. XIV-A) : 5 double axes, 1 bar-celt and 1 thick ring-like object. The length, breadth and thickness ofthe double axes are the following: (i) 36.5 by 28.5 by .5 cm.; (ii) 31.7 by 25.5 by .5 cm.; (iii) 27.5 by 24 by .5 cm.; (iv) 25.5 by 21.2 by .5 cm.; (v) 23.3 by 20.7 by .5 cm. The bar-celt is 28.1 cm. long, 2.9 cm. broad and 1.6 thick. It has not been possible to obtain weight of these objects, nor has it been possible to measure the ring-like object. However, all

these objects are quite heavy, generally conforming to the weight-pattern of the precisely weighed specimens from other sites listed here.

One of the present authors (AKN) could visit the sites of Bhaktabandh and Aguibani within a fortnight of the discovery of copper implements in December, 1976. The find-spots were not significantly disturbed till that visit. At Bhaktabandh the finds were made about half a metre below surface in an open field near the village. The immediate occasion was the construction of a road in that area. The deposit below surface (broken, compact, detrital laterite) where the implements were found, showed a reddish compact soil. At Aguibani too the finds were made about half a metre below surface, and the discoverer was a villager working in the land.

According to the villagers of Aguibani such hoards of copper implements have been discovered from time to time in this village and its vicinity. The implements thus discovered earlier are at present untraceable. According to one source in the village the number of celts discovered earlier in the village is not less than 30. Such a large number of artifacts and discoidal lumps of copper may suggest Aguibani to be a manufacturing centre, but nothing positive can be said at this stage.

At Bhaktabandh the implements were found carefully arranged. The procedure was perhaps to put the smaller objects over the larger ones. The patina marks on one of the celts from Bhaktabandh indicates the position of a smaller specimen kept over it.

At Parihati the available information suggests that the implements at the site were found in open field near the village, at not a great depth. A subsequent inspection showed unidentifiable pieces of pottery in the pit. Incidentally, both at Bhaktabandh and Aguibani some bits of unidentifiable potsherds were found lying scattered on the surface of the find-spots, but none was found inside the pits.

DISCUSSION

The total number of sites discovered to date is, thus, six : Tamajuri, Chatla, Kulghere, Bhaktabandh, Aguibani and Parihati. Except Chatla all these sites are in the extension of the Chotanagpur plateau in West Bengal. It is more than possible that other such hoards are waiting to be discovered in this region.

The basic tool-types are the following : (1) shouldered celt, with 2 broad sub-types made on the basis of the shape, of the shoulder—(a) reasonably straight (with only slight concavity) shoulder, without any upward kink at the beginning of the main body, and (b) concave-sided shoulder with an upward kink at the beginning of the main body; (2) bar-celt, tapering slightly from the middle to both end; (3) "pick"-like object, roughly pointed at the top and tapering toward the cutting edge—plano-convex in section and product of a single mould; (4) ring with two types—(a) usual "copper hoard" rings from Aguibani, and (b) the very distinctive ring from Parihati, the ends of which do not meet and are, in fact, considerably apart, but they terminate in solid, large, splayed out discs; (5) double axes—if these objects were really functional objects the hafting was obviously done in the middle, keeping both the axes free for action; (6) discoidal lumps of copper—as none of the objects has yet been cleaned by the institutions where they are preserved it is impossible to state if they are mere solidified lumps of metal (and thus perhaps ingots) or specific objects like shallow plates. We tend to believe from mere visual inspection that they are solidified lumps of metal.

None of these objects from West Bengal has yet been subjected to scientific analysis. On the basis of close visual inspection it may be said that all the objects except those from Parihati are crude in workmanship and products of single mould technique. The surface of non-Parihati objects is rough and shows porosity. In one specimen from Bhaktabandh we detect the presence of sand particles. The Parihati specimens are of better workmanship, and the Parihati ring may be considered a good example of double-mould technique. The weight of these objects is noteworthy : one shouldered celt from Bhaktabandh, for instance, weighs 4.25 Kg. This may cast doubt on the idea that these were functional tools. However, some specimens (e.g. the broken pick-like object from Bhaktabandh) show use-marks.

In a still unpublished paper P.L. Gupta has made it explicit that the "copper hoards" in Bihar, west Bengal and Orissa fall really in a small zone, in the districts of Palemau, Ranchi, Sighbhum, Hazaribagh, Santal Parganas, Dhanbad and the southern fringe of Monghyr in Bihar, in Mayurbhaj in Orrissa, and in Midnapur and Bankura in West Bsngal. The basic geographical local is the Chotanagpur plateau, in or around the rich copper seams of the region. The physical proximity between these find-spots and the local copper ore distribution is too close to be overlooked.

The most important aspect of P.L. Gupta's paper is that he drew up an inventory of "copper hoard" finds in West Bengal, Bihar and Orissa on the basis of earlier publications and the data available to him. It is useful to compare the West Bengal finds with those in Bihar and Orissa on the basis of this inventory. First, the shouldered celts are found all over the region, and also outside, and thus merit no special attention. Secondly, the only earlier reported occurrence of bar.celts in this region seems to be at Hami in Palamau district were 19 bar-celts were found in association with 6 flat celts. Some of them are in the Patna museum and have been examined by Gupta according to whom "these celts appear like a long chisel with a crescentic edge on one side and a pointed butt on the other and have nearly parallel but tapering sides". Parihati is the second site In this whole region to yield a bar-celt, but the Parihati specimen does not have any pointed butt. Thirdly, double-axes have hitherto been reported only from Bhagra Pir in eastern Mayurbhanj were three double-axes were found in association with a shouldered celt and an unascertained object. The second site to have yielded these double-axes is Parihati. Fourthly, the pick-like object is found only at Kulghera and Bhaktabandh in West Bengal; this type has not yet been reported from anywhere outside West Bengal. Fifthly, the Parihati ring the two sides of which end in solid discs seems to be the lone specimen of this type. Sixthly, regarding discoid lumps of copper it may be said that two pieces of unwrought copper were found at Kaharbari, Giridih (Pachamba) in Hazaribagh district. That a careful arrangement of objects as revealed in the recent West Bengal finds is not uncommon is suggested by the Bartola find of 21 flat celts in Ranchi district, where they were found lying one over the other. It should be more than clear that the recent finds in West Bengal fit in with the earlier discoveries in Bihar and Orissa.

Finally, a problem which has not hitherto been raised and to which no positive answer can be offered in the present stage of discoveries is; can these "copper hoards" in West Bengal be related to the chalcolithic tradition in West Bengal? The basic point to note is that the chalcolithic distribution in the region and the distribution of "copper hoards" do not *closely* coincide. The main concentration of chalcolithic sites seems to be in Burdwan and Birbhum districts, broadly to the north of Damodar. A few chalcolithic sites have recently been noticed in Bankura district which is also within the area of "copper hoards". If the chalcolithic sites are found extensively distributed in the "Copper board" areas of Midnapur and Bankura, the chalcolithic association of these hoards is a distinct possibility, but nothing more can be said in the present stage of knowledge. The only chalcolithic level in West Bengal to have yielded a copper object which fits in the general range of "copper hoard" objects in the eastern region is Mahisdal in Birbhum district, which has yielded a flat celt. But as a type this is not distinctive enough to establish a link between the chalcolithic horizon in West Bengal and the "copper hoards". As the Navdatoli find Indicates, "shouldered celt" as a type may be as early as chalcolithic but there is no shouldered celt in the chalcolithic context in West Bengal. The problem of chalcolithic-copper hoard relationship in West Bengal remains wide open.

What, however, lends these and other similar finds in West Bengal, Bihar and Orissa considerable theoretical interest is their association with the rich copper-bearing area of the region. The ore-implement correlation has not been attempted in any of these cases, but one would be surprised if the discovered implements were not made of the locally available ore. No speculation can be made on the antiquity of these copper objects, but the presence of a chalcolithic tradition in the region is suggestive, at least indicating that the metal-working tradition of the region stretches comfortably back to the middle of the second millennium B.C. It should be useful to undertake a field-programme with the specific aim of working out the distribution of "copper hoards" in relation to the copper sources, possible smelting sites and their contexts, and the metallurgical techniques involved in the making of the copper objects. It needs hardly any emphasis that the Chotanagpur plateau is among the richest metalliferous regions of the country, and there is enough historical evidence and suggestions that this region was a significant source of different types of metal in the historical period. What is needed, however, is a systematic investigation of the early metallurgical tradition in the Chotanagpur plateau.

ACKNOWLEDGEMENT :

Miss Madhusree Das supplied information about Kulghera finds. The Directorate of Archaeology, Govt. of West Bengal, and the Department of Archaeology, Calcutta University. gave permission to study the material. A.K. Datta discussed a few issue regarding Parihati finds.

(School of Archaeology, Archaeological Survey of India and Department of History, Delhi University)

A. K. Nag
and
Dilip K. Chakrabarti

REFERENCES

C. W. Anderson, *Catalogue and Handbook of the Archaeological Collection in the Indian Museum,* Calcutta, 1883.

S. C. Mukherjee. "Protohistory of West Bengal" *Exploring Bengal's Past,* Directorate of Archaeology, Govt. of West Bengal, Calcutta 1966.

A.K. Ghosh and Dilip K. Chakrabarti, Prehistoric metal stage in West Bengal, *Bulletin of the Cultural Research Institute,* Vol. 7 (1968), p. 112.

P.L. Gupta, Copper Hoards in India, *cyclostyle paper* (undated). We thank Dr. D.K. Bhattacharya for making this paper available to us.

An Early Warehoue on the Western Coast

The aim of the present paper is to describe and identify, if possible the vast structure complex which has been laid bare in the course of our excavations at Prabhas Patan (also known as Somnath Patan, District Junagadh, Gujarat). The circumstantial evidencal tends to show that the structure probably served the function of a warehouse. It is a unique structure the like of which has not so far been reportod from elsewhere in the country and hence its importance.

Before discussing the structure complex, it would be desirable to describe the culture background. The ancient site at Prabhas Patan is situated on the south-eastern coast of Saurashtra at the month of the river Hiran (Hiranya) near the port town of Veraval. The site was first excavated by late P. P. Pandya of the then Department of Archaeology, Saurashtra State in collaboration with late Dr. B. Subba Rao of the M.S. University, Baroda in 1955-56 and 1956-57 (*IAR* 1955-56 : 7-8 & 1956-57 : 16-17) and later by M.A. Dhaky of the State Department of Archaeology, Gujarat State and Dr. R. N. Mehta of the M. S. University, Baroda (Nanavati *et al* 1971). It was again excavated by Dr. H.D. Sankalia, Dr. Z.D. Ansari and the present writer in collaboration with the Gujarat State Department of Archaeology in 1972, 1976 and 1977 solely with a view to studying the Prabhas culture and laying bare the houses of the early settlement at the site (*IAR* 1972).

Our excavations at Prabhas have brought to light a five-fold sequence of cultures which is as follows :

Period I Pre-Prabhas culture (Circa 2200-2000 B. C.)

Period II Early Prabhas culture (Circa 1800-1500 B. C.)

Period III Late Prabhas Culture (Circa 1500-1200 B. C.)

Period IV Early Historic (Circa 4th Cent. B.C. to 1st cent. A.D.)

Period V Kshatrapa-Gupta (Circa 1st cent. to 6th cent. A.D.)

Of the five cultural periods, our main concern here is the Prabhas culture which is covered by Periods II and III (Dhavalikar 1977). The culture is characterised by its painted pottery. The vessels in this ware are of fine fabric and are treated with a pinkish or orange wash which, in several cases, has turned grey because of certain peculiar conditions of firing in the kiln. Over this are painted patterns in purple or dark brown. The range of the painted motifs is extremely limited because they are all geometric such as groups of vertical and oblique strokes, wavy lines, hatched triangles, lazenges etc. Another noteworthy feature of the Prabhas ware is that the design element is usually set in panels or registers. The most predominent shape is the sub-spherical bowl with a slightly incurved and featureless rim which is some time sharpened internally. The bowls are in all sizes, small and big, and one wonders why the Prabhas people required such a bewildering variety of bowls. Another important shape is a globular jar with outturned rim. The stud-handled bowl and the dish-on-stand were evidently borrowed from the Harappans.

The people of the Prabhas culture very rarely used stone blades and flakes in spite of the availability of suitable raw material in the surrounding region. But they do seem to be importing obsidian flakes of which a single specimen was found in the Late Prabhas levels. It probably came from Turkey which supplied obsidian to West Asian countries. It should also be stated in this connection that obsidian is found in Saurashtra at Osham Hill near Porbandar, but it is of a much inferior variety.

Copper implements may have been used on a wider scale, for excellent copper ore was available plentifully in the adjacent areas now in Amreli District (Lamberg-Karlovsky 1967 : 149) Although only a few bits of copper were found in the course of our excavations, earlier excavations at the site have yielded a few copper axes (Nanavati *et al* 1971 : 77, Pl. XI).

The people used beads of semi-precious stones such as chalcedony, carnelian, agate, etc. and faience and steatite as well. Among them the segmented beads of faience are quite common. They are either made locally or were obtained from the Late Harappan traders in Saurashtra. A unique seal amulet of steatite was recovered in the course of our excavations. It is engraved on both sides ; on one side there are seven stylized deer while on the other there are only five deer. Stylistically, the specimen is no doubt related to the Harappan seals. A gold ear ornament was recovered from the Late Prabhas levels. It is floral shaped and is provided with a loop at the back for suspension. It is certainly indicative of the prosperity of the Prabhas people. They also used cubicle chert weights exactly similar to those from Indus sites.

STRUCTURE COMPLEX

The structure was first encountered in the course of our excavations in 1972 whereas its extension was traced in the seasons of 1975 and 1977, and it is noticed that it has not yet been exposed completely. It is built of stone set in mud masonry. The stone used is the miliolite limestone which is plentifully available in the coastal areas of Saurashtra. What we have found is a number of walls running east-west and north-south, thus forming small squarish rooms, admeasuring 1.05 m square whereas some larger rooms measure about 3.50 m in length and 1 50 m in width. In most of the larger room and a few of the smaller rooms were found three or four flat stones set in mud mortar to form a sort of platform, usually near the entrance. It may be Stated in that in spite of three seasons' work we were not able to find out either the opening or the end of the structure complex. But unfortunately the structure has already been destroyed in the east and north by the citadel wall of the Early Historic period while in the west was dug a large trench by earlier excavators ; on south there are large banyan trees which make the excavation extremely difficult. Be that as it may, our work has revealed the following features of the structure complex :

1. For building the structure the Late Prabhas people first levelled the land surface by ramming stone rubble at places where some depression was noticed. This is clearly visible in the large room in Sq. B4 where in the wall we can see a number of courses of stone set in mortar whereas in the area enclosed by the walls—that is, within the rooms—we find stone rubble rammed into the earth.

2. The structure consists of a number of rooms averaging 2×1.50 m whereas some of the rooms are squarish (1.50X1.50 m). In some trenches where an attempt was made to trace the flooring, it was observed that in the area enclosed by the stone walls the people had rammed large lumps of black sticky clay. Thus it appears that they wanted to have a strong foundation not only for the walls but also for the area enclosed by walls.

3. A careful examination of the extant remains of walls and also of the area enclosed by them shows that there was no provision for any wooden post or uprights for supporting the roof as no post-holes have been found. This is indicative of the structure being roofless and exposed to the sky above. Another factor which provides corroborative evidence is the height of the walls which is not more than 60 cm at the most. In fact most of the walls have only one or two courses of stones. Only the central wall running north-south is a little high (60 cm), and two more walls parallel to it are also equally high but only at one or two points. We do not know whether originally they were so high or whether they appear so because of our deep digging in the area within for tracing the stone courses of the foundation.

4. The walls may not have been much higher than what we see them today because not many of the upper courses have fallen. If that had been the case, a number of loose stones would have been found in the debris. But this was not the

case and we can therefore be certain that the walls were low. In some of the rooms it has been observed that they were provided with a large flat stone in the northern wall probably to mark the entrance to the room.

5. In the earlier excavatlons it was observed that some of the rooms were provided with a set of two or three large flat stones set in black sticky clay. They form a sort of a platform.

6. A close examination of stratigraphy and a careful analysis of the artefacts recovered from within the structure suggests that it was not meant for residential purposes. No *chulah* or fire places, ash, bits of charcoal or clods of burnt earth and charred grains or any such evidence be token of the human habitation is totally lacking and one can therefore be certain that it is a specimen of public architecture.

Thus the only conclusion we could draw from the above discussion is that the structure was not meant for residential purposes. Since the site is located on the right bank of Hiran, hardly one and a half km from the sea at present, we wanted to ascertain whether the structure could have formed a part of an ancient port. We therefore invited Shri Vohra, the Port Officer at Veraval, with long experience of ports on the western coast, to inspect the structure complex. He was certain that it could not have served any function connected with port. Thus the structure have proved to be enigmatic. Since the structure does not apply any clue to its probable function, we began to examine the evidence furnished by the antiquties recovered from within the structure. The most noteworthy antiquities from the structure comprise the only steatite seal amulet, a solitary flake of obsidian, two huge storage jars of red ware, on plain and the other painted, some steatite and faience beads and a number of dentalium shells besides pottery, the yield of which is poor. These artefacts would suggest that the structure may be served as a storehouse. This surmise is further strengthened by the evidence from Tepe Yayha in Iran where such a structure complex with small squarish rooms measuring five feet square was exposed. This structure has been tentaviely identified by its excavator .as a storage place (Lamberg-Karlovsky 1972 : 174-83, pl. on p. 179). It is a labyrinthine structure with no entrances and hence it is suggested that the entry was provided from the roof. The Prabhas structure, as has been described above, probably had no roof of any sort and since the walls are low, entry into it may not have difficult.

An almost identical structure has been unearthed at Umm Dabaghiyah which, however, is much earlier in point of time as it has been dated to Circa 5500 B.C. It consists of an open court-yard surrounded on three sides by blocks of store room, some arranged along corridors, of regular dimensions (about 1.50 m to 1.75 m). These small rooms have mud floors and were usually entered from above ; few have doors leading into other rooms or corridors. None were provided with hearths and ovens, and they clearly did not serve a domestic purpose except when alterations took place later. The structure has therefore rightly been identified by James Melaart (1975 : 137, fig. 79) as a storehouse.

Nearer home, the evidence from Lothal is also significant. The large scale excavations at the site have brought to light a structure which has been identified as a warehouse. It is larger in area than the granaries of Harappa and Mohenjo-daro, and was erected on a massive podium of mud bricks in the southeast corner of the town. For proper haulage of goods intercommunicating passages and air vents were provided between cubical platforms (Rao 1973 : 56, fig. 15, Pl. IX. A).

Thus the circumstantial evidence from Prabhas Patan and the parallels cited lead us to infer that the structure was probably used for storage, and since it is located on the mouth of the river Hiran, it can be identified as a warehouse.

Deccan College and Postgraduate Research Institute Pune.

M.K. Dhavalikar

REFERENCES

M.K. Dhavalikar 1977 Sub-Indus-Cultures of Central and Western India, a paper read at the seminar on *Indus Civilization : Probiems and Issues*, Simla, 1977.

Indian Archaeology—A Review (abbreviated as *IAR*)

Lamberg-Karlovsky, C. C. 1967 Archaeology and Metallurgical Technology in Prehistoric Afghanistan, India and Pakistan, *American Anthr*. Vol. 69; pp. 145-62.

Lamberg-Karlovsky, C.C. & Martha 1972 An Early city in Iran. In *Old World Archaeology—Foundations of Civilization, Readings from Scentific American.* San Fransisco. pp. 174-83.

Melaart, James 1975 *Neolithic of the Near East.* London, World of Archaeology Series.

Nanavati, J.M. *et al* 1971 *Somnath—1965.* Baroda.

Rao, S. R. 1973 *Lothal and the Indus Civilization.* Bombay.

Romano-indian Rouletted Pottery in Indonesia

The presence of Romano-Indian rouletted grey ware in northwest Java provides evidence of trade between India and Jawa during the first two centuries A.D.. The pottery comes from precisely that region of Java which *ca*. 450 A.D. was known as Taruma and seems to have been a recipient of Sanskritic culture. Dr. Walker is a lecturer in the prehistory section of the Anthropology Department at Sydney University who also has published iately a major article on neolithic and copper age pattery from southeast Spain (Australian Studies in Archaeology No. 2, 1976). Mr. Santoso is on the staff of the Pusat Penelitian Purbakala dan Peninggalan Nasional, Jakarta (National Research Centre for History and Archaeology).

INTRODUCTION

In 1976 we conductsd investigations into earthenwares of the northwest Java 'Buni Complex' (Lutayasa 1972) and drew some 350 intact vessels at the Pusat Penelitian Purbakala dan Peninggalan Nasional and the Museum Pusat (Central Museum), thanks to the kind permission of R. P. Soejono at the former and of Professor Bambang and Mr. Sulaiman at the latter. A full study is in preparation for publication, Suffice it to say that the complex comprises buff, brown or grey cooking pots, pot lids, and shallow bowls or dishes, as well as occasional flasks with tall necks. Apart from these last, the ware is coarse and ill-fired with micaceuos or quartz filler and usually plain. The flasks often have incised concentric zonal decoration, and other vessels may have zonal incised chevrons, grids, and stamped decoration. One vessel bears stamped swastikas present on the upper part of cooking pots which have everted rims on which the colour is present inside as well as out. Pedestals and foot rings are very rare, but omphalos bases are not uncommon, likewise flat bases, although convex bases are the most frequent kind. The bodies of cooking pots are globular, sometimes carinated. Rims are usual, true necks infrequent. In some cases rims seem to have been added separately before firing, whereas in others rims were made of a piece with the body.

Most finds come from northwest Java, and particularly from that area now under paddy watered by the rivers Bekasi, Citarum, Parage and Cilimayo(ci=water, river), which have made a wide alluvial flood plain – Three groups of sites occur on it (Sutayasa 1972), one between the Bekasi and Citarum, a few kilometres from their mouths (near villages of Buni, Kedungringin, Bulaktemu, Kebon Klapa, Batujaya, Pulo Glatik), anoher 18 km northeast of Rengasdengklok (near Kobak Kendal, Dongkol, Cibutak, Pojoklaban, Tegalkunir, Babakan Pedes, Turi, Karangjati, Cilago), and a third at Cibango neat the month of the Cilamaya. The pots were found during agricultural operations by local people and later acquired by the Research Centre or the Museum. One trial archaeological excavation showed only that much disturbance and mixing of material had occurred at the place chosen, an unsurprising finding because agricultural irrigation and drainage ditches have been dug continuously for probably 1,500 years: an inscription of King Purnavarman of Taruma *ca*. A:D 450-500 tells of such operations (Taruma is identified by historians with the Tarum river region).

ROMANO-INDIAN WARE

Hitherto archaeology has not succeded in establishing clear links with India, despite Sanskrit inscriptions and Indian names (e.g. Purnavarman). Much Buni Complex material shows resemblances with Bengal vessels studied by Ms. J. Birmingham of Sydney University, and ceramic relationships do not seem to lie in the direction of the Sa-huynh/Kalanay traditions of Vietnam and the Philippines, although latter do the reach eastern Indonesia. In this article we shall cofine attention to import ware, which, notwithstanding its scarcity, alone among the Buni Complex vessels can be categorically said to be not made locally. We refer to Romano-Indian rouletted fine ware.

Fig. 1a shows a large piece of this from Kobak Kendal at in the Research Centre collection. The dish measured 300 X 6 mm and is of thin (6 mm) brittle ware which gives a bell-like ring when tapped. The body is grey in cross-section and on its inner surface, but the outher was treated with a red wash or slip (it is uncertain which). Microscopical grains of quartz or mica (the petrology has not been carried out yet, but is in hand) might represent materials present in the clay or else finely ground filler. Surfaces are very smooth, and perhaps were polished. No tell-tale striations indicate that a fast-wheel was used, though later treatment could have obliterated them. A circular band of rouletted dots is present on the inside, the impressions being somewhat blurred, perhaps also due to subsequent treatment. Fig. 1b shows another large piece at the Centre from the same locality. This dish measured 290X45 mm and is even thinner (4.5 mm). The ware is grey in cross-section and on the inner surface, but the outer surface is pink. There is no sign of wash or slip. Two concentric bands of rouletting are present, showing different patterns. There is also a shallow groove running around the upper part of the vessel. The third piece is an intact dish in the Museum Pusat (fig 1c) also with two concentric rings of decoration. It measures 275X50X6 mm. No cross-section of the fabric presented itself. The inner surface is grey, but the outer is red-brown and both polished and burnished, though not treated with a wash or slip. The rim is more complicated having an inturned beak and also milled decoration. The outside has running incised chevron decoration. Again, the rouletting shows two different patterns. Unlike the other vessels, the rouletting is sharply impressed. The piece comes from Cibutak.

Some other dishes which lack decoration seem to be made of very similar material. In one or two cases they have omphalos bases. They will be published along with the rest of the Buni Complex pots, since it cannot yet be stated that they are imports.

DISCUSSION

There is no doubt whatsoever that this ware is indentical to much of that published from many Indian locations, with the single exception of fig. 1 where exterior decoration is shown, a feature not characteristic of the subcontinent. Krishna Deva (in Wheeler *et. al.* 1946) described rouletted ware at Arikamedu, and his account was included along with accounts of Arretine ware and of amphorae under the general heading of wares imported from the Mediterranean, separated from the next heading "Local Wares". However, he wrote,

> "A characteristic pottery-type of Arikamedu is a dish (Type 1) sometimes more than 12 inches in diameter, with an incurved and beaked rim which usually has a facetted edge. The ware has a remarkably smooth surface, is thin, brittle and well-burnt, and has an almost metallic ring. The flat interior is normally decorated with two, occasionally three, concentric bands of rouletted pattern. This pattern is not an Indian feature and may be regarded as an importation from the Mediterranean region, but it has not yet been possible to ascertain whether the type itself is of similar origin. It may in any case be presumed that the varieties with distinctly inferior fabric and degenerate rouletted pattern were manufactured locally."

The ware was often slipped, the commonest of five slip types being "greyish pink ware, grey slip inside, brown to sepia outside. "The Arikamedu stratigraphy permitted further subdivisions to be made. Generally speaking the more incurved, less vertically walled dishes were associated with Arretine import ware, likewise dishes with pronounced beaked rims. However, both forms occasionally seem to have continued down to the end of the second century, whilst high external grooving (*cp.* fig. 1b) was never found before the appearance of Arretine ware (perhaps *ca.* A. D. 20-50), although rouletted ware did occur prior to that at Arikamedu. Burnished rouletted dishes there came mainly from pre-Arretine layers, but burnish was more often on inner not outer surfaces. Sharply impressed roulette motifs were said also to be early and not post Arretine in general. Those criteria could be used to argue an early first century date for fig. 1c. The running parallel chevrons of this piece might be parallelled in criss-crossing painted chevrons on russet-coated painted "Andhra" ware, whose forms include bowls just like those of rouletted ware, occurring often at the same sites as the latter, and being contemporaneous with it (Wheeler *et al.* 1946, 48 ; Wheeler 1947-1948, 236-7, 277-8, 308-99).

At Arikamedu rouletted ware occurs in pre-Arretine (pre-A.D. 20), Arretine, and post-Arretine levels, through to the end of the site *ca.* A.D. 200. Casal compared it with Etrusco-Campanian rouletted decoration (Casal 1949) but there the similarity ends. Rouletted ware is known from other south India sites, *viz.* Amaravati (Wheeler *et al.* 1946), Brahmagiri and Chandravalli (*ibid.*, Wheeler 1947-1948), Kondapur and Maski (Wheeler 1947-48), Uraiyur (*I.A. 1964-65*) and Maigramam (*I.A. 1961-62*). From north India it is known at Tamluk (*I.A. 1955*), Chandraketugarh (*I.A. 1956-57, 1957-58, 1959-60*), Rajghat (*I.A. 1963-64*), Sisupalgarh (Lal 1949), and Baral (*I.A. 1957-58*). Can we date rouletted ware at these sites ? Are there chronological divergences from Arikamedu ? The short answer is no. But it is hard to be precise. Tiberian currency found at Chandravalli was at first thought to come from layers which contained rouletted ware (Wheeler *et. al.* 1946), but subsequently it was said that the money could have been dropped as late as the second century (Wheeler 1947-48). Later excavations at Maski (Thapar 1957) did not find any more rouletted ware, but russet-coated painted ware was encountered. At Sisupalgarh rouletted in levels earlier than one in which there was a found of the second century Kushana monarch Huvishka, the site continuing down to *ca.* A.D. 350.

Despite occurrence of rouletted ware at Tamluk, it is conspicuous by its absence at Patna (*cp.* Altekar and Mishra 1959). At Chandraketugarh the first two periods do not have rouletted ware, and it appears either contemporaneously with (*I.A. 1956-57*) or somewhat after (*I.A. 1959-60*) the appearance of Northern Black Polished Ware, continuing during "Sunga-Kushan" times, and even into those of "early Gupta" (*I.A. 1957-58*). However the Gupta phase is characterized, as at other sites, by stamped ceramic ornament, not by rouletted ware. Plain flat base dishes of northern black polished ware have profiles like those of rouletted ware, and one (*I.A 1956-57*, 29, fig.14), has an internal circular motif from which radiate triangles, like the points of a compass, perhaps foreshadowing circular ornament of later rouletted ware, notwithstanding the Mediterranean inspiration of the latter. At Rajghat the single sherd of rouletted ware occurred in "layer 4" (*I.A. 1960-61*), but it is not stated whether this corresponded to pre-Gupta, Gupta, or later levels of occupation.

There is widespread occurrence in India of grey-pink fine ware dishes lacking decoration, but otherwise like rouletted dishes. We have found these too on Java. But as has been said the profiles have considerable antiquity in India, and it would be unwise to attribute these to foreign craftsmen. It seems likely that rouletted dishes were made in India rather than further west. Whether they were made by Meditteranean or local craftsmen we cannot tell. It does not much matter since if the latter were the case, they would have most likely been instructed by foreign potters, perhaps the same ones who copied Arretine ware at Arikamedu. That rouletted ware continued until the late second century suggests the type was adopted by Indian craftsmen as their own.

Distribution of rouletted pottery in India suggests dispersal from a central southern India in close contact within land towns, and trading up the coast as far as the Ganges delta. Classical sources refer to coastal trade known to the Romans and Greeks as far as the Bay of Bengal (Warmington 1974) though they themselves seem rarely to have penetrated far north. Arikamedu was probably one of their *emporia*, perhaps Ptolemy's Podouke (Casal 1949). Since knowledge of the southwestern monsoon was brought to the attention of Classical writers by "Hippalos", theoretically there was no obstacle to trade across the Bay of Bengal. However, Classical writers are vague about the geography of its eastern littoral, despite mentions by Pomponius Mela, Pliny, Ptolemy, and others. Indian sources are unhelpful about trade with southeast Asia, whilst it is unlikely the Chinese even had coastal trade as far south as Malaya in the first century A.D. and do not seem to have been capable of building and navigating ocean going craft for use in the South China Sea, let alone further west, until at least the fourth century (Wheatly 1961; Wolters 1967). Indonesian-Malayan sailors were very competent, however. Some scholars have even suggested they spread Austronesian languages to Malagasy on the far side of the Indian Ocean before the Birth of Christ ; at any rate it was not long after that date. Of course maritime trade was not necessarily direct. It could have been coastal or even overland. In support of the last-mentioned are perhaps the kettledrums of bronze from Indonesia which were probably inspired by soutwest Chinese examples. However they could have been made locally and a stone mould for the making of these is known from Bali (though it might be late). Van Heekeren (1958) has drawn attention to motifs on a drum from Sangeang island including houses on piles with sadle-shaped roofs (*cp.* modern houses from Sumatera, Sulawesi *etc.*), and humen figuress porting both clothes of Han China and Kushana India, and which argue for perhaps an early second century A.D. date. This article is not the place to discuss such esoteric possiblities as whether King Tiao-pien of Ye-tiao known to the Chinese *ca.* A D. 130 was or was not a rendering of a putative King Devavarman of Yavadvipa, that is to say a king bearing an Indian name of an Indonesian island known to Indians and Chinese by an Indian-type name. Many scholars firmly assert that even presence in Indonesia of Amaravati Buddha statuettes do not signify that Indianization was very marked. Certainly Chinese accounts of Indo-China from the third century testify to burial practices far removed from those of traditional Hinduism. Nor is this article the place for a full description of coarse pottery with Indian similarities from northwest Java, though such pottery does exist. Suffice it to say in that connexion that pot lids of upturned mushroom shape are the main Javanese type (we have only seen one convex pot lid) corresponding especially to Wheeler's types 36a (and less often 39a or 40c) Arikamedu. Type 33a was said to be "very rare" and was only known from pre-Arretine and Arretine layers at Arikamedu, whilst types 39 and 40 were from post-Arretine layears. (Wheeler *et at.* 1946). So-called "incised" ware (Wheeler *et al.* 1946, pl. XXXI C 2) is in fact the , very common mat / basket / raffia-impressed motif., caused by the type of fabric wrapped around the potter's paddle, which we have encountered in northwest Javanese "Buni Complex" pottery (also *cp. ibid.* pl. XXXII B 2). It was not common at

Arikamedu, but is found in some parts of eastern India. Stamp impressed and red wash/slip pottery of the post-Arretine layers at Arikamedu, and well-know from India in the secend, third, fourth, fifth and possibly later centuries is also well represented in north-west Java.

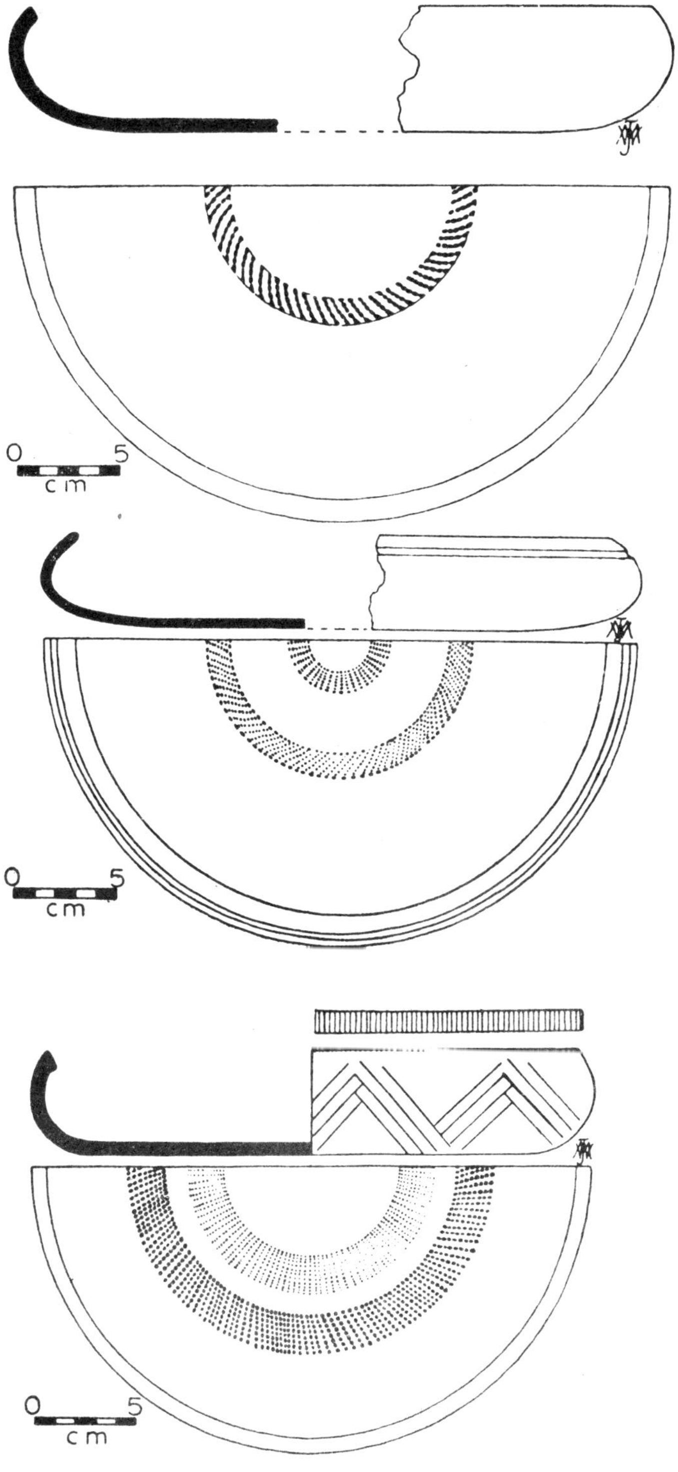

Fig. 1

Taruma was known to the Chinese in the seventh century as To-lo-ma, but scholars have pointed out that the name is parallelled in southern India at a place some 20 kilometres north of Cape Comorin (Coedes 1968, 54). Wolters was surprised that as early as the sixth and seventh centuries his historical investigations demonstrated considerable trade emanating from Java, especially with China (for which records are better than for India). The archaelogical evidence suggests that such trade goes back to the first century A.D. True, Indianization of Indonesia may have been a drawn out affair over many centuries, depending on awareness of Indonesian princes of advantages to be gained from adopting Indian culture and religions in terms of their own local politics. Yet finding of pottery in paddy fields, especially cooking pots with lids, feeding bowls and serving dishes, suggests the common people too may have acquired Indian inspired material things. Unlike Sumatera, Java is agriculturally rich though the dominant crop has been always rice. Not only burials, bur also food offerings to animistic spirits guarding the paddy fields might have been associated with the pottery—this is a guess at random. But Java is further from the mainland than Sumatera, and therefore was *terra incognita* to Chinese travellers for many centuries. It is not surprising we know so little about it from written sources. Historians have played down the importance of navigation in the Straits of Malacca and the Sunda Straits in early times on account of lack of documentary evidence. Perhaps the future will reveal archaeological evidence of maritime connexions which documents have not provided. At the present we know little about southern Sumatera and western Java in the first two centuries A.D. but evidence of statuary, especially from Sumatera, suggests a society with domesticated elephants, buffalo and horses, and various aspects of the material culture are depicted too, such as kettledrums show horses, also. One grave assemblage in Java provided remains of a goat. Bronze (mainly a copper-lead alloy) and very occasionally gold were known, as well as iron. Almost certainly horses were acquired from India, and perhaps were the most highly prized commodities of all that the subcontinent had to offer. Trade with Funan in the lower Mekong region may have been partly responsible for arrival of Roman material (coins and medals of second century emperors, a bronze lamp, a figure of Poseidon) though alternative routes involving portage over the Kra isthmus or even routes wholly overland from the Ganges delta might be envisaged. Hitherto sea-routes from the south to Funan have been dismissed by historians, but the discovery of Romano-Indian ware demands a reconsideration of these. At later times Srivijaya was a staging post where goods from India were transferred for export to China (Wolters 1967). Perhaps island Indonesia already played this role in the first and second centuries A.D. Our discovery of rouletted ware at very least means that such a possibility must be added to other possible routes of east-west trade.

Michael J. Walker and S. Santoso

REFERENCES

Altekar A.S. and Mishra V. 1959 *Report on Kumrahar 1951-1955.* (Patna).

Casal J. M. 1949 *Fouilles de Virampatnam-Arikamedu.* (Paris).

Coedes G. 1968 *The Indianized States of Southeast Asia.* (Canberra).

Indian Archaeology 1954-55—A Review, (New Deihi, 1955). pp. 19-20.

Indian Archaeology 1956-57—A Review, (New Delhi, 1957). pp. 29-30.

Indian Archaeology 1957-58—A Review. (New Delhi, 1958). pp. 51-52, 70.

Indian Archaeology 1959-60—A Review. (New Delhi, 1960). pp. 50-52.

Indian Archaeology 1961-62—A Review. New Delhi, 1964). pp. 26-27.

Indian Archaeology 1963-64—A Review. (New Delhi, 1967). pp. 59-60.

Indian Archaeology 1964-65—A Review. (New Delhl, 1969). p. 256.

Lal B.B. 1949 "Sisupalgarh 1948 : an early historical fort in eastern India" *Ancient India* 5, 62-105 pp. 86-87.

Thapar B.K. 1957 "Maski 1954 : a chalcolithic site of the southern Deccan" *Ancient India* 13, 4-142, pp. 72-76.

Sutayasa M. D. 1972 "Notes on the Buni pottery complex" *Mankind* 8, pp. 182-184.

Van Heekeren H. R. 1953 *The Bronze-Iron Age of Indonesia.* (The Hague).

Warmington E. H. 1974 *The Commerce between the Roman Empire and India.* 2nd. ed. (London).

Wheeler R. E. M., Ghosh A., and Krishna Deva 1946 "Arikamedu : an Indo-Roman trading station on the east coast of India" *Ancient India* 2. pp. 17-24.

Wheeler R.E.M. 1948 "Brahmagiri and Chandravalli 1947 : megalithic and other cultures in the Chitaldrug District, Mysore" *Ancient India* 4, 1947-1948. pp. 181-310.

Wheatly P. 1961 *The Golden Khersonese. Studies in the Historical Geography of the Malay Peninsula before A.D. 1500.* (Kuala Lumpur).

Wolters O. W. 1967 *Early Indonesian Commerce. A Study of the Origins of Srivijaya.* (Ithaca).

Ancient Indian Pottery-kilns

INTRODUCTION

Evidence of the earliest pottery-kilns in the Indian sub-continent comes from Mohenjo-daro. Remains of a number of kilns, in association with dumps of broken pottery, were unearthed at the site, while excavating the later phase of Harappan levels. A few of these structures were fairly well preserved. Extant remains of one of them, unearthed in the DK area in Block 9, enable us to visualize its shape and much of its technical feature. Mackay gives an illustrated description of it. The discovery of ancient Indian pottery-kilns has also been reported from a few other sites, such as Balakot and Inamgaon. But these oven-like structures are rather small.

COMPONENTS

There are three essential components in a pottery-kiln : (a) a fire chamber with one or more fuel-feed apertures, where fuel is burnt in a continuous supply of air, (2) vents to transfer the hot gases generated in the fire chamber into the baking chamber ; (3) a baking chamber which is an enclosed space, like an oven, where the sun-dried clay ware are carefully stacked and heated to the required temperature. Depending upon how the draught of hot gases moves within the baking chamber, the pottery-kilns are called : (1) vertical up-draught kiln, (2) vertical down-draught kiln and (3) horizontal-draught kiln.

MOHENJO-DARO EXAMPLE

The Mohanjo-daro example is a vertical up-draught kiln. It is a cylindrical structure (Fig. 1). At the bottom is the fire chamber, nearly three-fourths of which is below the ground level. It measures 2.25 m in diameter and 1.4 m in height. Above the fire chamber is the baking chamber, whose floor also measures 2.25 m in diameter. It is supported by the circular wall of the fire chamber and a hollow column of bricks at the centre. It is perforated with 14 holes, each of which measures about 11 cm in diameter. These are the vents. 13 of them are arranged in a ring near the edge of the floor and one at the centre which opens up through the hollow column that supports the floor from below. The enclosure wall of

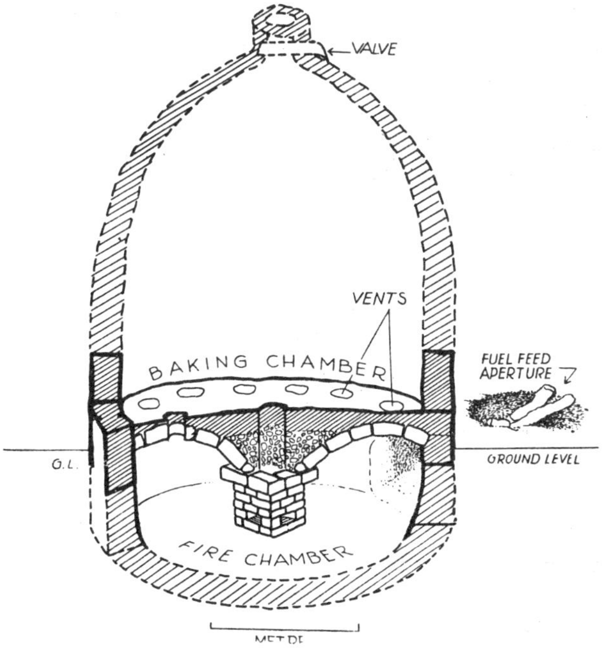

Fig. 1

the baking chamber is built of brick laid in mud mortar. It is plastered inside with clay. Much of it is broken. Its extant remains measure only 40 cm in height and within this height it does not show any vertical curvature. It therefore does not allow us to determine the height of the kiln. It was probably domed with a chimney, like the sixth century B.C. Corinthian pottery-kilns. A thin sheet of metal placed immediately below the chimney, that can be slid in or out, can control the aperture through the chimney. It acts like a valve to control draught.

KILN BAKING

While baking pottery in a vertical up-draught kiln, hot gases rise up in the baking chamber and pass out through the chimney, inducing a natural draught of air. This draught is controlled and the temperature within the baking chamber is raised, maintained or lowered by manipulating the aperture through the chimney. But in an up-draught kiln the heat within the baking chamber is not equally distributed. It is much higher near the bottom and becomes progressively less towards the roof of the chamber. Vertical down-draught kilns and horizontal–draught kilns are better for uniform distribution of heat within the baking chamber. In a vertical up-draught kiln the potter stacks the heavier thick-walled storage jars at the bottom of the chamber and smaller thin-walled vessels higher up in the pile. Thus he sees to it that the heating is adequate for all the wares stacked in the kiln.

When pottery is baked in a kiln there is not much wastage due to breaking of pots. They also get uniformly and adequately baked, free from smoke stains. But the process is not inexpensive. Kilns can be fired only by high-priced dry billets of hard wood or charcoal that produce intense, smoke-free flame. Also, the construction of a kiln involves a certain amount of capital expenditure. Kiln baking process, therefore, would become profitable only if continuously used to meet the demands of a large pottery market. It is uneconomic for a peasant potter working to meet the needs of his village.

OPEN-FIRE BAKING

Mohenjo-daro was a large Harappan town. Its pottery, like the pettery of other Harappan sites, is well made. Their uniform colour shows that the potter had considerable experience in his craft. But it is doubtful if much of the Harappan pottery was baked in kilns. It is likely that much of it was baked in open-fires. Mackay observes that the pottery of the present day Sindh potters, baked in open fires, is as good as the Harappan pottery, equally hard and strong and uniformly well baked. He therefore concludes that successful baking of pottery does not depend upon the structure of the baking device. In Kutch, near Bhuj, Professor R. N. Mehta has observed certain groups of potters using open-fires to produce pottery as good as that of the Harappans. This supports Mackay's observation. The rarity of ancient Indian pottery-kilns in the archaeological record suggests that more than 99 percent of the ancient Indian pottery was baked in open-fires. But unfortunately for the archaeologist, this baking device does not leave behind tangible evidence.

No clearly intelligible evidence of ancient Indian open–fires, used for backing pottery, has so far been discovered in excavations. However, the pottety baking technique used by the modern Indian village potter enables us to visualize the technique of ancient potter. It is simple, inexpensive and adequate. His openfire for baking pottery consists of a shallow, circular pit, 4 to 5 m in diameter, 50 to 75 cm in depth. It is loosely filled up to the brim with different kinds of easily available, inexpensive fuel like dry brush-wood, rice husks, dry grass or hay and cowdung cakes. Pots are carefully pilled up within the circle. The heavier, thick-walled storage jars are arranged at the bottom near the centre of the circle and the progressively smaller ware is placed one above the other in the pile. Thus the potter maintains the equilibrium of the pile by retaining its centre of gravity near the bottom. Cowdung cakes, hay and rice husks are put among the pots and also above them as they are placed in the pile. Finally, the whole stack is completely covered with brush-wood and hay and plastered with a thin layer of clay earth up to the crown of the pile. The crown of the pile is not covered with clay plaster, instead it is covered with broken pots. This open space acts like a chimney. Around the bottom of the pile. at the ground level are arranged 10 to 12 air inlets. These are made of rims of broken pots. While these holes are used to set fire to the pile and also as fuel-feel apertures, they primarily act like vents for a natural draught of air into the burning pile. Pl. XVA.

The firing may take 8 to 16 hours or even more depending upon the size of the pile and its contents. The potters continuously keep a watch on the pile to cover up any hole through which heat may escape. In an experiment at Vadodara, the temperature of an open-fire using cowdung cakes as the fuel, was found to reach 1000°c. A temperature of 800°c is adequate for baking pottery. The potters allow a sufficiently long time, two days or more, to cool the pile, so that the risks of breakage is minimized. Some of the important ancient Indian pottery like the Painted Grey Ware, Black Slipped Ware and Northern Black Polished Ware were baked in a reducing atmosphete. It is possible they were baked in *gajaputa*.

GAJAPUTA

Gajaputa is a well Known ancient Indian baking device. It is still used in the preparation of medicines and also for baking pottery. It is described by Vagbhata. It consists of a pit of about one cubicmeter. At the bottom, it is closely packed with cowdung cakes upto a height of 20 to 30 cm. The jar containing the material to be baked is placed at the middle of the pit, above the cowdung cakes. It is then fully surrounded with cowdung cakes and some more cakes are piled up above the pit. It is then set fire to and allowed to burn first, for a few hours, slowly, and then with strong intense heat for 8 to 12 hours.

There are groups of potters in the Ganga Valley and elsewhere in India who use the simple *gajaputa* for producing a shining black pottery. One such group lives near Vadodara. Originally, they came from the Ganga valley. These potters produced small decorative bowls, dishes and vases. They treat their wheel-thrown, sun-dried ware with a ferruginous clay slip whose composition they do not divulge. They stack the ware inside a large mouthed, thick-walled, well-baked, strong jar. The space inside the vessels and between them in the jar Is filled with cowdung cake powder and goat droppings., The jar is sealed with severel layers of clay and cloth to make it completely air-tight. The pottery in the jar is then baked in *gajaputa*.

Within the jar the pottery is babked in an atmosphere of excess carbon monoxide. Under this reducing condition haematite changes into magnetite which imparts a black surface finish to the pottery. It is likely that the Painted Grey Ware, Black slipped Ware and Northern Black Polished Ware were baked in a sealed saggar-like device, in an atmosphere of carbon monoxide, in a fire similar to *gajaputa*.

CONCLUSION

Not much of ancient Indian pottery was baked in kilns. They appear to be largely baked in open-fires. For baking in reducing atmosphere the potters possibly made use of *gajaputa*.

Maharaja Sayajirao
University of Baroda,
Vadodra.

K.T.M. Hegde

Book Reviews

S. P. Gupta with a forward by V. A. Ranov, U.S.S.R. ; Archaeology of Soviet Central Asian and the Indian Borderlands, Vol. I Prehistory. Vol. II Protohistory. New Delhi : B.R. Publishing Corporation, 1978 ; p.p. 600 illustrations 350. Price : Rs. 400, U.S. Dollars 80, for the set.

These two volumes span the entire length of the period before history of the countries known as Turkmenia, parts of the western Mongolia, north-eastern Iran, Tadjikistan, etc., and now collectively called 'Soviet Central Asia". These volumes have been rightly or appropriately called "Prehistory', and "Protohistory", respectively. For, as I have been repeatedly saying for the last 20 years, it is not advisable for academic as well as practical reasons of everyday life, to designate the entire period before the known historical period in any country as "prehistory". Not only the methods and data for the earliest periods—known as "Stone Ages" popularly and rightly, quite different, but there are various gradations, or stages of economic and cultural manifestations which the use of these two words "Prehistory" and "Protohistory" immediately reveal when read or heard.

As Dr. Ranov, one of the most well known Russian archaeologists (prehistorian), says in his Foreword, "the book is the result of the visit of Dr. S.P. Gupta to the Soviet Union and Mongolia under Cultural Exchange Programme between India and USSR and between India and People's Republic of Mongolia." And it must be said at once that Dr. Gupta has not only utilized the opportunity well but performed an indeed herculean task, and with his characteristic dash published the results of his labour in an admirable publication when one sees such works, one wishes other scholars who went on such visits had done half as much.

Not only the printing is good, but the numerous half tone blocks are very well printed. And the entire get up of the book is artistically laid. Thus we should congratulate the author as well as the adventurous Publisher-distributors.

The contents of the book as Dr. Ranov says, "give a full picture of the present idea of the given subject—the various divisions and sub-divisions, the regional and sub-regional cultures of this vast region."

The work should be of special interest to Indian archaeologists. For the Soviet Central Asia and India are close neighbours, and there must have been considerable exchanges of goods and ideas by various methods—diffusion, trade or even actual migration of people.

Some years ago when I had an occasion to discuss the origin of the Middle Palaeolithic in India, and West Asia, I could lay my hands only on the report of tools and burials in the famous cave at Teshik-tash. Now Dr. Gupta tells us that there are no less than 78 sites reported since the initial discovery in 1938, of which 21 are in this region.

Hence Ranov says, as I had predicted, "one would not completely rule out the marginal impact of (the) great Central-Asian Mousterian Culture on the still not adequately studied Middle Palaeolithic Culture of India." Ranov would also see some resemblance between the Lower Palaeolithic Karatau (south Tajikistan) and the Soan. Interestingly this region has yielded handaxes as well, though so far very few. And it is surmised by Gupta that the handaxe-makers came (possibly) from Caucasia, and the chopper-using from the sub-Himalayan Zone. However, as in Kashmir, the tools of the true handaxe type are few. Hence the picture is hazy. That of the chopper-chopping is slightly better. And here, as is in the Kangra Valley, these tools are found even with the Neolithic.

The same thing is true of the Upper or Late Palaeolithic. Countries on India's frontier—both Pakistan and Afghanistan have given very recently some evidence of it. This has been included by Gupta, thus makig his account absolutely up to date.

Likewise his detailed treatment of the various aceramic, and ceramic Neolithic, Chalcolithic and the Bronze Age Cultures—too numerous to mention individually in a brief review,—would help in our understanding the origins of the Chalcolithic cultures of India. A persual of Gupta's detailed review shows that only Iran and Afghanistan could have provided the models for the goblets of Navdatoli (so far no other site, even in Malwa, has yielded such distinctive pottery).

Equally interesting is Gupta's discussion of the Harappan contact with Shoturgai on the Oxus.

While discussing the Neolithic and Chalcolithic cultures, Gupta consistently uses the world "microlithic blades." This usage is wrong, unless the tools are really microliths. For during the Chalcolithic period, though the blades were smaller when flint or chert was not available, more than 55% of the blades were parallel-sided. Lunates were very few and points still fewer. Evan at Mehrgarh one might be able to distinguish between the Mesolithic microliths and the Neolithic-Chalcolithic blades.

While discussing the role of Baluchistan and Afghanistan Gupta thinks that Gordon Childe and his "children" (including the reviewer) had "overplayed", this because we have now evidence from Mehrgarh (Baluchistan) and a cave in Afghanistan. Such a view is hardly justified. The earlier writers had no hindsight and the conditions were made all the worse by numerous surface collections made through scrappy excavations. *We must not forget that Baluchistan has by and large remained a transit region*, hence it could not develop or sustain a culture or ruling dynasty during the last 2300 years. And in Afghanistan even now as the *Time* magazine has said recently there are very few highways. And the country remains undeveloped, because it is mountainous (*Time* December 15 1978, p. 17). This underlines the need of a historical perspective and the fact that any inference based on archaeological evidence is true upto the moment when it is made. This I had said as far back as 1934. Even now the discovery of Mehrgarh does not completely alter the situation. Since this site is on the perennial flowing Bolan river it might have given rise to the aceramic and ceramic Neolithic culture, but would it be possible *everywhere* in Baluchistan ? What we should do in any region, and particularly in Baluchistan, is to group the known cultures, according to their degree of environmental suitability and then proceed to discuss their role. In Baluchistan no prolonged work has been possible because of political and climatic factors. But this can and should be attempted in India, as I have already said elsewhere.

Gupta is justified in rejecting the attribution of the PG Ware to Early Aryans. This pottery—its shapes and fabrics—is quite different from the Gandhara Grey Ware. It is however probable that the PGW belongs to the later Aryans. For, as *Rigveda* says the Sarasvati was drying up and this was the reason why the Aryans were migrating westwards. Now this has been again confirmed, as pointed out by Dr. Rafiq Mughal in his latest communication by a German Professor Herbert Wilhemy *(Zetscrift fur Geomorphologie* 1969, pp. 76-91, band 8). This scholar also has in veiw some seismic disturbance which might have created the "present" Ganga system. According to one Puranic tradition, the Ganga is post-Sagars, that is, its occupation by man is considerably later than elsewhere. One wonders whether this has reference to tha migration of the Aryans from the Punjab.

In short, these two volumes prepared with great labour and scholarship by Dr. Gupta are to be used, read and re-read, by Indian prehistorians and protohistorians, and not merely admired, and put on the shelf

Deccan College H.D. Sankalia
Pune

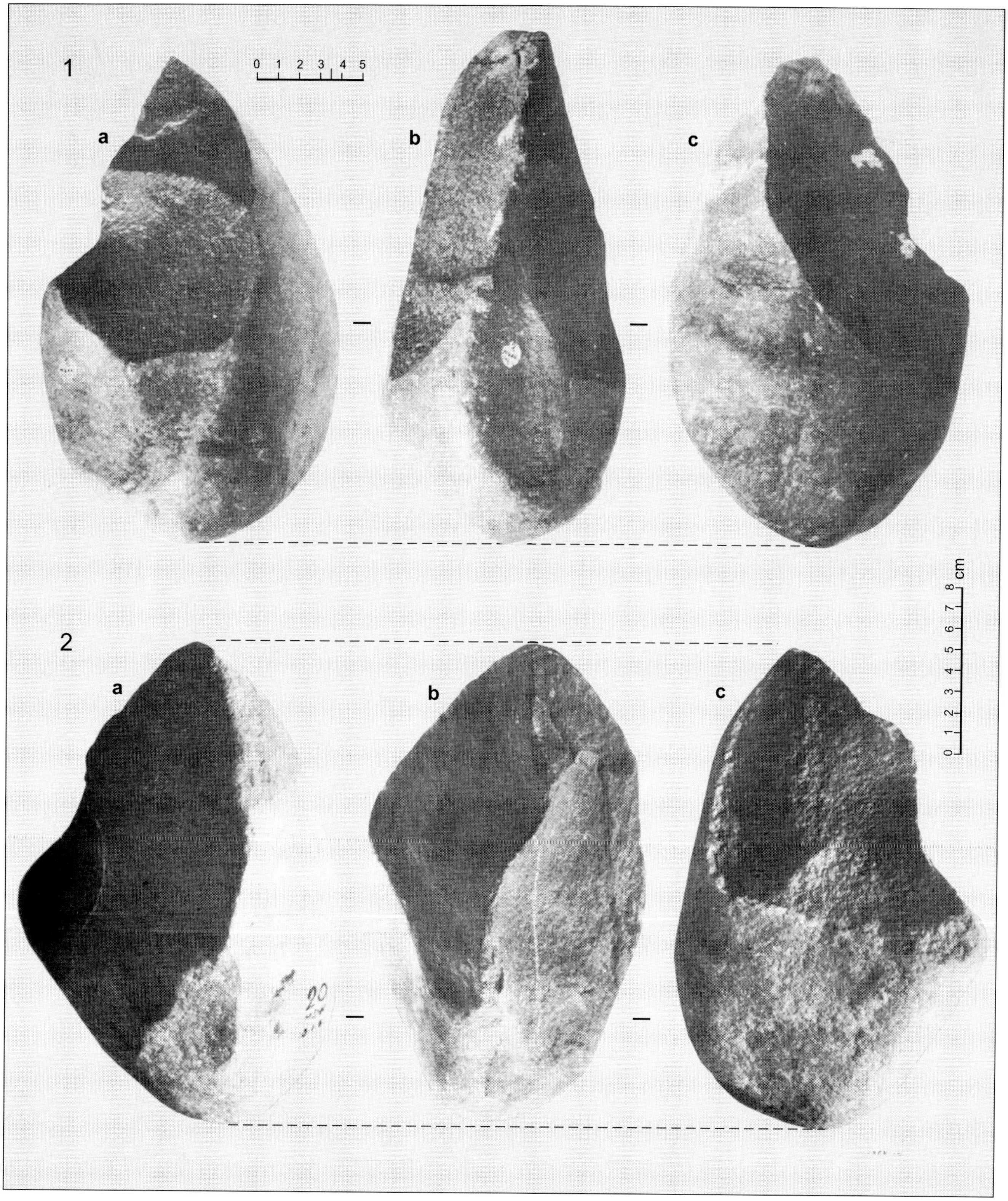

Mahadevian Pebble Chopper/Chopping Tool Industry, Narmada River, Central India.

[Courtesy : A. P. Khatri.]

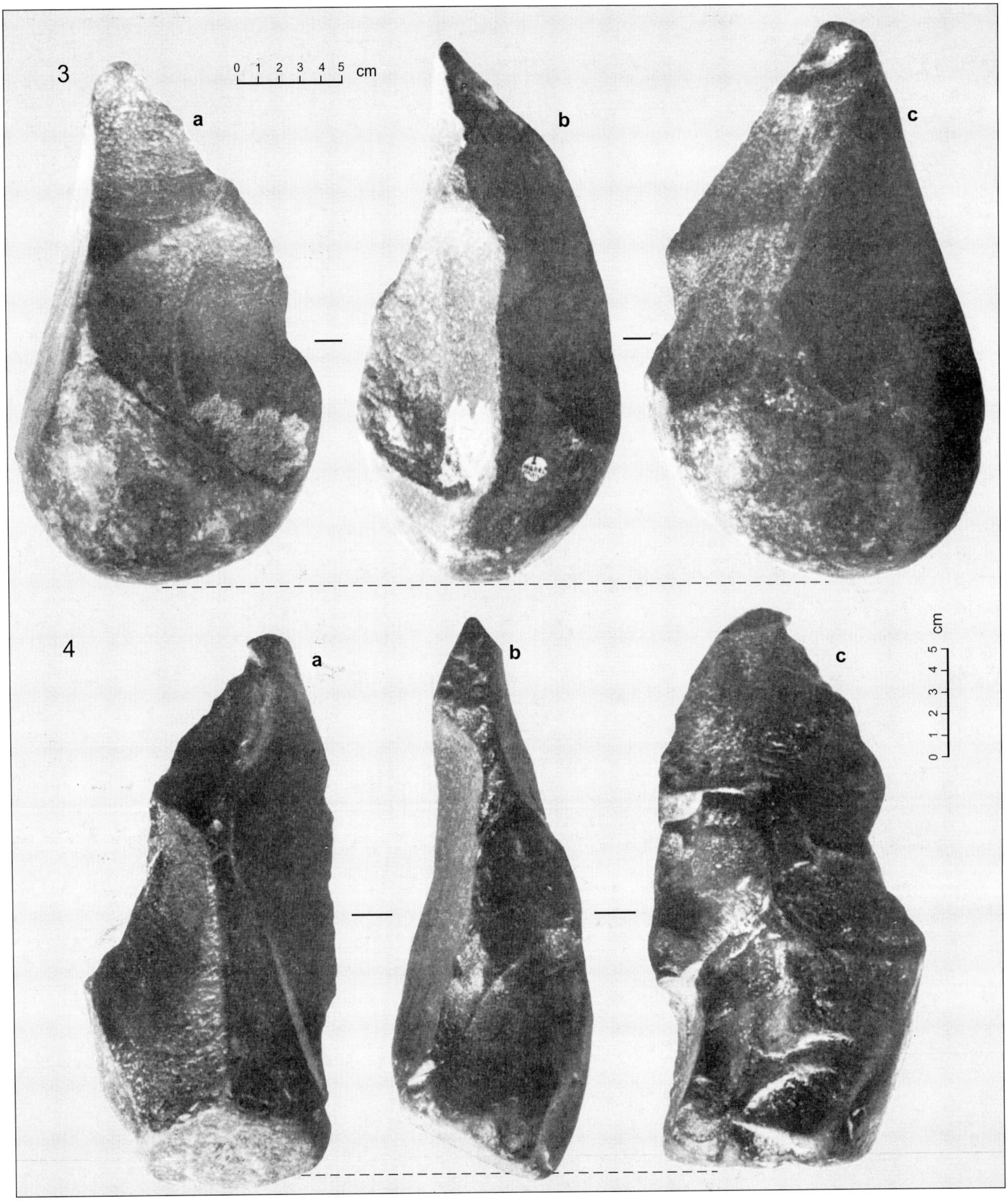

Mahadevian Pebble Chopper/Chopping Tool Industry, Narmada River, Central India.

[Courtesy : A. P. Khatri.]

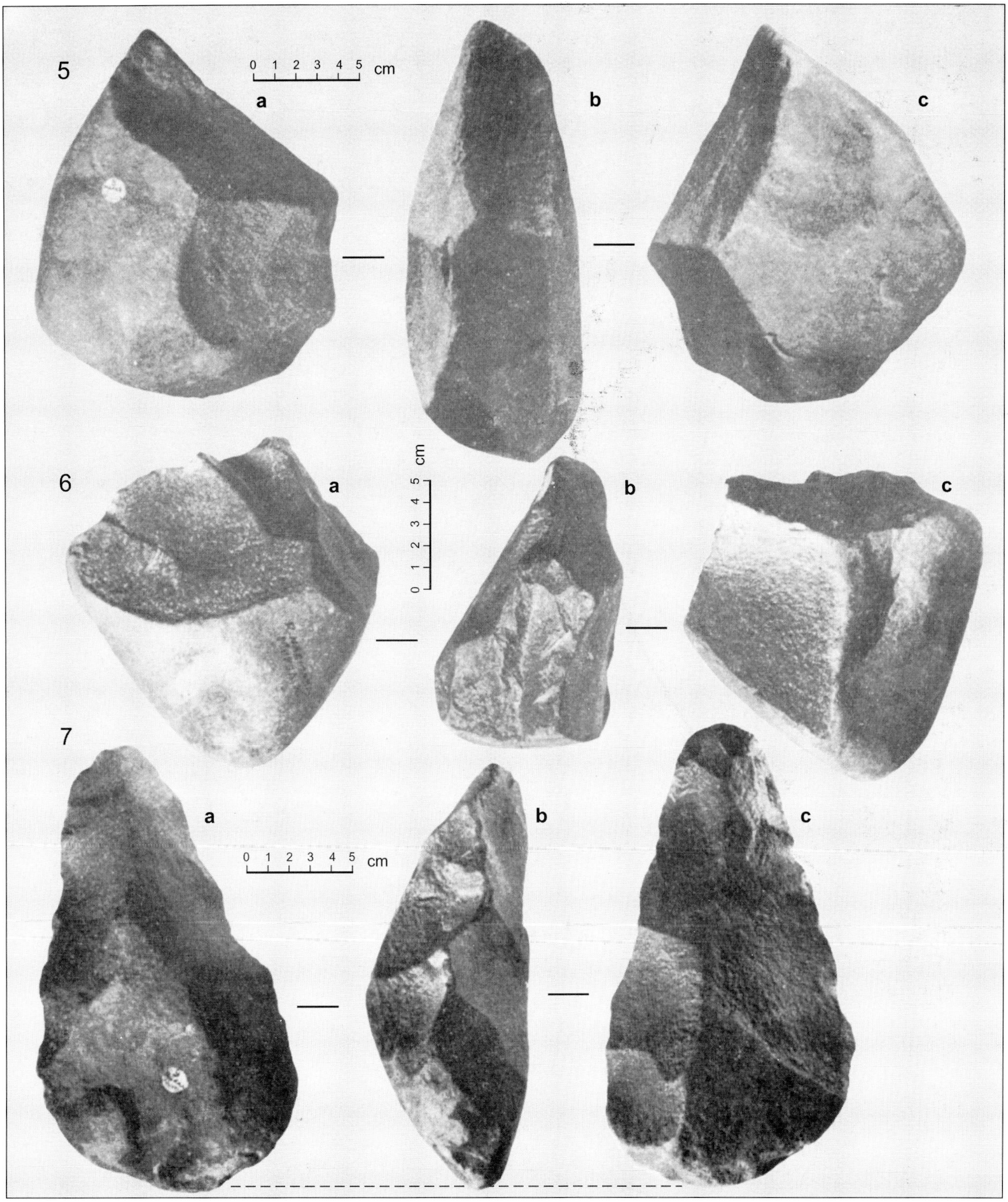

Mahadevian Pebble Chopper/Chopping Tool Industry, Narmada River, Central India.
No. 7 is incipient Handaxe.

[Courtesy : A. P. Khatri.]

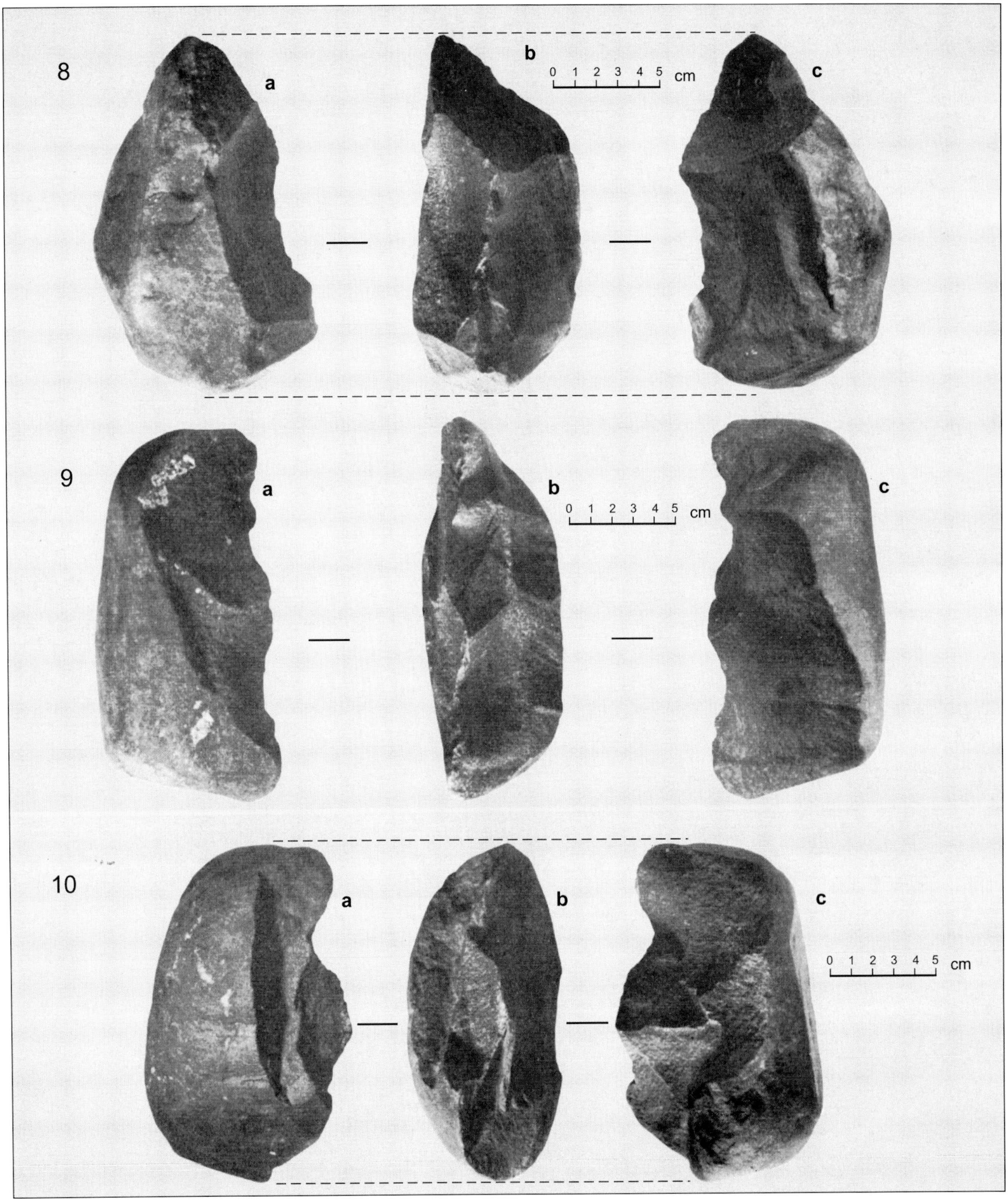

Mahadevian Pebble Chopper/Chopping Tool Industry, Narmada River, Central India

[Courtesy : A. P. Khatri.]

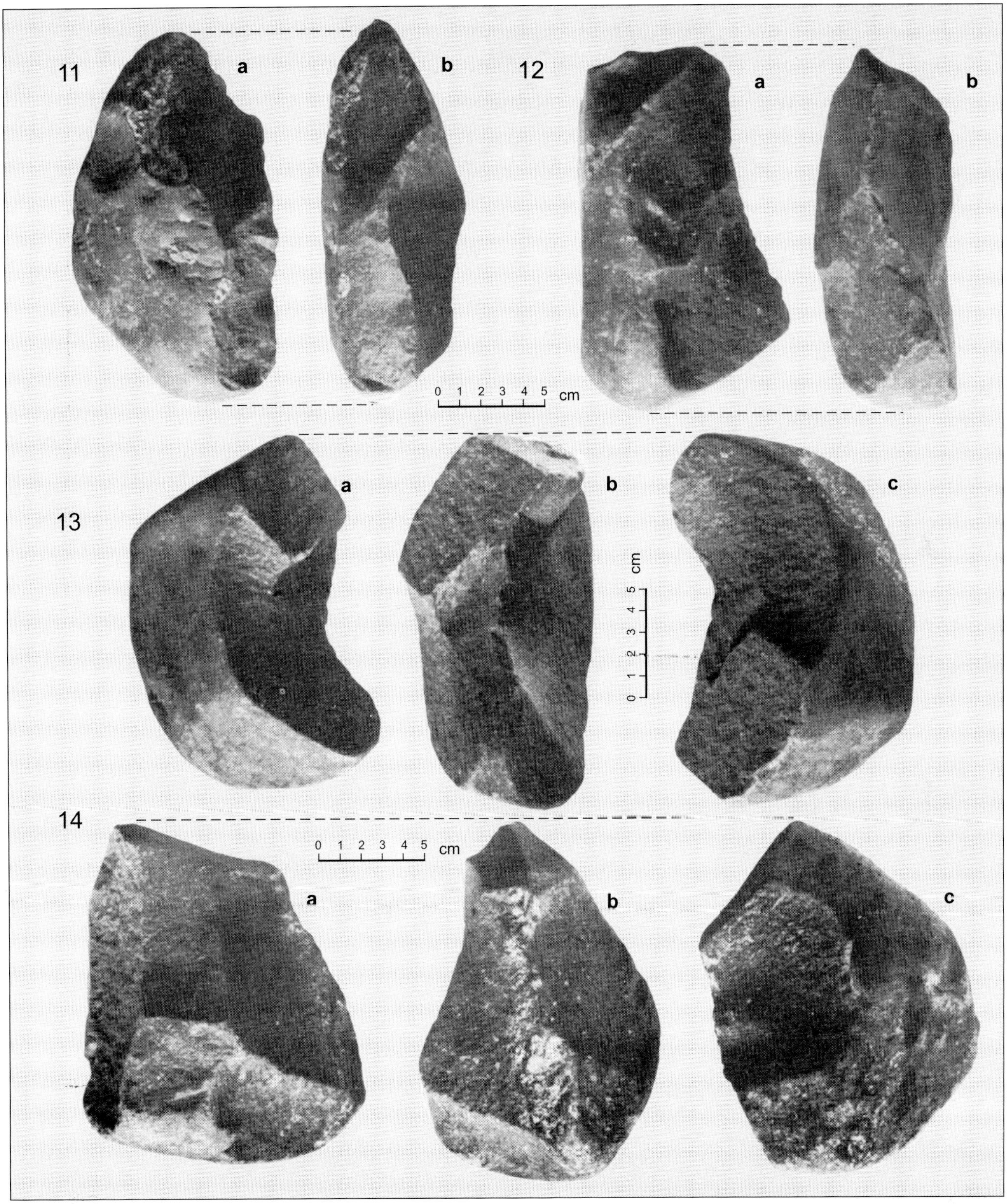

Mahadevian Pebble Chopper/Chopping Tool Industry, Narmada River, Central India

[Courtesy : A. P. Khatri.]

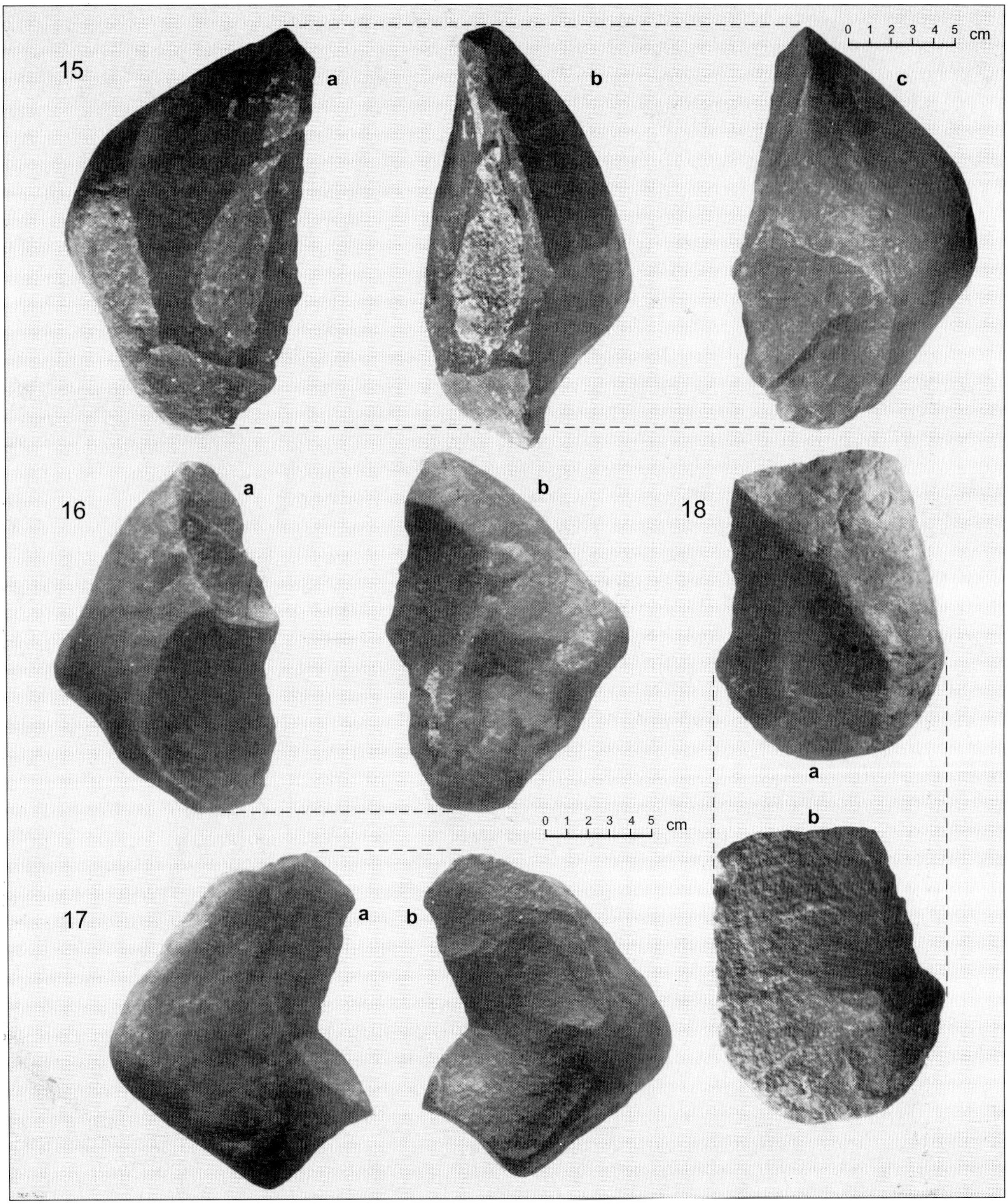

Mahadevian Pebble Chopper/Chopping Tool Industry, Narmada River, Central India

[Courtesy : A. P. Khatri.]

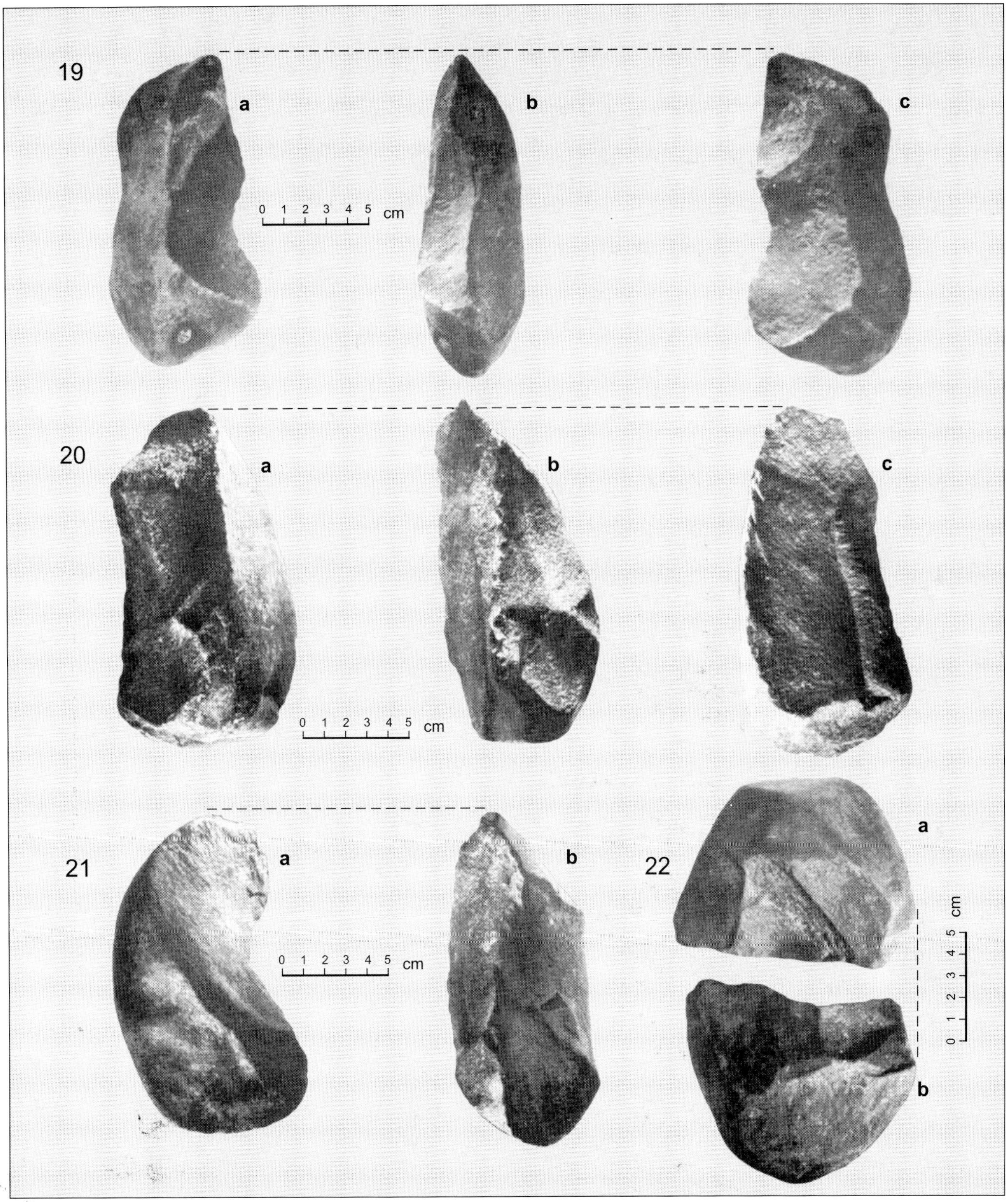

Mahadevian Pebble Chopper/Chopping Tool Industry, Narmada River, Central India

[Courtesy : A. P. Khatri.]

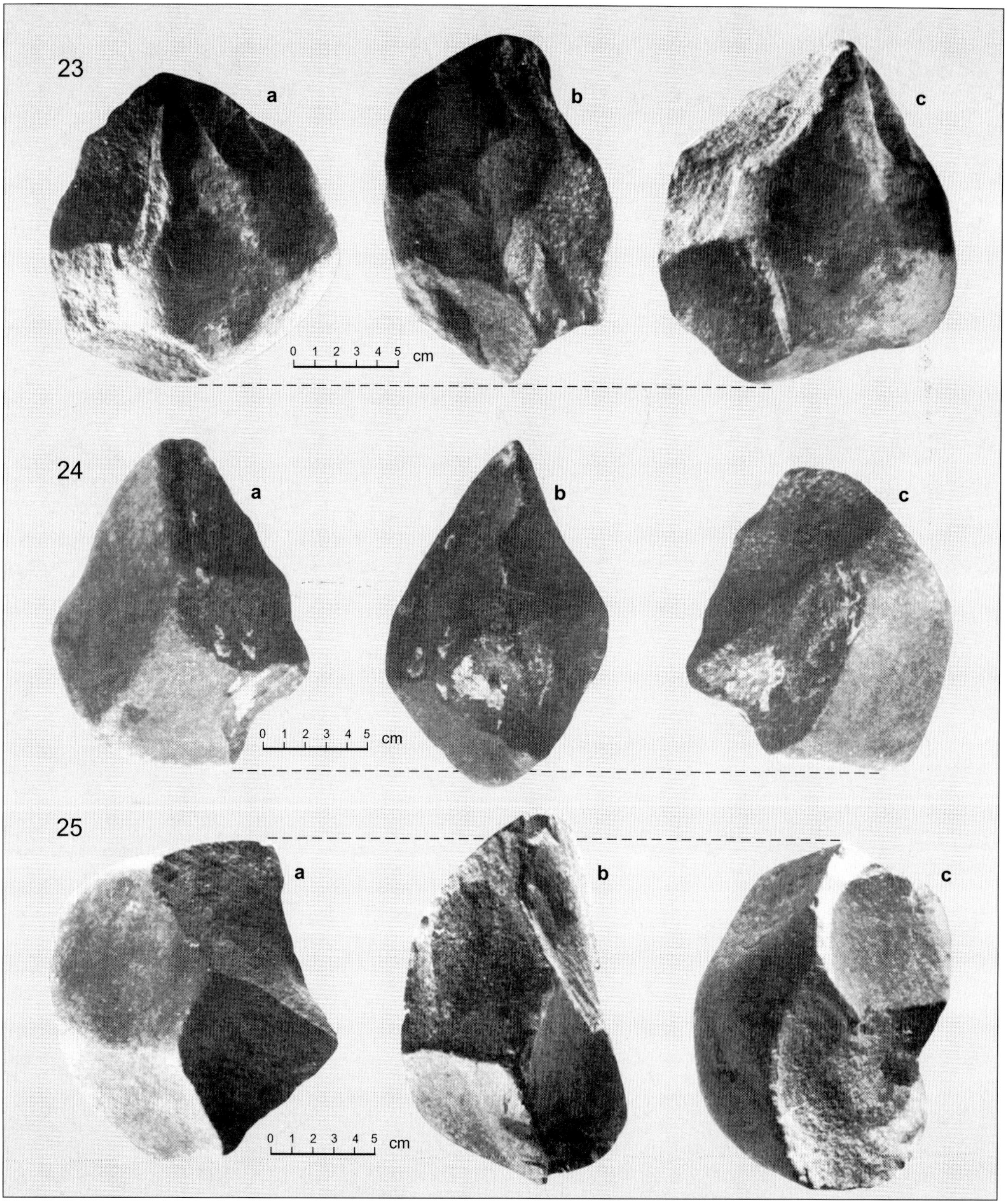

Mahadevian Pebble Chopper/Chopping Tool Industry, Narmada River, Central India

[Courtesy : A. P. Khatri.]

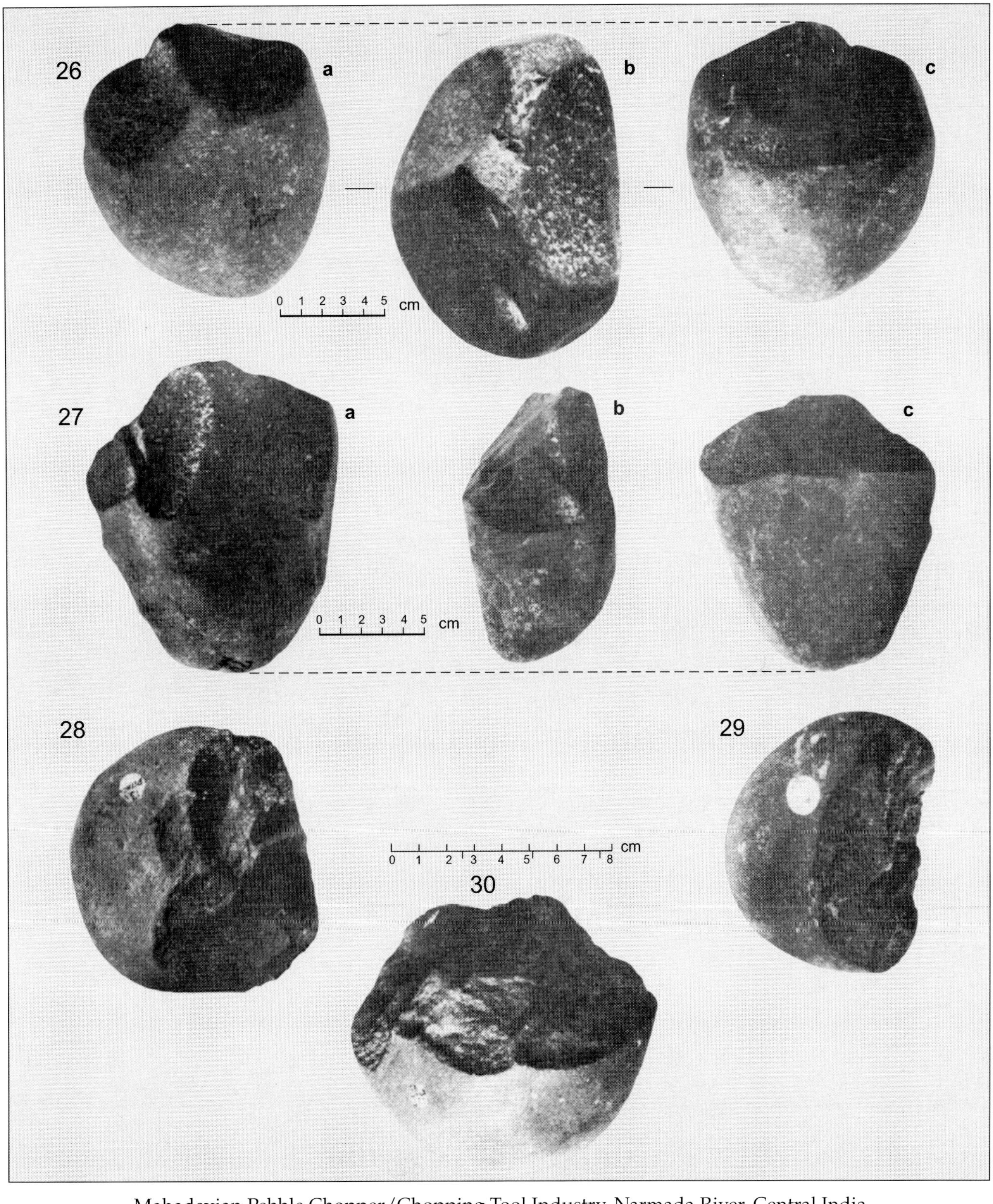

Mahadevian Pebble Chopper/Chopping Tool Industry, Narmada River, Central India

[Courtesy : A. P. Khatri.]

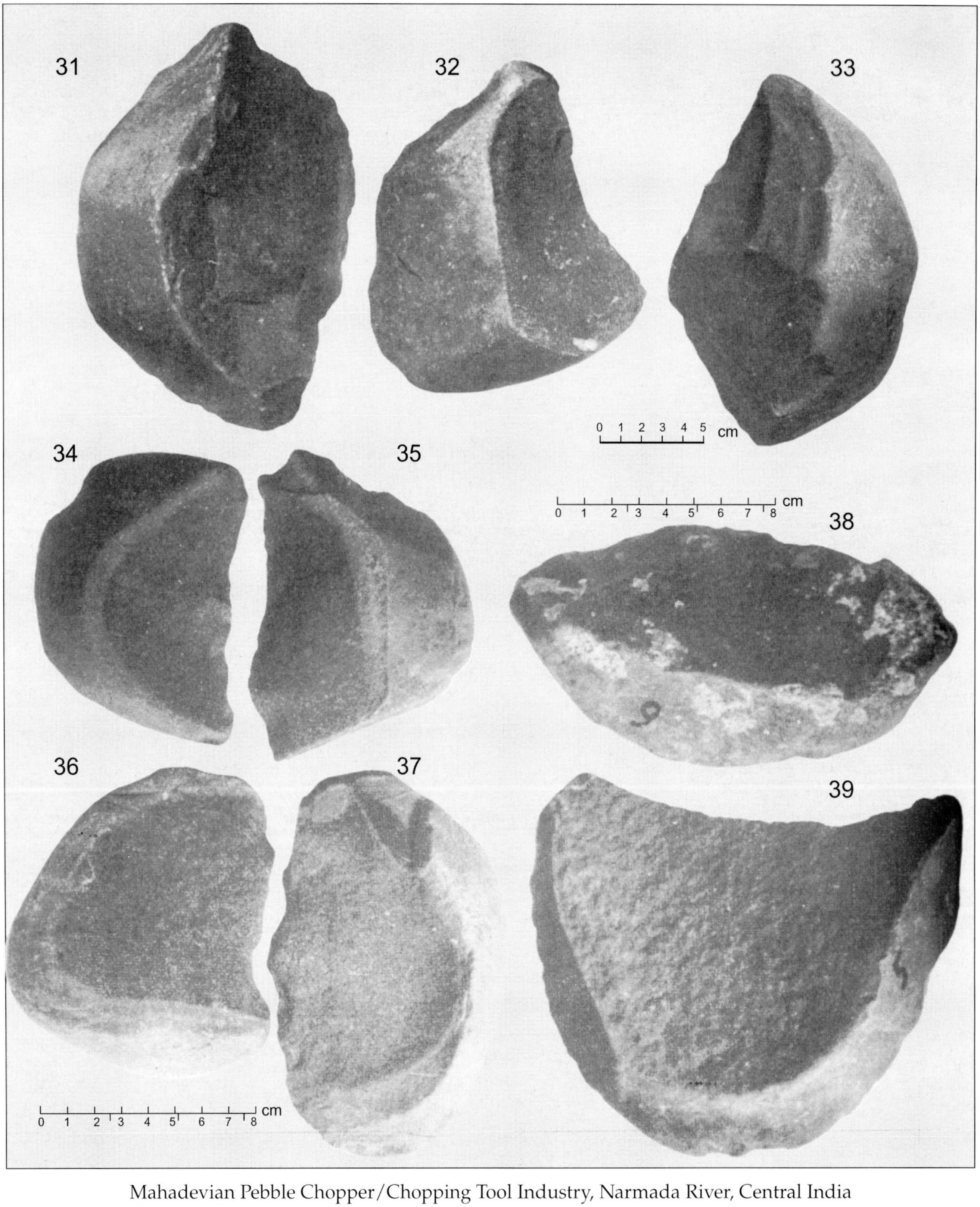

Mahadevian Pebble Chopper/Chopping Tool Industry, Narmada River, Central India

[Courtesy : A. P. Khatri.]

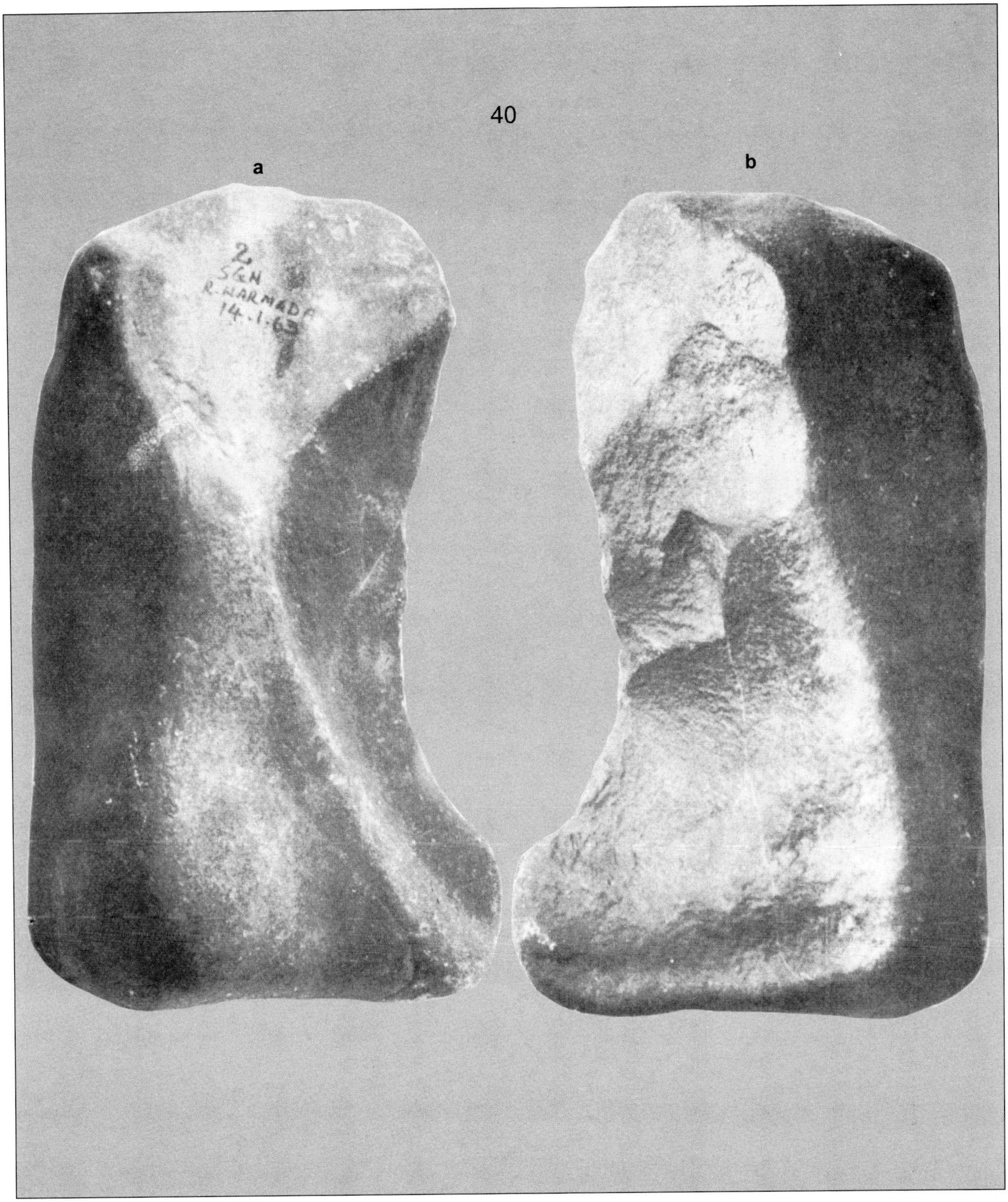

Mahadevian Pebble Chopper/Chopping Tool Industry, Narmada River, Central India

[Courtesy : A. P. Khatri.]

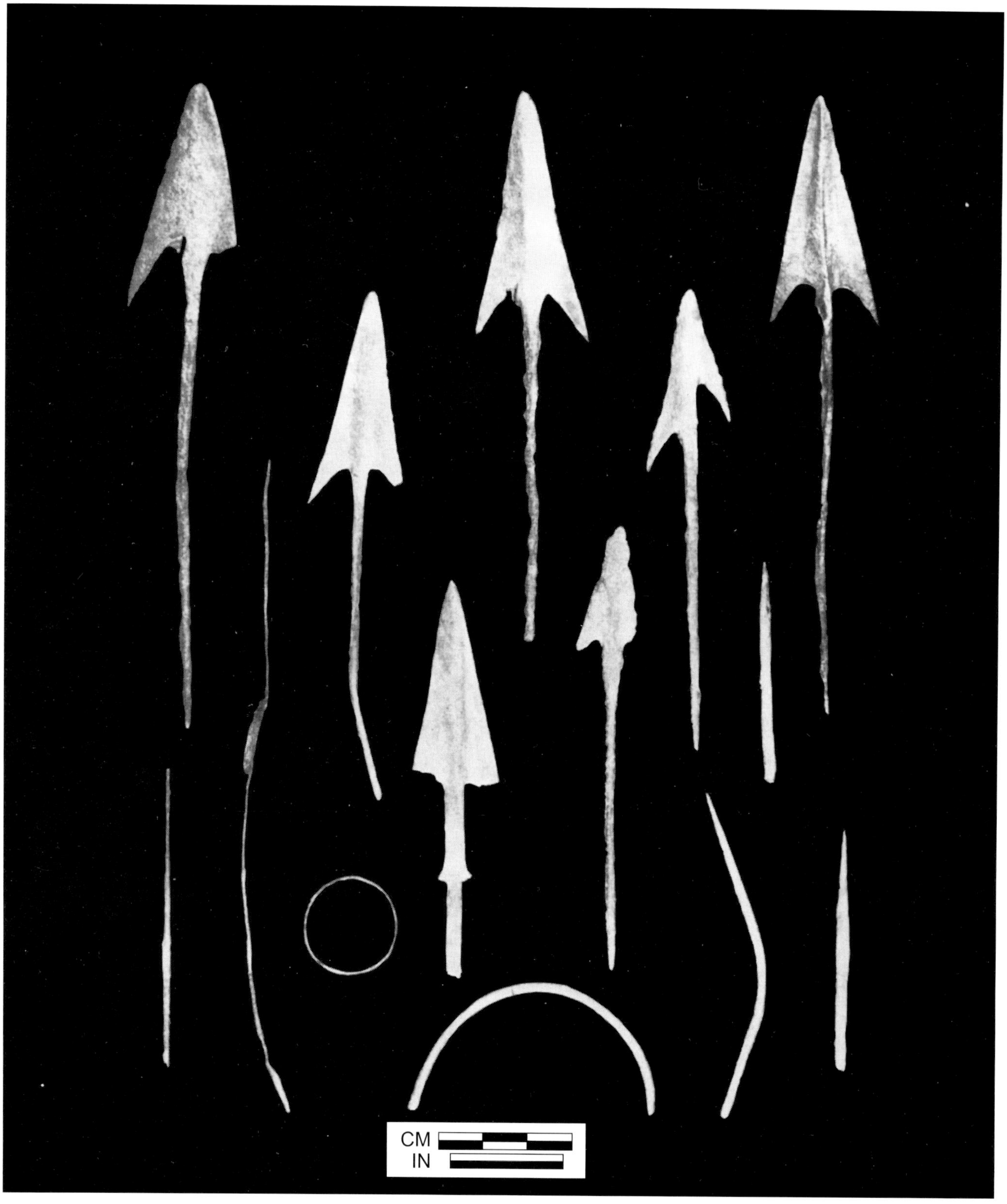

Copper objects from Burzahom, Period II

[Courtesy : Archaeological Survey of India.]

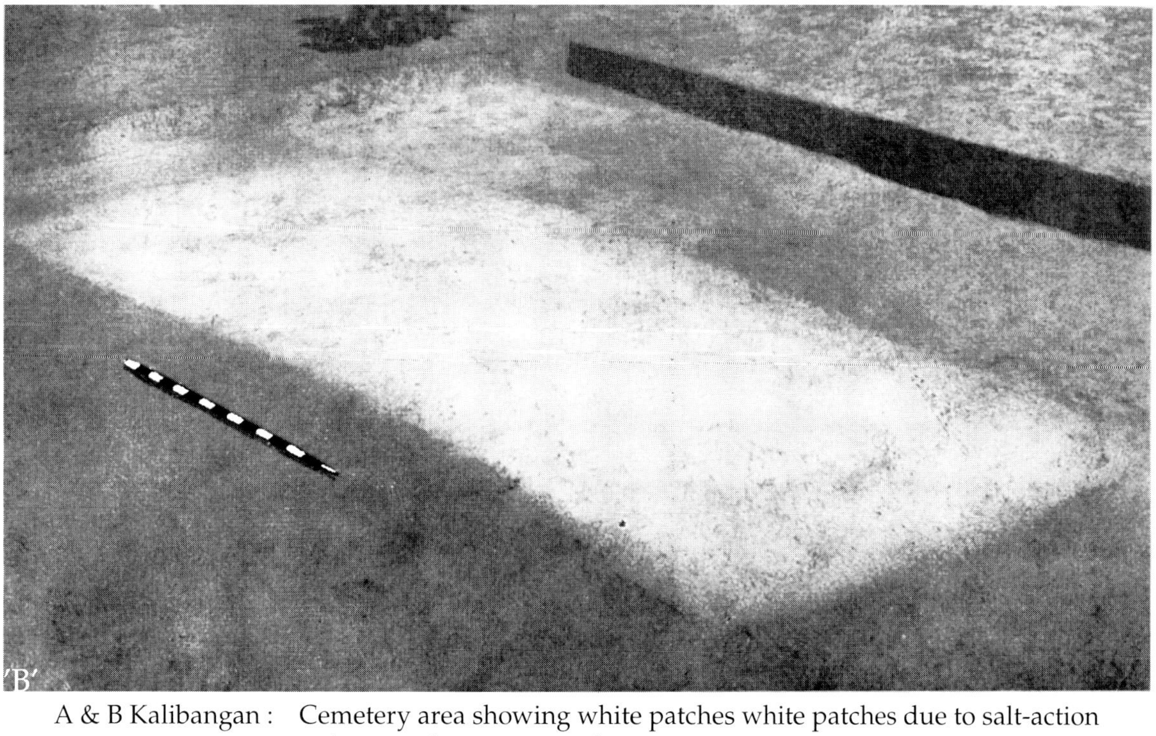

A & B Kalibangan : Cemetery area showing white patches white patches due to salt-action indicating the existence of graves.

[Courtesy : Archaeological Survey of India.]

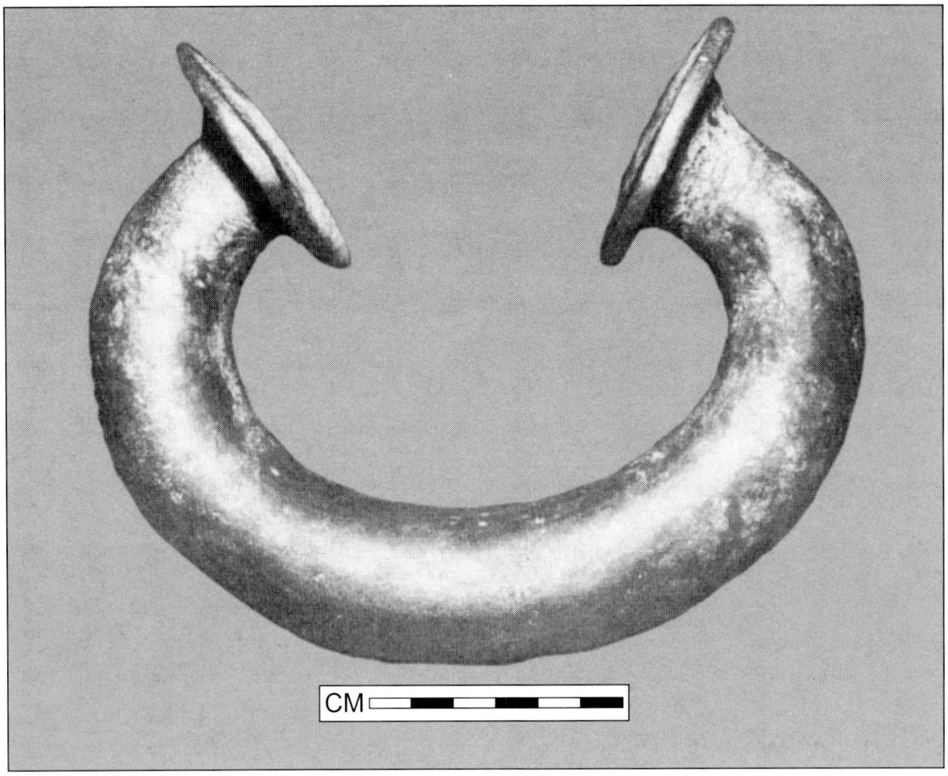

A. Copper Hoard Ring from Parihati (West Bengal).

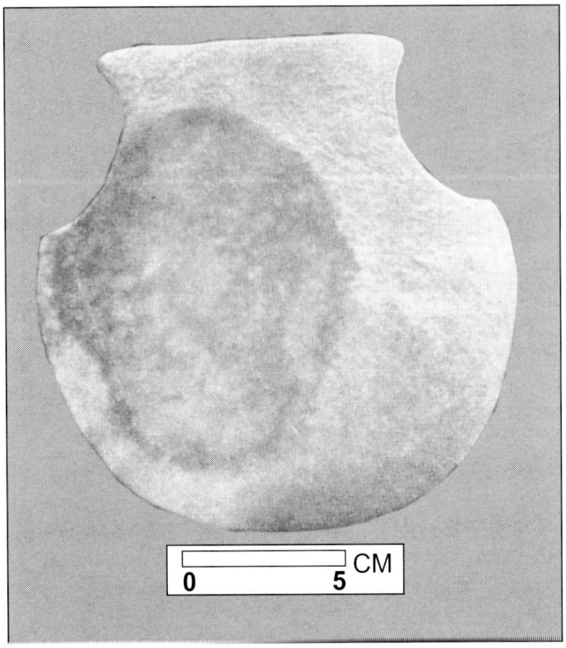

B. Copper Hoard shouldered celt from Bhaktabandh (West Bengal).

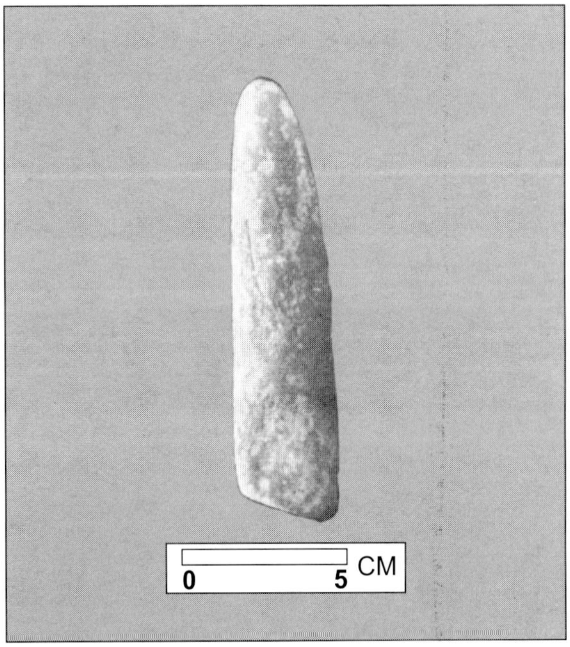

C. Copper Hoard Pick-like object from Bhaktabandh (West Bengal).

[Courtesy : Dilip Chakrabarti.]

A. Pottery baking in the open fire. [Courtesy : KTM Hegde.]

B. A dome under construction at Yard in Iran.

[Courtesy : Archaeological Survey of India.]

A. Tile work on the outer Face of the mosque at Balkh, Afghanistan.

B. The Dome on the mosque at Balkh, Afghanistan.